Lake Michigan Shipwrecks
South Haven to Grand Haven

SAUGATUCK

MARITIME SERIES

Book 4

by Kit Lane

PAVILION PRESS
P.O. Box 250
Douglas, Michigan 49406

International Standard Book Number
1-877703-03-6

Cover: The Graham & Morton Company's steamer **Argo** struck the bar at the entrance to Holland harbor on November 20, 1905, and went aground north of the pier. Here she stayed until spring, but was eventually pulled off the beach and returned to service.

Lake Michigan, Friend and Foe

Each of the five Great Lakes has its own sailing characteristics and problems. The shoals and islands of Lake Superior are a hazard to navigation especially in stormy weather, the shallowness of Lake Erie makes it quick to respond to wind. Lake Michigan sits basically north-south a north wind has full play for its entire length, sweeping across 360 miles of water to roll up backbreaking seas. Once a vessel gets south of the Manitou Islands there are no islands to hide behind in a storm and few natural harbors.

The coast of Lake Michigan is made up of sand. Before the government began work as early as the 1830s, shifting sands could change the entrance to a harbor by a half a mile or more at the whim of any big wind. Despite the best work of the Army Corps of Engineers most West Michigan harbors are still at the mercy of the shifting sands.

Harbor entrances on the east shore of Lake Michigan face west, the source of the prevailing winds. Manmade structures have been built at the mouths of all of the active harbors to channel the river water into Lake Michigan with sufficient speed to carry its sand and silt away from the channel, but deposits still tend to form shallow bars just north and south of the entrance making it important for vessels to enter the harbor straight down the channel. When the strong winds blow across the harbor mouth, and especially when the wind is directly from the west, water exiting the channel strikes a combination of wind and crashing waves and the fallout of sand occurs at the end of the improvements causing a bar to form directly across the entrance to the main channel.

Lake Michigan is also a narrow body of water, less than 100 miles at its widest point. Many a vessel which has failed to enter Racine or Milwaukee has ended its career wrecked and ashore near Grand Haven driven by the prevailing winds.

Only an occasional commercial vessel enters west Michigan ports today. All over the Great Lakes the number of boats has declined, while their size makes only the largest and most sophisticated harbors accessible to them. But the few that still come, and a continually increasing fleet of pleasure boats, still respect Lake Michigan.

Although a great many sources, vessel registration records, newspapers, insurance records, and other materials were used in the compilation of these accounts, no claim is made that it is comprehensive. There remain at least a dozen accounts that could not be confirmed in any of the usual ways and had to be omitted. There are probably also wrecks along the shore that were never recorded.

The reader will notice that there are extensive quotations from old Life Saving Station reports and newspapers. Especially after the advent of the telegraph the old accounts were written in such colorful, dramatic style that printing the story as it would have appeared to contemporary readers is the best way to convey the excitement, the occasional horror and the sense of awe that surrounded navigation on Lake Michigan.

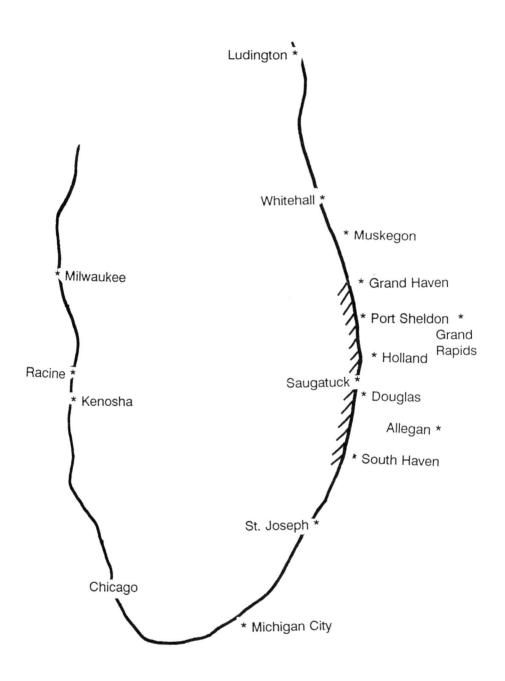

Ludington *

Whitehall *

* Muskegon

* Milwaukee

* Grand Haven

* Port Sheldon   *
              Grand
        * Holland Rapids

Racine *

Saugatuck *

* Kenosha

* Douglas

Allegan *

* South Haven

St. Joseph *

Chicago

* Michigan City

Southern Lake Michigan

First Recorded Wreck, A Capsized Canoe

1821
Near Grand Haven

Although settlement did not take place along the eastern shore of Lake Michigan until at least fifty years later, the first boat which stopped in at the mouth of the Grand River other than Indian canoes and trader's boats, was the British sloop **Felicity** which anchored a short distance up the river Sunday, October 31, 1776. The captain later reported that the harbor was 70 to 80 yards wide, and 2 to 4 fathoms (12 to 24 feet) deep. The first recorded wreck along the coast was a capsized Indian canoe in 1821. An Ottawa chief, his wife and son were returning from the Chicago Treaty powwow when a storm developed. Their canoe capsized and the wife and son were drowned.

The **Andrew** Leaves a Mystery

October, 1826
Mouth of the Grand River

In October of 1826 the schooner **Andrew** was driven ashore at the mouth of the Grand River after a failed attempt to enter the unimproved harbor. In the ship's cargo were 20 barrels of whiskey on their way to the trading post of Rix Robinson, near the intersection of the Grand and Thornapple rivers, where the settlement of Ada would later be constructed. Robinson salvaged the barrels that floated to shore following the wreck and buried them in the sand near the beach on what he hoped was safe ground. Some time later when he returned to claim his goods the dunes had shifted enough to obliterate the landmarks that he remembered and he failed to locate his goods. Legend had it that the barrels are still there, under the sand near the harbor mouth, waiting to be discovered by modern-day treasure hunters.

Riverboat on the Lake

1836
North of the Kalamazoo River

In 1836 a group of Kalamazoo businessmen built a vessel that was to be half of a daily service of freight and passenger traffic from Kalamazoo to the mouth of the river, where the goods and passengers could connect with boats that could carry them around the Great Lakes and beyond. If the boat had a name it has not been recorded.

She was built in 1836 by Lucius Lyon, Thomas C. Sheldon, Justus and Cyren Burdick, all investors in the plat of the town of Kalamazoo, and three storekeepers, Hosea Huston, Caleb Sherman and George W. Winslow. None of the owners had much nautical experience but they hired a Kalamazoo carpenter to construct a flat bottomed boat that could negotiate the shallow portions of the river and the rapids near Otsego.

The vessel was powered by steam and its primary task was to tow scows and log rafts to the mouth of the Kalamazoo. In addition to lumber and other wood products the Kalamazoo area was an early producer of flour. The prairie-like landscape of much land near the city did not need as much clearing as most Michigan land and was able to go into production with less delay.

The new river boat was launched in early 1836 and, according to early histories, one successful round trip was completed with Captain Albert Saxton in command, and part-owner George W. Winslow aboard. They experienced only minor difficulties with snags and low water. On the second journey the captain decided to test the craft on Lake Michigan possibly with his sights set on the settlement at Port Sheldon, near the mouth of the Pigeon River. If the boat was as flat-bottomed as county histories describe it is no wonder that the captain stayed near the shore on the trip north. There he either went aground on a bar or ran into enough difficulties that he beached the craft between the mouth of the Kalamazoo River and the mouth of the North Black River to the north (where Holland was later built). The boat was not salvageable, but the crew and passengers got safely ashore.

Because of the financial Panic of 1837, the investors were not in a position to make further attempts at navigation on the river and the idea of a powered vessel was abandoned for several years. Barrels of flour were sent downriver on poled flatboats. A poet named Drummond offered the following advice to river men who would attempt the larger waters:

> Now all good steamboat sailor men,
> Take warning by that storm
> And go and marry some nice French girl
> And live on one big farm.
> The wind can blow like hurricane
> And suppose she blow some more,
> You cannot drown on Lake Michigan
> So long you stay on shore.

Schooner **Laporte** Beached at South Haven

Fall, 1838
Near South Haven

The 150 ton, three masted schooner **Laporte** was wrecked in the fall of 1838 near where the south pier of South Haven harbor was later built. The vessel was commanded by Captain Webster. The settlement of South Haven was just getting underway, but the wrecked boat was discovered by Clark Pierce who had arrived in the area with his family earlier that year. A road between South Haven and Paw Paw had been opened in 1835 and Pierce carried the baggage of the sailors in his wagon to Paw Paw while the men traveled there on foot. The boat lay on the beach at the mercy of the waves all winter. In the spring what was left of the **Laporte** was burned by the owners for the iron fastenings. The schooner was nearly new at the time of her accident having been built at Buffalo, New York, in 1835.

Gov. Mason Unable to Navigate Big Lake

May 3, 1840
Mouth of the Grand River

In 1835 Lucius Lyon, one of the founders of Grand Rapids, and several friends and business associates including N. O. Sargeant and Richard Godfrey had a small riverboat constructed to establish regular steamboat traffic between Grand Rapids and the mouth of the river. The vessel was named **Gov. Mason** and her namesake, Michigan's governor Stevens T. Mason presented the boat with her first set of colors. She made her first run down the Grand River July 4, 1837, commanded by Captain William Stoddard.

In 1838 an early spring flood inundated most of downtown Grand Rapids and the **Gov. Mason** was carried inland and left high and dry about where the Union Depot was later built. At great effort and expense the vessel was repaired and returned to the river, but was never a success financially.

On May 2, 1840, the **Gov. Mason** had completed the run to Grand Haven and had on board several passengers eager to pay passage onward to Muskegon. After an overnight stay in Grand Haven she set forth on Lake Michigan but encountered a severe storm. The hapless river boat was washed back until nearly at the mouth of the Grand River she went ashore on a sandbar and was dashed to pieces by the wind and waves. The passengers and crew escaped uninjured.

Schooner Florida, Apples Ashore in Storm

November 18, 1842
North of South Haven

According to Captain O. W. Rowland, who wrote an account in the 1912 *History of Van Buren County*, the two masted schooner **Florida** went on the beach just to the north of the mouth of the Black River on the 18th day of November, 1840 (the captain missed in his recollecting by two years). The vessel's home port was Buffalo, New York, and she was attempting to deliver 700 barrels of apples and hardware when she was caught in a November snow storm. The **Florida** became disabled in the storm and was washed ashore just north of the river. The crew managed to get ashore, but nearly perished in the cold and snow attempting to find their way to Bangor.

The December 9, 1842, issue of the *Grand Rapids Enquirer* states tersely, "The schooner **Florida** went ashore at South Black River. No lives lost."

W. H. Hurlbut, who lived at Bangor at that time, afterwards planted an orchard of seedlings from apples procured from this vessel. One of the trees proved to be very valuable producing a large yellow fall apple with a slight blush on the sunny side and having a pleasant sub-acid flavor. Hurlbut named the apple the Floridan in honor of the wrecked vessel.

Mutiny Wrecks the **Milwaukie**

November 17, 1842
North of the Kalamazoo River

When the three masted schooner **Milwaukie** anchored off the mouth of the Kalamazoo River in mid November, 1842, the storm that would be her undoing was already brewing to the northwest. But, since it was impossible to enter the unimproved harbor, the captain insisted on casting off to reach the relative safety of Lake Michigan. The story of that night was later told in an 1891 issue of the *Lake Shore Commercial*, having as its source S. A. Morrison, who played a key role in events.

On the 16th of November, 1842, the **Milwaukie** anchored off the mouth of the Kalamazoo River, having received a partial cargo of flour at St. Joseph, and proceeded to take on between 400 and 500 barrels more that had been brought down the river from Kalamazoo.

The crew of the ship were incensed at the captain for stopping at this place on account of the danger of severe storms common on the lake at that season of the year. . . but no particular note was taken of the circumstance until later developments recalled it to memory.

The loading of the flour consumed all day, and it was long after dark before the **Milwaukie** hoisted anchor and set sail for Buffalo. About this time the wind suddenly shifted to the west and northwest and the temperature as suddenly fell below the freezing point. All night the cold wind whistled and shrieked about the old stone light house that sentineled the primitive harbor and just about the time the light of another day was breaking the inmates were aroused by an alarm at the door. A curious sight greeted Lightkeeper Nichols as he opened the door in response to the summons. Six forms that might have been taken for anything but human beings stood before him. Yet, human beings they were! Half insensible from the hardships they had undergone, uncouth, misshaped masses covered with ice and flour -- these were the only survivors of the crew of the ship that had loaded here the day before.

Stopping at the light house at this time was a young man named Alex Henderson. . . and he immediately started down the lake shore to ascertain the extent and location of the disaster, which the appearance of the survivors betokened. Some two miles north of the river he saw the big ship driven hard on the outer bar, and already beginning to break beneath the blows of the heavy seas. Here he also found another of the crew who had succeeded in reaching the shore, but was too far gone to make any effort to save himself, and who died soon after.

A short time before this an Indian squaw, travelling from Grand Haven to Saugatuck along the lake beach had noted the disaster and made haste to seek Mr. Morrison . . . who was familiar with the Indian dialect. To him she related what she had seen and a party was organized to go to the scene to render what assistance was possible. Nothing could be done, however, until the sea subsided and then it was found the captain and seven of the crew had perished from exposure on the boat.

According to a brief account in the December 2, 1842, *Grand Rapids Enquirer*, reprinted from the *Kalamazoo Gazette*:

> We understand that the ship **Milwaukie** left the mouth of the Kalamazoo, on Thursday, the 18th inst., for Buffalo, but the wind, which blew a gale, prevented her either from making an offing, or returning to the port, the channel being difficult of access. The vessel was driven ashore, a short distance from the mouth of the river where she broke in two, the sea making a complete breach over her. The crew comprised fifteen men, six of whom only were rescued; the other nine were either drowned, or perished from the cold. The names of the sufferers we have not heard.
> The **Milwaukie** had on board 1300 barrels of flour, 900 of which were owned by Mr. Walbridge of this town, and 400 by Mr. Bush of Allegan. A portion of this was insured.

While the snow still swirled George W. Holt of Buffalo, one of the owners of the **Milwaukie**; the agent who had loaded the flour at St. Joseph; and Henry Bishop of Schoolcraft, whose sister was the wife of Daniel C. Whittemore, the captain of the **Milwaukie**, headed for Singapore to learn the condition of the ship, to determine if anything could be salvaged and to see what disposition had been made of the bodies. Bishop reported events in a letter to an Allegan newspaper in 1894:

> We traveled in a light two-seated cutter, with a pair of good horses and were three days in making the journey from Schoolcraft to Saugatuck [where] we found the ship had been driven on to the beach sidewise and was embedded in solid ice up to the main deck.
> Six sailors had been saved by getting a line on shore by one of them, while Capt. Dan C. Whittemore, the first and second mate and six sailors had perished on the vessel . . . . The sailors that were saved all had on oil cloth overalls and jackets. This kept their bodies dry and is an item well worth knowing to others liable to be exposed to severe storms. We could get but little information from the sailors that were saved about the accident. It was evident that they had worked hard and long in getting the flour on board and had subsequently refused to work at the proper time to save the ship. I gathered some items from one young sailor who had assisted the officers in trying to get the ship started. This sailor informed me that they objected to leaving St. Joseph (sailors are apt to be superstitious). One reason he assigned for the sailors not wanting to leave St. Jo. was that the rats left the ship in large numbers whilst laying at the dock in the harbor. The sailor said they did not think it so strange until an old gray rat left, when they expected

something would happen to the ship if they continued on their voyage.

Another theory concerning the grounding was advanced by Captain Charles M. Link of the scow-schooner **Trio** who lived south of Saugatuck. He said, "The Captain of the **Milwaukie** wanted to make sail and get out to sea that night when the storm came on, but the crew were timid and would not move the ship. No doubt the Captain was killed by a man named Williams, one of the crew, for he was never seen again."

The flour was packed in barrels and much of it was only slightly damaged in the accident. A portion of the cargo was packed in a warehouse and later sent on to its destination. But another part of the cargo was salvaged by the residents near the mouth of the Kalamazoo River at Singapore and Saugatuck, who claim that if it were not for the food provided by the wreck of the **Milwaukie** many of the pioneer families would not have been able to survive the hard winter of 1842-43.

The sailing ship **Milwaukie** was built in 1836 at Grand Island, New York. She was enrolled at Buffalo, May 16, 1836, and measured 113 feet in length and 285.85 tons. Her owners were Bronson, Holt & Dousman. A steamer, also named **Milwaukie** was launched the following year at Grand Island and enrolled for the first time November 11, 1837, measuring 172 feet in length and 401.40 tons. This vessel was wrecked near Milwaukee in 1841. Because of the similarity of names and dates, the two vessels are often confused. It was the full-rigged ship that called at Singapore.

The Pathway to Safety

November 19-24, 1842
At the Mouth of Grand Haven Harbor

The storm that sank the **Milwaukie** and **Florida** was seriously felt farther north. A dispatch from Grand Haven, dated November 24, 1842, was printed in the December 2, 1842, issue of the *Grand Rapids Enquirer*, which reported, "Such a storm has never before been recorded in the annuals of the Peninsular State. It commenced on the 17th ultime., and continued for several days. The snow fell rapidly and the wind blew almost a hurricane the first 48 hours, since which the snow has continued to fall, occasionally, and is now probably three feet deep on a level." Through the snowflakes the residents of Grand Haven watched the drama:

> The first vessel that made her appearance here was the **Wave**, Capt. Butterfield. She came in on Saturday, the 19th, from Southport, which place she left on the Monday previous for Muskegon. Capt. B. says he never experienced a gale more severe. The snow falling in such quantities, prevented his making harbor before, or even discerning land.
>
> On the following day a vessel was seen making for this port, which proved to be the **Columbia**, with lumber from Muskegon for Chicago. She sprung a leak the first night of the gale, off Southport. The crew consisted of two men and a boy. The men stood their regular tricks at the helm and bucket. They were able to keep her free by bailing constantly, until the last day they were out, when it rapidly increased

upon them. Discovering land at this place they shaped their course for the river, but coming in, owing to the heavy sea and her unmanageable condition struck the bar and went ashore. Capt. Noyes of the **Crook** and Capt. Butterfield, with some of their men, true-hearted sailor-like, at the risk of their own lives, put off in a boat to the relief of their brother sailors, and brought them ashore in safety. . .

On Tuesday of this week we saw for the first time from this place, a vessel that had been dismasted, driven about by the wind and sea, the only sail her topsail, hung to a jury mast, which the crew had rigged during the gale. They could not make the harbor, the wind not being fair for them, as they were obliged to keep before it. They anchored a little south of the mouth of the river. Capt. Noyes and Butterfield went out to them, found the vessel to be the **Solomon Juneau**, Captain Jeffries, Master. They made another effort to get into harbor, but failed; cast their anchor, but not holding them, they drifted off. For the last two days they have been near here, with no very pleasant prospect before them. This afternoon the wind changed to westward and brought then safe into port. The vessel's masts were thrown out by the heavy sea, on Wednesday night (the 16th) near Twin Rivers, eight days since. I should think no one would envy the sailor after viewing the condition of this craft, shattered and covered with ice, without masts, anchor or sails. . . the vessel was loaded for Chicago, St. Joseph and Michigan City with apples and salt.

Whitney Capsized by Spring Storm

March 17, 1844
Near the Kalamazoo River

The merchant schooner **Daniel Whitney** (some accounts call it the **David Whitney**) in command of Captain Crooker, was lost in March of 1844, but the details of her fate were slow in being confirmed. The April 5, 1844, issue of the *Cleveland Herald* reported only:

The gale of Lake Michigan on March 17 not only wrecked several vessels, but also probably, destroyed numerous lives. The extent of the damage to the shipping by the gale cannot be estimated, as many vessels ventured out on the day previous to the storm from Chicago, Milwaukee and other ports on the lake.

Capt. Jackson of the schooner **Warren** arrived at Chicago before the **Margaret Helm** left. He stated that the schooner **Whitney** left Grand River ahead of him, but had not been heard of and is supposed to be lost.

Another week passed as the family of the crew members anxiously scanned the horizon and the newspapers. The August 14 issue of the *Chicago Journal* had further news:

> Schooner **Daniel Whitney**. Capt. Crooker (formerly of Bath, Maine) from Kalamazoo with bark, is supposed to have been capsized in the squall last Friday night, and all on board lost. The vessel's galleys, bulwarks, hatches, etc., have drifted ashore, also one of the seamen's caps.

Confirmation came the following week when the *Journal* noted:

> Schooner **David Whitney** -- The schooner **Lafayette** fell in with this vessel bottom up about six miles northwest of Kalamazoo on Wednesday last, and with the assistance of the **Margaret Smith**, succeeded in righting her and towing her into Kalamazoo. The body of Mr. House, a passenger, was found under the deck in the hold of the vessel, and that of the cabin-boy under the cabin floor. There were four persons on board, all of who have perished. From appearances, the **Whitney** must have been hove to under a close-reefed mainsail and jib at the time she capsized. The mainsail was split, which probably caused the accident.

Adventures of the **Mint**

November, 1844
Near the mouth of the Kalamazoo River

The notes of a 1907 interview of Captain Charles M. Link of Pier Cove with local historian Henry Hudson Hutchins of Ganges, talk of another shipwreck, and a boat with a history. The handwritten notes read:

> Late in November, 1844, I was a passenger on board the schooner **Mint** bound from the mouth of the Kalamazoo River to Chicago. There was a strong west wind blowing and we had to make northard until off Port Sheldon. The wind blew so stormy we turned back for the Kalamazoo. Missed the river and were blown high and dry on the beach just south of the mouth. Two other schooners the **Jessie Smith** and a scow had gone ashore there the same night but previous to our return. The **Mint** was a gun boat during the War of 1812. Was sunk at Sacketts Harbor, Lake Ontario, either in battle or to prevent capture and was not raised until 1839. Said to have been stranded and broken up south of the entrance to the Calumet harbor in 1850.

Because of the handwriting it is hard to be sure if interviewer Hutchins is writing

Mint or Mink. No record of a schooner **Mint** can be found in accounts of the War of 1812, but a schooner named **Mink** owned by the Northwest Company, was captured in 1814 by a fleet under the command of Captain Arthur Sinclair. The **Mink** was transporting a cargo of flour from Mackinac Island to St. Mary's, at the foot of Lake Superior, with plans for eventual shipment of the cargo to forts on Lake Superior. With intelligence gained from the capture of the **Mink**, Sinclair went on to capture the schooner **Perseverance**, which was first burned by the enemy, then seriously damaged in an effort to take her over the falls at St. Mary's and eventually burned by American forces to keep her out of the hands of the English. One list of boats notes that a schooner, **E. Mint**, was in commission 1845 but lost in 1850.

Marvin Capsizes, All Lost

May 23, 1851
Off Grand Haven

The merchant schooner **Sylvanus Marvin**, was not far off the mouth of the Grand River at Grand Haven when she filled with water and capsized taking all nine aboard to a watery death.

An enrollment dated May 27, 1844, lists her as having been built at Milwaukee and measuring 65 feet in length, 18.10 feet in beam and 64.63 tons. Later sources list her as built at Little Fort (Waukegan) and 73 tons. In 1847 she was owned by John F. Guyles, Mordecai J. Brown and Jeremiah G. Brown, all of Little Fort, Lake County, Illinois. She sailed on Lake Michigan from Muskegon to Chicago, then, after 1848, from Manistee to Milwaukee in the lumber trade.

Schooner **Helena** Driven Ashore

October 2, 1851
Near the Mouth of the Kalamazoo River

Improvements to the harbors of western Michigan came only slowly and after many petitions. In the October 15, 1851, issue of the *Grand River Times*, a weekly newspaper published at Grand Haven with Democratic leanings, the editor chides the party in power:

> We learn that the schooner **Helena** was driven ashore near the mouth of the Kalamazoo River, on the night of the 2d inst. and completely destroyed by being broken to pieces. Passengers and crew all saved with more or less suffering. When will our Whig Administration give us harbors? We pause for a reply.

Two Saved After **Mary Margaret** Wrecks

May 30, 1853
North of Grand Haven

In the spring of 1853 the captain and a passenger were rescued after two days in the partially submerged cabin of the **Mary Margaret**, a schooner from Michigan City, Indiana. Two crewmen were less fortunate. According to an account in Leo C. Lillie's *Historic Grand Haven and Ottawa County*:

> On June 1, 1853, a peculiar lake disaster occurred about eight miles northwest of Grand Haven. A schooner was founding lying on her beams end. When she was discovered by the crew of the **G. H. Roberts**, a voice was heard from the cabin. An opening was immediately cut through the vessel's side. Her Captain Andrew Bergh and Mr. Lukas A. Farnsworth, a passenger and part owner of the boat, were saved from a lingering and horrible death.
>
> The schooner proved to be the **Mary Margaret** of Michigan City. which left Muskegon Sunday evening May 29th, with six persons on board on its way to Grand Haven. At 12 o'clock Capt. Bergh had left the deck in charge of Joseph Ermity and William Johnson, with strict orders to be called on the least change in the weather. The wind was then light and the weather clearing up.
>
> About 2 o'clock he was awakened by a noise on deck, sprang from his berth, and reached the deck just as his vessel was capsizing. She turned bottom up, carried Capt. Bergh over her deck, but he succeeded in working his way into the cabin. The vessel was 4 or 5 miles from land when she capsized. Capt. Bergh found Mr. Farnsworth and two of the crew, Zacharius Nelson and Charles Plumb, in the cabin. In order to keep their heads out of the water, the four were obliged to huddle themselves into one berth where they could with difficulty maintain their position. On Monday Nelson and Plumb became exhausted, released their holds, fell into the water and were drowned. The other two remained in their precarious situation until Wednesday noon when they were rescued.

The rescuing boat was unable to take the schooner in tow and the vessel floated around Lake Michigan for more than a week until it was rediscovered by the **Telegraph**. The **Mary Margaret** was then towed to Stoney Creek, about 35 miles north of Grand Haven, where the bodies of the two drowned crewmen were removed from the cabin and buried.

The schooner was later salvaged and returned to service.

Sloop **Ritchie** Capsizes, One Dead

July 25, 1853
Near Holland

In 1847 the Rev. A. C. Van Raalte determined to set up a new home for his congregation near the head of Black Lake, and thus began the West Michigan town of Holland. It grew very rapidly, by 1853 there were several thousand people in Holland and several other communities around it, which were also founded by large groups of people seeking to avoid the religious persecution of the homeland. Although "the colony" voted early in the process of settlement to purchase their own boat, the **Knickerbocker** the transportation of goods and passenger service to this large, and growing settlement, attracted many independent operators. That was apparently the intent of the sloop **Ritchie** when she was lost near the mouth of the Black River on July 25, 1853. The August 3, 1853, issue of the *Grand River Times* describes the incident:

> On Monday of last week the sloop **Ritchie** capsized near the outlet of Black Lake. Three persons were on board, one of whom, Rufus Aton, formerly of Pennsylvania, was drowned. The **Ritchie** is a small coaster and had sailed on that day from this port [Grand Haven] to Black Lake.

After the accident, the sloop **Ritchie** was salvaged, repaired, and returned to service.

French Anna Loses a Passenger

September 22, 1853
Off Port Sheldon

Great Lakes fishing boats had to go where the fish could be caught. In the early fall of 1853 a trip around the lower peninsula of Michigan was fatal to one Lake Huron fisherman. The *Grand River Times* for September 28, 1853, tells his story:

> On Thursday, the 22nd inst. Henry Merriman of Flint, Genesee Co., was accidentally drowned in the lake a few miles from this place. Mr. M. and two others left this port for Chicago in the **French Anna**, a small fishing vessel from Saginaw. In the evening, about 9 o'clock, when three miles off Port Sheldon, he was struck by the boom and knocked overboard. -- The wind was blowing fresh, the sea was rough and all attempts to discover the lost man proved unavailing. The vessel and those on board had recently come from Saginaw. The deceased was about 21 years of age. His parents reside in Flint. The body has not yet been recovered.

The Three Lives of the **Rocky Mountain**

November 16, 1853
Near Grand Haven

The schooner **Rocky Mountain** was frequently in trouble, but always seemed to bounce back. The November 19, 1853, issue of the *Grand River Times*, printed a story copied for the *Chicago Democratic Press*:

> The schooner **Rocky Mountain** of Cleveland, Capt. O. Stentam, lost her rudder off the mouth of the Kalamazoo River on Wednesday last in a blow and went ashore near the mouth of that river. The Captain and crew had hard work to run her ashore as she was half full of water when she struck. She was *"flying light"* and was insured for $2,000. A protest has been entered for the recovery of the insurance.

But the schooner was apparently raised instead, because in April of 1854 the *Grand River Times* again reported that she was ashore. This time near Grand Haven. In the same storm the schooners **Henry Clay, Maine, Traveler, President** and **Baltic** had gone ashore at Muskegon. Before paying claims on the insurance for the vessels several Chicago insurance companies sent the tug **Eclipse** up the coast to see if the schooners could be refloated. By the time of the report the **Henry Clay, Maine** and **Traveler** were already afloat and the others waiting their turn.

The tug must have succeeded with the **Rocky Mountain** as well because the April 28, 1854, issue of the *Chicago Journal* reported the final demise of the schooner. She had missed Chicago harbor with a load of lumber and struck the breakwater near the American Car Works "and was ground almost instantly to pieces." The final owner of the **Rocky Mountain** was John B. Weir of Chicago.

Schooner **Hunt** Aground and Abandoned

November 23, 1853
Mouth of Grand River

A quick turn of the weather could easily spell curtains for a beached schooner, in mid-November it was the schooner **Hunt**. According to the November 23, 1853, issue of the *Grand River Times*:

> The schooner **Hunt**, which went aground at the mouth of the river, a few days since, has been stripped and abandoned. She was owned, as we have been informed, by a firm in Chicago.

The **Humming Bird** Explodes

September 2, 1854
On the Grand River

Humming Bird was a little steamer built by Henry Steele at Steele's Landing (later Lamont), a small town downriver from Grand Rapids, specifically for river use. The boat was the forerunner of the modern catamarans. It was constructed on two canoes (some accounts say scows) that were decked over to prevent swamping, with a paddlewheel between them. Motive power was furnished by an engine that had been salvaged from the State Salt Well below Grand Rapids. The **Humming Bird** was launched in August of 1847 and commanded by Captain Willard Sibley.

She became part of the riverboat fleet on the Grand River in 1847, the year a canal was built around the rapids. For several years she ran upriver, from Grand Rapids to Ionia and Lyons, with the **Empire** and **Algoma** supplying the downriver route from Grand Rapids to Grand Haven. The little steamboat was purchased in 1849 by Robert S. Parks who later constructed boats for the Illinois Canal. In 1853 the **Humming Bird** began work on the downriver run. In 1854 there was low water in the river and the larger **Algoma** which ran to Grand Haven could only get as far upriver as Steele's Landing.

On September 2, 1854, the **Humming Bird** had picked up passengers from the **Algoma** and was headed for Grand Rapids when there was an explosion. The day was described in the September 6 *Grand Rapids Inquirer*:

> Many of our citizens were startled about five P. M. on Saturday last by a report which sounded like a cannon, and apparently some distances from the city. A messenger soon arrived from Capt. Collier of the steamer **Algoma** stating that the steamer **Humming Bird,** Capt. Grady, on her upward trip had exploded her boiler about seven miles below the city, nearly opposite the Bemis farm and requesting immediate assistance. The fact that many of our prominent citizens who were engaged down the river and in Chicago lumbering generally return on Saturday from their week's avocations caused a feeling of anxiety and gloom to spread over the city until the particulars were learned. Immediately after the dispatch arrived Mr. Gall of the G. R. Trans. Co. dispatched teams and physicians to the scene of disaster and others of our citizens also drove down in order to render any aid that might be required. On examination the result was found not as disastrous as at first supposed. The **Humming Bird** was steaming at her usual rate, having a scow in tow, and on board about twenty-five passengers taken from the **Algoma** at Steele's Landing, that being as far up the river in the present stage of water as the **Algoma** can with ease run.
>
> From Mr. Damon Hatch of this city, we glean the following particulars: Mr. H. with Captain Collins and others were seated on the bow of the boat and had noticed what appeared to be some disarrangement in the top of the steam chest and the bubbles were

playing around the centre, which was apparently very hot. At about the same time a boy supposed to be the one killed, was observed to move the weight that balances the safety valve, *to the extreme end of the lever*, almost immediately a report ensued, and Mr. H. found himself in the river in water over his head. After scrambling on board of the scow with the assistance of the pilot, Mr. James Marshall, himself with Capt. Collins and others, applied themselves to the work of ascertaining the extent of the damage.

Most miraculous to relate only one was killed, John McMunn, aged about sixteen, who with the pilot were standing at the wheel. He was blown about eight rods forward into the river and taken out dead. Marshall was also blown into the river, had his collar bone dislocated, and was scalded somewhat. The impression is prevalent that there was little or no water in the boiler and the explosion, the result of gross negligence on the part of the engineer. At all events the Transportation Co. owes it to themselves and the public to fully investigate the cause of the disaster, and promptly discharge from their employ, those by whose carelessness the accident occurred. Many of the passengers were either forced by the concussion, or jumped, into the river, but all were rescued. Mr. Damon Hatch lost one wallet containing thirty dollars and another with some two hundred more in, was fished up by one of the boat hands, Mr. Robbins, a lad some sixteen years of age, and restored to the owner.

This is the first explosion that has taken place on the river, during the eighteen years in which steamers have plied upon its bosom and it is truly miraculous that this was no worse, in fact, the wonder is that all on board were not instantly killed.

The incident has become part of Grand Rapids' legend. According to Grand Rapids historian Charles E. Belknap, "There is a tradition that the engineer of this boat made a practice of hanging his hat on the safety valve and one day in a burst of speed it blew up just before it reached the city. On board was a cargo of Illinois Red Eye and Cyclone Buster from Missouri. Some of this stuff blazed when it came in contact with the river water and the next run of mullet, the story ran, had red noses. The fishermen claimed it was due to the spread of the **Humming Bird's** cargo; others said it was a fish story circulated by John B. Goff a temperance advocate who was stirring up the people about that time."

Stuart Breaks in Two

November 6, 1854
North of Grand Haven Harbor

At Grand Haven it often happened that a boat stuck on one of the bars near the harbor's mouth had plenty of company. That's how it was on November 6, 1854. The *Grand River Times* for November 8, 1854, reported:

During the gale on Monday night of this week four schooners, the **Lizzie Throop** of this place, the **Twin Brothers** of Chicago, the **Eno** of Detroit and the **Ellen Stuart** of Chicago went ashore at the mouth of the river on the north side.

The **E. Stuart** was owned by A. H. Covert of Chicago and is hopelessly lost being broken in two and sunk so as to be mostly under water. She was insured to the amount of $3,000. Her cargo consisting of iron, coal and water lime, was partly insured. The crew remained on board from the time she sunk in the forepart of the night until ten o'clock of the next day, at which time they were taken off with the life boat belonging to the propeller **Ottawa**. The sea was very rough at the time, and several ineffectual attempts had previously been made to reach them with a yawl and Mackinaw boats. Those who finally succeeded in making the rescue, Robert Getty and three others whose names are not known to us, receive, and most deservedly too, the highest praise for their skill as well as daring with which they accomplished the perilous achievement.

The **Eno** was pulled off the bar on November 12, the **Twin Brothers** and **Throop** were saved the following day. Nothing could be done for the **Stuart**.

May Flower Sinks in the Kalamazoo

October, 1854
Kalamazoo River

Without a picture, or a more complete description, it is hard to tell what made the wreck of the river steamer **May Flower** so difficult to deal with. The accident was reported in the October 17, 1854, issue of the *Grand Haven News*:

> The steamer **May Flower** owned by Harwood and Bentley of Muskegon, running on the Kalamazoo River, struck a snag sixteen miles below Allegan and sunk in twelve feet of water.

Sixteen miles below Allegan would put the accident in the bayou between Bear and Swan Creeks. Records are unclear whether the entire boat was later raised, or only the engines became part of a new **May Flower** that was launched in Muskegon in the early 1860s and used as a ferryboat around the Muskegon harbor.

A Stormy Day at Grand Haven

October 26, 1855
Entrance to Grand Haven Harbor

Unlike Saugatuck and Holland, where the settlements are several miles upriver from the point where the river actually enters Lake Michigan, portions of the early settlement of Grand Haven was within sight of the harbor mouth. The travails of boats attempting to enter the breakwaters in bad weather were often witnessed by a large crowd. In the October 31, 1855, issue of the *Grand River Times* the editor describes a stormy time as the very life of a schooner, and sometimes even her crew, depended on a single favorable toss of the surf at a crucial moment:

Lake Michigan has had another scathing. Only a week ago a terrible gale swept over it, and again on Thursday night and Friday night another hurricane lashed it into foam. Our lumbering fleet have this time suffered severely. The howling of the storm on Thursday night called loudly for sympathy for those exposed to its fury and early Friday morning anxious eyes were watching the entrance to our harbor.

As soon as it was light enough to see, we found that three vessels had entered the harbor safely. The schooner **Julia Smith**, next the brig **Susan A. Clark**, next the schooner **Magic**. On the north bar, the heavy sea making a clean sweep over them, were the schooners, **Two Charlies**, Capt Lalotte, **Lady Jane**, Capt. Henderson, and **William Tell**, Capt. Steketee. Nine vessels and one steamer were in the offing, struggling against a sea that rolled fearfully, occasionally burying them from sight by the lashing foam and spray. The wind was "close" to use sailor parlance, for entering the harbor, but the attempt must be made.

The schooner **Helgoland**, Capt. Loutit, came first, under all the sail that she dare show to the storm. It was an exciting scene to see them near the bar against fearful odds. Three already on, and a narrow channel to keep, or share their fate. The sea on the bar repeatedly buried the **Helgoland** from sight, but she weathered it and came in all right. The schooner **Liverpool** followed in her wake closely, but was short of sail -- if we can judge of such matters -- and stemmed the contending elements slowly, when nearly in she touched the north bar, payed off and dashed ashore near the **Two Charlies**.

The steamer **Ottawa**, Capt. Dalton, next made the attempt; but on nearing the harbor and witnessing the dangerous struggle she must encounter, stood out again to get a heavy head of steam before making the attempt; a part of her smoke stack had been blown off -- a kind of reef not to her advantage in a struggle for life -- soon she was pointed to the harbor; twice she was deluged to her pilot house, but she made a straight wake into smooth water, much to the credit of the judgment of the commander. The **Henderson**, Capt. Peterson, (an old Salt) and the **New Hampshire**, Capt. Tart (one of our boys) made for the harbor in company. They were both managed skillfully making port in safety. Captain Peterson afterwards said, "an old Salt like me, should not receive credit; but when a boy can handle a vessel as the **New Hampshire** was handled, *he* deserves it."

The **Illinois**, Capt. Burke, came next; gallantly she dashed along, came over the bar, struck, payed off and was hurled against the **Two**

Charlies, carrying away her stanchions by the action of the sea, endangering both vessels. Being in deeper water, by timely setting sail as the sea lifted her around, Capt. Burke brought her in with only the additional loss of the topsail, that being blown from the bolt ropes in attempting to set it. Schooner **Frances**, Capt. Mathes, was too far north, and could not fetch, and was piled up near the **Lady Jane**. Schooner **Home** struck about half way in, payed off and went ashore. Schooner **Ocean**, Capt. Miller, with his usual good luck made good weather of it, and went flying up the river with a "hurrah for Harry Bluff." The schooner **Falcon**, too far north, could not make the harbor, went ashore near the **Frances**, and broke in two. The **Little Belle**, Capt. Payne, found he could not make a sure thing of it, stood out, and though carrying a heavy press of canvass could not weather the beach, went ashore near Point au Sauble, five miles north of this place. Schooler **Telegraph**, Capt. McNamara, came on to the bar, struck and by skillful seamanship her topsail was set aback when she payed off, heading out into the lake, and slowly worked off into deep water and stood down the lake, coming into port in the afternoon. The **Lizzie Throop**, Capt. Furlong, stood out and down the lake and came in all right next morning.

It has been a fearful time for sailors. At this port there were no lives lost. Seven vessels now lie on the bar.

There was similar carnage all over Lake Michigan during the storm. Seven vessels were reported the same day ashore at Muskegon. The schooner **Kitty Grant** capsized on the lake, losing a crew of four.

Of the boats run aground at Grand Haven the only ones that occur on later lists indicating that they were totally lost that day were the **Home**, **Falcon** and the **Liverpool**. The others were eventually salvaged.

Rescuing the Crew of the **Lodi**

November 22, 1855
South of Grand Haven

Before the U. S. Life Saving stations were established on the Great Lakes the government assistance was limited to the placing of life boats at established ports, usually in the charge of a specific caretaker. It was one of these boats that figured in the dramatic rescue of the crew of the schooner **Lodi**. The story unfolds in the *Grand River Times* for November 28, 1855:

The schooner **Lodi**, which left this port on Tuesday last, freighted with lumber for Chicago, after being driven by force of adverse wind and wave to the opposite shore of the Lake to her imminent peril, and unable to reach her destination, was at length obliged to return hither, and in attempting to enter the harbor she struck upon the south

21

bar, having become unmanageable on account of the frozen condition of her sails.

After striking the bar, the sea, which was rolling in tremendous swells, made a clean sweep over her decks, filling hold and cabin to their utmost capacity, so that her crew, consisting of five men, were obliged to seek refuge on the most elevated part of the stern, as she lay in a careening position, and then, with the foam-capped surges dashing over them in their fury, did these unfortunate men with suppliant gestures beckon to our citizens for succor; nor was the appeal in vain.

Capt. Dalton, of the propellor **Ottawa**, immediately manned the life boat belonging to the steamer, and though the attempt appeared futile and fraught with extreme peril, yet he boldly started to the rescue. But the breakers proved too much for a craft so light, and notwithstanding the most vigorous exertions of her crew, she was carried with immense velocity far to the leeward of the stranded vessel, and no effort on their part could enable them to reach those who were watching with most intense interest and agonizing suspense, every motion made for their relief; and as they saw the utter failure of this attempt, hope had well nigh fled, and the dark waves look to them like a pall about to be thrown over their lifeless forms. It was even whispered among the brave Captains and sailors on shore, who were witnesses of the abortive attempt to reach those whose lives were in such fearful jeopardy, that all further attempt was useless, and though the vessel had now drifted within a few yards of the shore, yet those brave and warm-hearted comrades must perish.

"But no," says Capt. Harry Smith, "I will rescue them or perish in the attempt. It shall never be said that I saw five bold hearts thus pleading for succor and turned my back upon them and left them to find a watery grave."

The Government life boat is manned with as bold a Captain and crew as ever trod the vessel's deck, and with strong arm and determined spirit they pull to the rescue; now rising high on white crested wave, now sinking from view in the deep troughs of the tumultuous waters. At length the wreck is gained. Though benumbed with cold, and wearied with the almost superhuman efforts to retain their hold upon the sinking wreck, joy seems to quicken their feeble pulse and their stiffened limbs receive new strength, as with the assistance of their deliverers the unfortunate sufferers reach the boat. And now the strong oar vigorously plies for the shore, and the life boat, though filled with water by the dashing surges, bravely buffets them and reaches her destination in safety with her precious burden. They are rescued.

Many a one amid those anxious spectators stands ready to grasp the hands of those whose hearts failed them not in time of peril, but freely risked their own to save the lives of their comrades. Such noble bravery, such disinterested benevolence, truly merited a reward. And our citizens with their characteristic benevolence bestowed upon them a tangible memento, assuring them that a deed of daring like that just accomplished, was duly appreciated by them, and should not go unrewarded. A purse of ninety dollars was immediately made up for the Captain and crew. This, in addition to the consciousness of having saved five of their fellows from the yawning waves, must be a source of gratification of the most pleasing character to those favored with its possession. The names of the *braves* are as follows:

Capt. Smith, Commander of the life boat, James Marvill, John Dailey, Ralph Coventry, Eli Duvernay, James Prindle, and Mr. Lucas, mate of schooner **Transit.**

Vermont Gets Lost in a Storm

December 10, 1855
Near Pigeon Creek

The schooner **Vermont** was used largely in the tannery trade, transporting raw hides to be tanned from Chicago to Grand Haven, and the finished product back to market, when she lost her way during a fall storm in 1855. The incident was reported in the December 12, 1855, issue of the *Grand River Times*:

The schooner **Vermont**, owned by C. B. Albee, Esq., of this village, was run ashore on Sunday afternoon last, about six miles south of the mouth of Grand River. The **Vermont** left Chicago on Saturday at 1 o'clock P. M., with a fair wind for this port. She made the light at the entrance of the harbor some time in the latter part of the night, but the wind blowing a fearful gale, it was impossible to keep the light in view without danger of a too near approach to land. In the morning, owing to the unfortunate condition of the atmosphere for an extended view, no land could be descried. Not knowing, therefore, the exact position of the vessel, in respect to the shore, and the wind suddenly veering to the northward, accompanied with a fearful tempest of snow, it was judged dangerous by the owner, who chanced to be on board, for the vessel longer to retain the position she then occupied. By the consent of Captain Getty it was resolved, in order to save life, to head her for the shore, enter the harbor if possible, if not, to run for the nearest point thereto, where there existed the best possible chance for saving the lives of passengers and crew. She was accordingly headed for the land and ran on the beach near Pigeon Creek. A line was immediately taken ashore and as securely fastened as possible, to enable those on board to reach the shore in safety, which they succeeded in effecting by means of a smaller rope and basket, and arrived at our village on Sunday evening about 5 o'clock P.M., in an exhausted condition.

The **Vermont** was very heavily laden, having on board 2700 bushels of corn, for Messrs. White of Grand Haven, and Hopkins & Brothers of Mill Point; 1000 bushels of oats, some $2,000 dollars worth of hides, a quantity of pork and beef, besides other articles of merchandise less valuable, belonging to Mr. Albee. The grain will prove a total loss, most of it having already been washed out of the vessel into the lake. A portion of the hides will doubtless be recovered. No hopes are entertained of saving the vessel. No insurance on vessel or cargo.

The life line, which allowed all on board to reach shore safely, was set by First Mate Richard Connell who dove into the surf and swam ashore with a rope. Eleven years later Connell became the first captain of the Grand Haven Life-saving Station.

Caledonia Goes Over; Six Die

September 17, 1856
Off Grand Haven

The schooner **Caledonia** capsized attempting to enter Grand Haven in a gale. The intriguing thing about the newspaper story, which reads like an eye witness account, is that there are no reports about the people on shore seeing, even for a brief time, any of the six crew members that were lost with the boat. In September often the water was still warm enough to give men a chance for survival if they were good swimmers, or managed to catch something that would float. The *Grand River Times* describes the day:

> On Wednesday evening last, commenced one of the fiercest gales that has ever visited Lake Michigan. The wind breezed up freshly from the west, during the afternoon of Wednesday, and ere midnight had risen to a furious gale, which increased in violence as the morning of Thursday approached the dawn, and continued with unabated vigor, not only through that day, but the following night, and manifested but little abatement till Friday morning.
>
> On Thursday morning the **Ottawa** presented herself in the offing to the view of hundreds of anxious spectators watching with intense interest the unequal contest of the gallant boat with the madly surging waves that were furiously tossing their foam-capped crests high in air, and though like mountains they rolled threateningly along striking the noble craft with the force of a maddened giant -- yet under the guidance of her skillful captain and crew she conquered every impediment, surmounted every danger, and was moored safely at her dock.
>
> During the day a number of vessels, outgeneraling the fury of the gale, came into port, none of them having suffered material damage.
>
> About four o'clock the schooner **Caledonia** of Chicago, in attempting to enter port struck the bar and was almost instantly capsized when within a few yards of the mouth of the river. The captain and crew, consisting of six men, as nearly as can be ascertained, were drowned. She was owned by Captain Day, then on board -- was a new boat -- had been engaged in the Lower Lakes trade -- was at the

commencement of the gale a little to the north of us, taking in a cargo of wood, but to escape the fury of the elements directed her course to this harbor, where the melancholy accident occurred. In an hour or two after the disaster the vessel was broken up by the fury of the waves, and portions floated ashore.

Just at evening the schooner **Storm** was beached a little north of the mouth of the river. The crew succeeded in reaching the shore in safety next morning.

Also in peril during the storm was the propeller **J. Barber** which had left Grand Haven Wednesday and sought refuge at St. Joseph after damage to her steam pipes and the propeller **Foss** which sprang a leak on Thursday and was run ashore near the mouth of the Kalamazoo, where the brig **Sandusky** was also grounded.

Hull of **Forest City** Found in Lake

November 22, 1857
Near Pier Cove

According to the *Allegan Journal* for November 30, 1857:

On Sunday, the 22nd inst. came ashore at the first bar about half a mile south of Ganges (Pier Cove) pier. Her name is the **Forest City** and she was loaded with grindstones, fish, &c. She was from Port Huron and when she came on shore had not a soul on board -- probably all hands lost. Her masts and rigging are mostly carried away. A skiff was obtained when she grounded and R. B. Robinson with great difficulty boarded her but the sea was so violent at the time that a close examination was impossible. She was probably bound for Chicago.

The same paper notes that, "A body came ashore at the mouth of the River last week -- name unknown." Broken pieces of grindstones are sometimes still found in the Pier Cove area after storms and during low water.

Schooner **Globe** Founders

December 14, 1858
South of Saugatuck

Prior to 1859 when the Goodrich steamer **Huron** began regular passenger service, the most common way to go to Chicago and elsewhere on the Great Lakes was to book passage on a schooner. There were several passengers when the scow-schooner **Globe** went to pieces in Lake Michigan near Newark (Newark is an old name for Saugatuck). The story is told in the *Allegan Journal*:

25

After our paper had gone to press last week we received from F. B. Wallin, Esq., of Newark, the particulars of the loss of the Schooner **Globe**. It appears that this vessel left the Mouth of the Kalamazoo River Saturday night, Dec. 14th, with the Captain and owner of the vessel, Nelson Olsen and his brother, of Newark, one seaman, a single man and a married man with wife and two children as passengers on board.

She had as freight, lumber and lath, belonging to Mr. Parish of Silver Creek, and about $850 worth of leather from the tannery of C. C. Wallin and Sons. Mr. S. A. Morrison had also placed $100 in the Captain's care for some person in Chicago. As soon as fears were entertained of the Schooner's safety Mr. Wallin started in search along the beach for the wreck, and after he had proceeded a short distance found fragments of the vessel which had drifted ashore. It is thought the vessel must have been unseaworthy, though the Captain supposed she was strong and tight. All the circumstances seem to indicate that she split during Saturday night or Sunday morning, as the wreck was on the beach early Monday morning.

Mr. W. informs us that the Captain had been in America and on the Lakes seven years and was a man of good character. The brothers came with their parents from Norway last Summer. But little is known of the other persons.

Schooner **Minnesota** on Bar

March 29, 1859
At Mouth of Grand River

Two more boats on the infamous Grand Haven bar made the newspaper columns after a storm in March, 1859. It was reported by the March 23, 1859, *Grand Haven News*:

Vessels on the Bar -- Standing on the dock this morning we noticed two vessels on the South bar, at the mouth of the river. The brig **Portland** and the schooner **Minnesota**. The brig had on board a full load of lumber, and is reported to be much injured, full of water and it is a matter of doubt whether she can be saved. The schooner will probably be got off without material damage.

Enterprise Returns to Start of Voyage

April 15, 1859
Mouth of River, Grand Haven

The schooner **Enterprise** was on her way to Michigan City, Indiana, with a cargo of seasoned lumber and plaster loaded at Grand Haven on April 15, 1859 when she encountered high seas in a heavy gale.

According to an account in the Wednesday, April 20, 1859, *St. Joseph Traveler*:

> In the heavy gale of Friday last the schooner **Enterprise** of Wilkinson City (near New Buffalo) ran ashore making the harbor at Grand Haven and broke in two. She was heavily laden with plaster for Michigan City. The gale struck her opposite this port, and forced her back to Grand Haven where she ran ashore as above stated. The vessel and cargo are a total loss. The crew was saved.

Even after the grounding there was some hope that the vessel might be saved. However, the *Grand Haven News* for May 4, 1859 reported:

> The schooner **Enterprise** -- beached at this port a few days since -- has been abandoned after an unsuccessful attempt to get her off. Two steam pumps; vigorously applied had no available effect. She is a total loss.

Sole Survivor Rescued From **Euphemia**

May 26-28, 1859
Off Black Lake

The schooner **Euphemia**, wrecked in a gale on Lake Michigan the last week of May, 1859. The wreck floated along the shore and was finally spotted off Black Lake, at the head of Holland harbor on May 28. Fortunately the season was sufficiently advanced that the water was already warm enough to allow one member of the crew to survive the ordeal and tell the tale. The story was reported in the June 2, 1859, *Detroit Free Press*, reprinted from the May 31 issue of the *Holland Register*:

> On Saturday, May 28, the crew of the schooner **Commencement** which was beached during the late gale, descried some floating wreck in Lake Michigan off Black Lake. One of them on going to the mast head, made it out to be a vessel, and thought he saw a man on it. Although the lake was still rough, the **Commencement's** yawl was immediately manned and started out as soon as she could be got ready; Vinke & Bosman's fishing boat and the **Swallow** of Mr. P. Boot, followed which, returning to shore took the yawl in tow. On reaching the wreck it proved to be the schooner **Euphemia**, Capt. Claussen, which left here loaded with lumber Thursday morning. Only one man was on her, being the sole survivor of a crew of six persons. The sailor who was rescued was in a most pitiable state and could not have survived another night. He was badly bruised, his limbs were very much swollen and he was nearly exhausted with cold and starvation. He was brought to Holland at once and is now slowly recovering.

The survivor knew only portions of the crews' names, but the *Detroit Free Press* obtained a list of the crew from the Detroit shipping office. Captain and owner of the vessel was Captain Frederick Claussen, aged 65, a Hollander belonging at Black Lake, Michigan; John Griffin, mate, age 24; John Briebiling, a Swede, aged 22; Peter Reeves from New York, aged 29; Peter Hammitt, the sole survivor, and "a cook shipped by the captain and name unknown." The Holland paper described the cook as "belonging to Detroit and whose mother is a blind woman depending on her daughter for support." The newspaper continued:

> Capt. Claussen bought the schooner which he has but just purchased from Detroit having shipped his crew at that port.
>
> They loaded deep with lumber nearly all on deck and cleared from Black lake at about 9 o'clock Thursday morning. It soon commenced blowing a gale from N.N.W. Between 3 and 4 P.M. the wind shifted to S.E. and E. About 11 P.M. they reefed their sails and at 1 A.M. of Friday night they got in all their canvas and wore ship. At about 6 A.M. saw land. They had lost the center-board chain so that the center boat was down to full depth and they could not get it up. 8 A.M. the vessel capsized and lay only about five minutes on her beams-end when her masts broke away, and came alongside and she went over bottom up. When she first capsized the crew hung to the weather side except the cook and another who were washed off by the sea, but caught pieces of lumber and floated off. As she went over bottom up, the captain and Hammitt caught in the fore-rigging and held on, and the two remaining men got on the keel. They did not stay long but caught pieces of lumber and he saw them still floating for an hour or more. He thinks one of them was still in sight as late as 1 o'clock P.M. The main boom fell on Captain Claussen's thigh and left arm and injured him very much perhaps breaking his thigh though he could not tell. Hammitt got him out as well as he could and lashed him fast. He died at Hammitt's side about three hours after receiving the injuries. Some time after he was dead, the main mast was thrown round by the sea and crushed him, and not long after the lashings gave way and his body washed away.
>
> At night they were near shore. A black boat with three men in it came to the wreck and commenced plundering it taking off the mainsail and some ropes. H. begged them to take him off, but they rowed away, and left him without replying. Saturday morning a boat he thinks the same came to her again -- he says the wreck was near a dock or pier -- and they again commenced plundering, and again left him to perish. The wreck drifted off and about 10 A.M. he was rescued as first stated, having been exposed to the sun and storm, without food, about thirty hours.
>
> We can hardly believe there are beings, in human form, who would refuse to rescue a fellow man from death, and hope it will prove otherwise, but if this is true and the villains are found, their case ought to be summarily tried in Judge Lynch's court.

Buffalo Aground, Horse Lost

September 12, 1859
At Grand Haven

A horse was the only victim when the brig **Buffalo**, under the command of Captain William Loutit, failed to make the piers at Grand Haven. According to the *Grand Haven News*:

> The brig **Buffalo**, Capt. Loutit, from the lower lakes, laden with a cargo of coal for the Detroit and Milwaukee Railway Company, went ashore near the end of the pier, at this place, on Sunday last. Four of the crew, while attempting to land in the yawl, were swamped, and only escaped with their lives by the timely assistance of spectators who were on the beach; the remainder were rescued from their perilous position by the prompt and noble efforts of Messrs. Matthews and Walker, fishermen, who fearlessly, with their boat, encountered the foaming billows of the lake. A valuable horse belonging to the captain was drowned while attempting to bring him ashore. We understand the vessel and cargo were insured in responsible companies, and that there is not much hope of salvaging either.

Steam Ferry in Frequent Trouble

1859
Grand Haven Harbor

A small steam ferry boat, no name ever recorded, operated at Grand Haven by William Ferry and Myron Harris, provided an efficient way to cross the river at points far removed from a bridge. Because she ran across the traffic there were frequent collisions.

On July 15, 1859, a schooner hit the vessel and the ferry sank without loss of life. She was quickly raised and continued her cross-river task.

In October of the same year the little ferry was victorious in a collision with one of the river boats on the Grand Haven to Grand Rapids run. The October 19, 1859, *Grand Haven News* reported:

> The steamer **Pontiac** as she was leaving here on Friday last swung around against the steam ferry boat and stove a hole in her side and after proceeding a short distance sunk -- the water covering her upper deck. There is now but one boat, the **Michigan**, Capt. Gano, running regularly between this place and Grand Rapids.

In November the **Pontiac** was raised, repaired and refitted. The following spring she was converted into a freight and towing vessel under Captain John Parks.

Notter Burns, Engineer Lost

When the steam tug **George Notter** of Milwaukee grounded on the bar outside of Grand Haven Harbor in April of 1861 it was the precursor of a bad year for the vessel. After lying on the bar for several days, filled with water, and cabin washed ashore, she was raised and repaired. The rest of the year went well until her final trip, August 30, 1861. The story is recorded in the September 4, 1861, issue of the *Grand Haven News*:

The tug **Notter**, Capt. J. Sims, left this port on Friday last for Milwaukee, with the dismasted schooner **Toledo** in tow. At 3 o'clock P.M., when out about fifteen miles, she caught fire, and, notwithstanding the earnest work of her crew, it gained so rapidly among the dry piles of wood around the boiler in the hold, that they were unable, unaided, to extinguish it. The engine was therefore stopped to allow the vessel to range up alongside, that the men on both vessels might fight the flames. But all proved unavailing. Capt. Sims called off the men, and supposed all were on board the **Toledo**. As the tug drifted away the Engineer came up out of the engine room, and had he jumped would have reached the vessel, or at least so near as to have been reached by a rope, but instead of that he attempted by backing the engine to bring the tug near enough to the vessel to ensure his escape. Quite a heavy sea was rolling and the vessels gradually drifted away from each other. The Engineer than lashed a number of sticks together and dropping them over the stern let himself down into the water, and clinging to the wood was for some time kept afloat. His shipmates kept watch of him as he rose upon the top of the waves, on the wood, until they had drifted apart about a mile. That was the last they saw of him. They suppose he lost his grasp and sunk.

The **Toledo** was without the usual yawl belonging to such vessels and no help from the vessel could reach him. The **Notter** burned down to the water line and sunk. A jury-mast was rigged on the floating vessel, a small sail set, and next morning she was picked up and towed back to this port by the propeller **Barber**.

The Captain of the propeller **C. Mears** offered to go in search of the missing man with his steamer with the hope that the Engineer might yet be floating on his raft, and with Capt. Sims and N. H. Ferry, on board as "lookouts" ran out and cruised around nearly six hours in the locality of the casualty, but found only the drifting wood. The Tug **Notter** was owned by Capt. A. Sims of Milwaukee and was a powerful tug, but old. No insurance.

Peoria Sinks Fishing Boat

December 17, 1861
Near Grand Haven Harbor

Schooner captains and fishermen were often at odds. It was always a tricky maneuver to exit an east shore harbor under sail. When fishing boats were in the way, the situation was even more difficult. The reporter hints that there may have been malicious intent when the schooner **Peoria** sank a fishing boat on her way out of Grand Haven. The report was carried in the December 18, 1861, *Grand Haven News*:

> SAD OCCURRENCE. -- As the schooner **Peoria** was outward bound, on the morning of yesterday, from this port, either intentionally or for some unaccountable reason, she struck a fish boat, in which were four men engaged in taking in their nets. The boat was instantly shivered into fragments and three of their number were drowned, the fourth barely escaped by clinging desperately to a piece of wreck that floated within his reach. The deceased were very worthy, industrious young men, Hollanders, of whom our village was suddenly yet sadly deprived. What excuse can be rendered by those who had charge of the vessel, for this lamentable disaster, it is impossible to conceive. The atmosphere was remarkably clear, the sun shone brilliantly, the wind gentle and fair, and the water was as placid as the stillness of a summer's evening.

Revolving Light Saved, Lost

November, 1864
Off Grand Haven

Following a November storm two schooners that had been on the beach were reported rescued in a report in the November 16, 1864, *Grand Haven News*:

> The schooners **Emmeline** and **Revolving Light** which went ashore just outside our pier a week ago last Saturday night, are in port. The **Emmeline** was brought in Friday afternoon last, all right, loaded forthwith and left for Chicago Saturday night. The **Revolving Light** was partially unloaded while on the beach -- so that she was got afloat and towed inside the harbor. The cargo has been discharged and two steam pumps have been brought over from Chicago to set her afloat again. The **Abigail** that went ashore about the same time that the other two vessels above named were beached is still in her old position with the prospect of proving a wreck.

The following week the **Revolving Light** was sent on to Milwaukee for repairs to her storm-damaged hull, but she must have been more seriously effected than was apparent. The November 23, 1864, *Grand Haven News*, reported:

> The schooner **Revolving Light**, of which we made mention in our last issue, left this port on Thursday morning last, in tow of the steamship **Detroit** -- destination, Milwaukee -- the steam pump in constant operation to keep her afloat. But, the pump becoming disabled, she was abandoned about 30 miles out from Milwaukee in sinking condition. The tug **J. P. Ward** was sent to search for her, but nothing was found of her except one of the cabin doors and the tool chest belonging to the pump. A heavy sea was running at the time.

Two Drowned Off Tug **Waukazoo**

October 12, 1866
Kalamazoo River Mouth

On October 12, 1866, the tug **Waukazoo** from the Grand River was attempting to enter the mouth of the Kalamazoo River when she met with difficulties, probably trying to cross the bar that frequently blocked the entrance to the river during and after stormy weather. At least two passengers, children of the Rev. John Wesley Cawthorne were drowned. According to Michigan Methodist church records the accident happened in the evening and the survivors were forced to remain on the wreck, partially submerged in the water, until daylight when the rescue could be affected. In addition to losing a son and a daughter, according to the obituary of Mrs. Cawthorne written in 1900, "this exposure brought on sickness and for 35 years she has been a patient sufferer."

The Rev. John Wesley Cawthorne was born in England and was married, July 26, 1853, to Jerusha Marie Calkins of Erie, Pennsylvania. He had preached in England as a young man and served church meetings in Canada before being received into the Methodist Episcopal Conference of Michigan in 1854. In Michigan he had served churches at Lapeer, South Albion Laphamville, Sparta, St. Johns, Flat River, Kelloggville and Lamont. It was during the transfer of his goods and family on the tug **Waukazoo** from Lamont, just downriver from Grand Rapids on the Grand River, to Saugatuck near the mouth of the Kalamazoo River that the accident occurred.

The boat was brand new at the time of the incident, and may have been on her test or maiden run. She was salvaged and returned to Grand Haven. The October 17, 1866, issue of the *Grand Haven News*, makes no mention of the tragic incident to the south and reports, "The new steamer **Waukazoo**, Capt. James P. Brayton, left port on her regular trips last Monday night." Another paragraph notes, "Her movements give general satisfaction to the owners, Messrs. Brayton and Farr."

Pastor Cawthorne went on to serve congregations in Saugatuck, Ganges, Flowerfield, Monterey, Salt River and Millbrook before his death in 1896.

Cushman Fireman Dies in Port

March 21, 1866
At Grand Haven

Early steamers had exposed machinery that was often a hazard to the unexperienced or unwary. John Souter, who may have been a new hand was assisting his brother with the engines aboard the **Gov. Cushman** which, in 1866, was offering regular service between Milwaukee and Grand Haven for the Detroit and Milwaukee Railroad when a misunderstanding had fatal consequences. The story is told in a brief paragraph in the March 23, 1866, issue of the *Grand Haven News*:

> John Souter was accidentally killed on board the propeller **Cushman**, the 21st inst. The boat had just arrived from Milwaukee and the engineer gave orders to close the draft. Souter was acting as fireman, and understood the order to be "throw it off the center." While endeavoring to execute the order in that direction, the engineer, his brother, reversed the engine, let on steam and the crank key cut and fractured his skull in a most shocking manner, causing instant death. He was in the army in the Mexican war, was in the late rebellion and fourteen months a prisoner in Charleston. He had no family.

The **Gov. Cushman**, a steam-driven propeller vessel, had been launched in 1857 and undergone a lengthy rebuilding in 1865. On May 1, 1868, the boat was preparing to leave the port of Buffalo with a load of grain from Milwaukee bound for Port Colborne, Ontario, when there was a sudden explosion. The entire stern of the vessel was blown away killed 11 of her crew and leaving the boat a total wreck.

Commerce Washes Ashore

August 1867
Near South Haven

The schooner **Commerce**, bound from Chicago to South Haven was washed ashore near South Haven and became a total loss in August of 1867. According to a compilation of the U. S. Coast Guard Records, 1867-1873, in the National Archives the vessel was owned by D. G. Wright of Chicago. It was registered at 324 tons and valued at $6,000. A portion of the value of the **Commerce**, $3,500, was covered by insurance. After the schooner went on the beach the cargo was saved.

Two Lost as **Travis** Capsizes

September, 1868
Near Grand Haven

The **J. A. Travis**, was a schooner, in some accounts called a scow schooner, built at Pentwater in 1867 by W. Arnold for S. Graham and other Pentwater interests. She was originally 72 gross tons.

The vessel was only a year old when she was blown down and capsized near Grand Haven in September of 1868, with the loss of two lives.

The **Travis** was later righted and repaired and, in 1874, was lengthened and rebuilt to 101.28 gross tons. After her disaster near Grand Haven she sailed for another 25 years before meeting succumbing to Lake Michigan. She was on her way from Icke Pier to Milwaukee on November 16, 1893, when she was wrecked at Cana Island. All five members of the crew were rescued.

Milwaukee Aground, All Saved

October 8, 1868
North of Grand Haven Piers

The **Milwaukee**, a sidewheel passenger and package freight boat serving as one of the Detroit and Milwaukee Railroad "Black Boats," on the Milwaukee to Grand Haven run, grounded on a bar trying to enter the harbor of Grand Haven in a storm on October 8, 1868. All aboard, 104 passengers and a crew of about 25, were eventually rescued. The story, full of exciting detail, was told by one of the passengers in a letter to the editor of the *Grand Rapids Eagle*:

> A few facts concerning the last twenty-four hours' history of the beautiful boat that now lies a wreck on the beach, at the mouth of our river -- the sepulcher of so many lives -- may be of interest to many of our people, many of whom have so often trusted their own lives and the lives of those dear to them to her strength, without a question as to her ability to ride out any storm that might arise, even upon our tempestuous Lake Michigan.
>
> We left Milwaukee on Thursday evening, at 11 o'clock, with a passenger list numbering 104, and a crew of about 25, under care of noble Captain Trowell. The boat was loaded heavily -- though not overloaded -- with corn, flour and wool. As the boat left the dock at Milwaukee and steamed out into the lake, everything to an inexperienced eye, betokened a quiet, beautiful night and a safe voyage. No thought of fear or of a coming storm seemed to be entertained by any one on board and many had retired to their state rooms at an early hour -- before the boat left the city -- with as perfect a feeling of security as they would in their own homes. About 12 o'clock the storm

began; the sky was covered over with clouds that seemed filled with snow, and everything assumed a dreary and uncomfortable aspect. The noble boat, however, seemed to pass along through the rising angry waters with ease and grace, apparently conscious of her past ability to overcome all obstacles and her present ability to take her precious cargo to a place of refuge. As we neared the eastern shore the storm increased and the waves continued to gain in size and power until as we neared Grand Haven it seemed that no steamer, however strong and seaworthy, could stand it long unless harbor was soon reached.

Our captain, fearing that the breakers would carry us upon the bar, after nearing the pier put out directly into the lake for a mile, at least, in order to come into the channel from a more southerly course, but it did not avail. As she entered the channel, or that which had heretofore been the channel, but during the late storm had been filled in with new accumulations of sand, the ship struck, and at once all headway was lost, and control over her from that moment ceased. The jar was so terrible, the noble boat quivered and groaned at every joint, seemingly mindful of her ultimate fate. She trembled even as a strong man will in the presence of death. The jar and crush brought every one from their state rooms to the cabin -- even those who had been suffering all night from terrible seasickness forgot it entirely in the anxiety for the preservation of their lives. The fear of immediate peril was soon relieved by the calm, courageous bearing of Captain Trowell and a few other noble men who put to shame others who would have caused a panic among all the rest. Her engine, that beautiful piece of mechanism, that so many have admired, still kept about her work; the ponderous beam still lifted itself high in the air, but no strength of even that wonderful machinery backed up by a full head of steam could avail against the fury of the wind and waves. The elements were against us. We could but acknowledge that we were powerless in the hands of Him who holdest the winds and waves in His control, and at whose bidding only would they ceased from their work of destruction and death. Let those who scoff at and make light of that power that upholdeth us all, pass a day and night upon the deep with death staring them in the face continually; let them look upon the calm faces of weak women with helpless children, still strong and hopeful because of their faith in that unseen, yet nevertheless ever present power, which so many ages ago spake unto the winds and they were still, and they will cease to scoff and learn to be better and truer men.

But a few moments elapsed ere the captain, aware of the inability of the boat to clear herself from the bar upon which she had struck -- the breakers each moment carrying her still harder on and causing her to labor more and more fearfully -- ordered her engineer to stop his engine and to fill her with water, thinking that by so doing she would settle down into the sand and rest comparatively easy. This seemed for a time to have the desired effect and she gradually worked herself down, where the breakers lost part of their power over her. The storm, however, instead of lessening in its strength and terrible force gathered new power as the morning passed away, until about noon she turned almost directly around with her broadside to the waves. She began at this time to show that she could not long stand the action of the breakers upon her side -- first floated away portions of her paddle box, then gradually the stronger portion of her framework began to loosened, her engine broke loose from the woodwork that surrounded it, and at every wave that broke over her, her cabin floors would rise and fall, bending like a willow in your hand. In the midst of all these hours the passengers, many of them ladies with little children, all strangers to each other, manifested a courage and calmness that to me now seems wonderful. About 3 o'clock it became evident to Captain Trowell and others who were in consultation with him, that the boat could not long bear up; confident as they had been until this time that she could remain there safely even for days. You may remember that she was on the bar some years ago. She then remained on nineteen days and was taken off safely.

Efforts were at once made to get a line ashore. The signal of distress was hoisted and one of the life boats lowered. Meantime the bow had broken off, just in front of her wheel house, and all that portion of her ceased to be safe for any one to remain in a moment. Those who had their state rooms in front of her engine, sought refuge in her after cabin, and there the anxious, though silent passengers, gathered, some with life preservers around them, others with ropes, securing their children to them; all nerving themselves for the final struggle. Everything seemed to depend now upon the success of those having the life-boat in charge, in getting a line ashore, by the aid of that, the boats could get back to us again safely. Meantime, hundreds of the citizens of Grand Haven gathered upon the beach, building fires and awaiting the life-boat now nearing them. As she approached the shore, scores of them rushed into the angry waters at the peril of their lives, in order to save the boat from swamping among the breakers near the shore. Finally came the signal that the rope was fast; that the boat had reached the shore safely. The Lord be praised! was the exclamation that burst from many a bursting heart. Some light now began to dawn. Almost at the same time other life-boats were seen coming to our rescue from the town, and our salvation seemed possible. A few anxious moments more -- the waves all the time breaking over us, and our position growing each moment more perilous -- and one of the boats was ready for its precious load. One by one the women were lowered by a rope, until all were at last received into five different boats. As each boat struck out on its perilous way the prayers of those left behind went with them for their safety. Husbands stayed behind; for the "women and children must go first," was the universal expression and wish. So without crowding, and without panic, they all left us. All but one, and of her I must speak. Maggie, the chambermaid, pale but calm, would not go until the children were all safe. Then the old men must go first, and it was not until all the helpless ones were safely on their way toward the shore that she would consent to leave her post.

Milwaukee

Soon the cry went up that some had reached land safely; carried through the last breakers in the arms of strong men. Not a moment too soon had the trial of the life boats commenced, for now the darkness began to gather and it was nearly nine o'clock before Captain Trowell and his 2nd mate, the 1st mate being helpless from a fracture of the collar bone, left their pride and pet, the beautiful **Milwaukee**, and turned their shoes toward the expectant anxious multitude upon the shore. The cheers that went up when all were safe, might have been heard above the roar of the sea. "All are safe," was the cry that sounded above all the noise of the wind and water, I thought if all things else were lost, it was enough.

I can not say too much in praise of Capt. Trowell -- calm and thoughtful -- he was at all points of danger alike capable and assuring. That he was deceived in the strength of his boat, is now too apparent . . . . Although built but nine years ago, many of her timbers were rotten, as a score of men will testify that on Saturday examined portions of her frame work that floated ashore for two miles along the beach . . . I will not intimate that there was knowledge of the weakness of the steamer **Milwaukee** on the part of those having her in charge, *but should there not have been?*

In conclusion let me say that the Captain and crew, with a few exceptions, deserve and will ever have the entire confidence and esteem of those committed to their charge. . . may they never pass through such an experience again. . . H.J.H.

The **Milwaukee** was a sidewheeler of 1,039 tons, 247 feet in length. She had been launched at Buffalo in 1859.

Schooner **Blue Bell** Lost

October 8, 1868
Near Grand Haven

The same storm that doomed the steamer **Milwaukee** cast several other Lake Michigan boats up on the beach. The small schooner **Blue Bell** was washed ashore near Grand Haven with a load of timber and railroad ties. Her crew scrambled to the beach and were saved but the vessel was considered a total loss. According to the October 10, 1868, *Grand Rapids Daily Eagle*, she was insured for $4,000.

Other boats ashore near Grand Haven in the same historic storm were the schooners **Clipper City, Coaster** and **Flora**. The newspaper notes, "The **Flora** was taken off by the **Tempest** today, and the others await suitable weather for their relief."

Green Ashore After Hard Season

November, 1869
Near South Haven

The year 1869 proved a difficult one for the sailing scow **Grace A. Green**. Shortly after navigation opened, she was attempting to get into the harbor at Chicago during a gale and, according to the May 19, 1869, issue of the *Muskegon Chronicle*, she "was thrown on her beam ends, but righted again and got inside with three feet of water in her."

Later in the season she wouldn't be so lucky. The **Green** was bound from Chicago to South Haven in November of 1869 when she went ashore near South Haven and was a total loss but most of the cargo was saved.

The **Green**, a scow of 54.41 gross tons, was enrolled at Detroit in 1860 and later owned by L. H. Gale of that city. In April of 1862, her registry was moved to Chicago. At the time of her loss she had just been purchased by A. Maywood of Chicago, with William Johnson as master. The value of the lost boat was recorded at $1,300.

Man Lost Off **F. Foster**

July 7, 1870
Off Holland Harbor

The schooner **F. Foster** lost a crewman while the vessel was off Holland, July 7, 1870. In the rescue attempt two more crewmen were lucky to be alive after a long row. According to the July 9, 1870, *Lake Shore Commercial*:

> Last Thursday at 1 p.m. as the schooner **F. Foster** was reefing her mainsail, fifteen miles off Holland, D. Grimes was thrown overboard by the main sheet. The boat was immediately lowered, and half filled by a sea; the mate and one of the crew were in her before she touched water, and made every effort to find the lost man but were unsuccessful. The two men in the boat, after pulling about until almost exhausted tried to regain the schooner, but could not. They then pulled for Kalamazoo River, lost their oars in the heavy breakers and were thrown on the beach by the surf.

A Bad Month for the **Daylight**

Saugatuck and Grand Haven
October, 1870

The small steamboat **Daylight** was one of the first boats owned by Saugatuck's Captain R. C. Brittain. In October of 1870 she had just begun regular service, according to the Saugatuck newspaper for October 1, 1870 "The steamer **Daylight** leaves docks at Saugatuck 3 p.m., arrives at Holland 4:40 in time to catch the 4:55 train to Allegan, or the 7:55 train to Grand Haven or Muskegon. Any going by this route will have a good view of our Lake Shore scenery, such as they will not be able to get in any other way, while, under Capt. Brittain's care, the ride by lake, though short, is sure to be pleasant."

The October 7 paper carried the unpleasant news: "The steamer **Daylight** left this place about 5 p.m. Monday on her way to Holland. When about half a mile from the end of the pier her whistle pipe blew out. Her steam quickly ran down, leaving her helpless. Luckily the wind drove her inshore so fast that she struck the north side of the pier and was saved from going ashore. The **Ira Chaffee** was lying at the pier, and by the prompt aid her crew and others gave, she was towed out of danger. One of her wheels was disabled."

She had barely had her wheel repaired and returned to service when another disaster descended. The October 15 newspaper reported: "On Thursday morning last the citizens of Spring Lake, Ferrysburg and Grand Haven were aroused from their slumbers by the shrill whistle of Messrs. Cutler & Savidge's large steam mill at Spring Lake, at about two o'clock caused by the burning of the steamer **Day Light** lying at the dock of Col. Wm. M. Ferry's foundry. The fire originated where the smoke stack passed through the upper deck, and in a very short space of time, the whole upper works were wrapped in flames. The upper deck was entirely consumed, with but little damage to hull and machinery. The vessel is insured."

Steamer **Orion** Strands on Bar

October 17, 1870
Near Grand Haven

The **Orion**, a sidewheel passenger and freight steamer, was fighting a gale coming in from astern when she attempted to enter Grand Haven harbor on October 17, 1870. She struck a sand bar and jammed on it. With her engines running full steam the side wheels were raised out of water in the high waves. An October 18 story from Grand Haven was printed in the October 19, 1870 edition of the *Grand Rapids Daily Eagle*:

> The **Orion** will prove a total wreck, the sea last night breaking her up badly. The schooner **Two Charles** went ashore at this place last night and the barge **Mary Amanda** near Saugatuck. The former was pulled off today by the combined efforts of the revenue cutter **Andy Johnson** and the tugs **Tempest** and **St. Mary**.
>
> The **Orion** was a fine boat that had done good service in the popular line to which she belonged. She was built at Manitowoc for the Goodrich Transportation Company in 1866. She was 200 feet in length, 500 tons burden and worth $80,000. She was insured for $24,000. Her engines will probably be saved.

The **Orion** was officially 185 feet in length, 494 tons and had been launched at Manitowoc in 1866. She was under the command of Captain John Richardson. As workers fought to salvage all they could from the wrecked schooner the small schooner **Little Georgia** of Sheboygan went ashore in nearly the same place losing 250 of her 400 barrels of lime. The engines of the **Orion** were raised and placed in Goodrich's new sidewheeler **Muskegon**.

Guido Survives Wintry Ordeal

December 6, 1871
Grand Haven Harbor

The small two-masted schooner **Guido** which had been built at Manitowoc, Wisconsin, in 1856, was struggling to reach Milwaukee in a gale during the early part of December, 1871. However, the vessel had suffered damage in the high wind, the sails were torn and some of the rigging blown away. The anxious crew worked their vessel to within sight of the lights of Milwaukee, but did not have enough sail left to permit them to maneuver her into Milwaukee harbor.

At the mercy of the northwesterly winds, the powerless schooner was blown back across Lake Michigan eventually entering Grand Haven harbor.

The men had not eaten in several days and were suffering from severe frostbite and exposure. One had been struck by a flying jib sail and it was feared he might lose an eye.

But the crew was nursed back to health and the **Guido** went on to work on the lake another 50 years, remaining on the rolls until 1939, an active service of 83 years.

Tow Line Tangle Fatal for **Boole**

October 9, 1872
Near South Haven Piers

The little tugboat **L. H. Boole**, 30 tons, was built in 1858 at Milwaukee. She was known around her home port of South Haven as a vessel that would risk her own safety to help other boats in need. The August 7, 1869, issue of the *South Haven Sentinel* reported:

> On Monday morning last during quite a blow the scow **Wm. Bates**, Capt. Jas. McDonald, was seen to the north of this port, the supposition that she was trying to get in here. The tug **L. H. Boole** went and took her in tow and brought her safe to port notwithstanding the gale.

In October of 1872, trying to assist other boats unable to enter the harbor as the result of a severe storm, the **Boole** got her propeller wheel fouled in the tow line of a vessel she was aiding. Powerless to save herself she drifted ashore becoming a total loss. Her crew was rescued.

Schooner **Delaware** Ashore in a November Gale

November 30, 1872
North of Holland

The story of the schooner **Delaware** which went ashore near Holland in 1872 was later dramatically related by Edith Souter Kardux in the August 15, 1947, *Holland Sentinel*:

> One stormy November morning as my father was starting his day's work, a neighbor's daughter, on her way to school, told him a large three-masted ship was on the bar a little way north.
>
> "My brother wants you to come and help get the sailors off," she said.
>
> Father dropped his axe and joined the neighbor and other men he had sent for to rescue the crew if possible.
>
> The vessel, the **Delaware** of Buffalo, N. Y., had been disabled

on the East shore and had drifted before the wind which was blowing a gale and when toward morning it turned cold, and began to snow, it rapidly developed into a regular blizzard.

The crew realized the ship would be lost and they would have small chance of being saved in the terrible storm. As their anxious eyes were trying to glimpse shore, the ship struck the bar and began to swing around and settled.

Members of the crew hurriedly lashed themselves to the rigging, so as not to be washed overboard as the waves swept over the doomed vessel. She had struck on the outer bar, opposite what is now known as Kardux beach, lately developed into a thriving resort colony.

The men gathered on the beach decided they could do nothing without a boat and the nearest boat would be at "the mouth" (the entrance to Black Lake) so eight of them started to get a boat. When over half way to the mouth they found the yawl boat of the wrecked ship. It had washed overboard during the night. The men turned it upside down on their shoulders and, walking and staggering along the uneven beach with their heavy load, they finally reached the place nearest the ship.

One can imagine the agony of that crew as they caught an occasional glimpse through a rift in the storm of men on shore and see them walk away. They gave up all hope of being saved and then, after what seemed an eternity, they saw the men returning with a boat.

Then began a terrible struggle with Lake Michigan. To launch the boat, they would run through the waves with it and try to get in only to have a giant wave tear it from their grasp and toss it back on the beach. Then they would try again and again, finally succeeding. After a terrible battle with the waves, they reached the ship and brought one man and a line to shore, making the line fast. Having that to hold to they made several trips to the ship, saving all the crew, one was a woman, the cook. They were in a bad way, completely exhausted, hands and feet frozen and their clothing frozen stiff.

Kindly hands carried them up the bank to a farm home where women had prepared beds and blankets, plenty of hot coffee and food. All suffered terribly from the exposure, but after a few days were able to leave Holland for their homes in distant cities. Three remained and went to work in the woods, later buying land and marrying lake shore girls. They had had enough of sailing.

The ship was taken off in the spring by a salvage company. It broke in two when it struck the bar.

The **Delaware** was loaded with wheat which covered the beach several inches deep in the spring. During the winter she was completely covered with ice and, with other girls and boys, we went out over the icebergs, and were actually on the ship,

Another account of the disaster, written in 1939, by George H. Ogden who also lived nearby relates that one of the farmers later died of injuries received when he was crushed during the launching of the lifeboat.

The December 7, 1872, issue of the *Holland City News* reports that Captain Henderson of the "barque **Delaware** wants to thank citizens for their help when his vessel wrecked near the mouth of the harbor." He estimated the cargo as 33,000 bushels of wheat, worth $40,000. The schooner was repaired and continued on the lakes for many years, carrying cargoes of lumber, coal and other non-perishable goods. She was finally retired about 1926.

The "D" from the ship's name was nailed to a sapling by Nels Ogden and remained there until the sapling became a large tree. It was taken down by George Ogden and is now in The Netherlands Museum.

Steamer **Ironsides** Misses Harbor

Grand Haven Harbor
September 15, 1873

The wooden passenger and freight propeller **Ironsides** sank in a furious gale near Grand Haven, September 15, 1873. She had been built at Cleveland in 1864 by iron industry pioneer Eber Ward to haul ore on the Great Lakes during the Civil War. She was 1,123 tons, 233 feet long, 38 feet in beam with two boilers which fed steam to two pistons that drove her two four-bladed propellers. She had been purchased in 1869 along with her sister ship, **Lac la Bell** by Nathaniel Engleman of Milwaukee. The two vessels were used as cross-lake ferries for the Detroit and Milwaukee Railroad, the route under contract to the Engleman Transportation Company. Both vessels had been overhauled in the winter of 1872-73 for passenger service.

The **Ironsides** left Milwaukee bound for Grand Haven Sunday night, September 14, 1873 with winds out of the southwest. She had aboard 19 passengers, 33 crewmen and a varied cargo. During the night winds increased to gale force and switched to the west. The seas increased as they reached the eastern shore.

Monday, September 15 the **Ironsides** approached Grand Haven at 7 a.m. with winds blowing at full gale force. Captain Harry Sweetman made two attempts to enter port and narrowly missed going on the beach. He aborted the third try and backed off two miles hoping that the storm would subside. However the vessel had struck bottom several times in her attempts to enter the harbor and water was pouring in the cargo gangways and through seams opened by the pounding.

The water in the hull overwhelmed the capacity of the pumps and by 9 a.m. the ship began to sink. The **Ironsides** lost control of her machinery and a flag of distress was run up, but no aid was near. At 11 a.m. five lifeboats were put over the side and all passengers and crew made it to them safely. Captain Sweetman was the last to leave, he entered a lifeboat about noon just in time to watch his vessel plunge to the bottom of Lake Michigan.

The lifeboats tried to gain shore, but the waves and wind made it difficult and only two succeeded. The other three boats capsized casting their passengers in the lake. The occupants were lost in plain sight of those on shore. The newly organized volunteer life saving crew was on hand under Captain Richard Connell, but could do little.

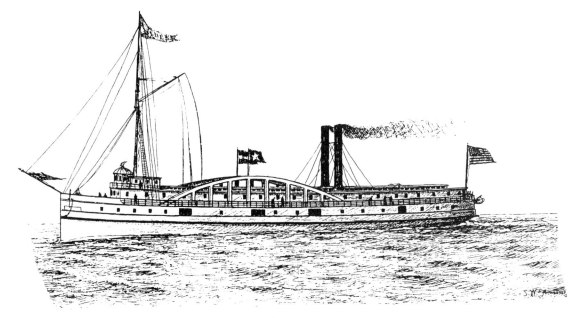

Ironsides

Twenty eight, some accounts say 23, lives were lost including Captain Sweetman, Chief Engineer Robert McGlue and the Steward, Dan Drescoll. The bodies of Harry Hasebarth and his bride later washed ashore in each other's arms. Gerald Smith, a Grand Haven cigar maker, was another victim.

The wreck was relocated for the first time in April of 1878 when fishermen brought in two sections of brass machinery that were identified as being from the boat. The *Grand Haven Herald* commented, "The two [pieces] supposed to belong to some steamboat and quite likely the **Ironsides**. The amount of this class of jetsam lying on the bottom of the lake is immense, and it is only occasionally brought to the surface."

In August of 1887 Michael Engelmanne of Manistee, owner of the **Ironsides** announced that he would make an attempt to raise the vessel, but did not succeed.

In 1966 divers Gene Turner and the late David Groover found the remains of the **Ironside** southwest of the Grand Haven pier in 120 feet of water. Painted scroll work could still be seen on her two pistons, named Jack (starboard) and Jill (port). Artifacts recovered from the wreck are on display at Tri-Cities Museum. The wreck was relocated in 1990 through the efforts of Doug Welsch and fellow divers.

Three Drown as **Throop** Breaks Up

October 17, 1873
North of South Haven

The schooner **Lizzie Throop** was on her way from Muskegon to Chicago with a cargo of slabs on October 16, 1873, when she struck by high winds. According to a report in the October 25, 1873, *South Haven Sentinel*:

> The schooner **Lizzie Throop**, Captain Robert McKee, left
> Muskegon at about 6 o'clock on the afternoon of the 16th inst., bound
> for Chicago with a cargo of slabs. About ten o'clock in the evening she
> was struck by a squall, the wind being high all night. At three o'clock in
> the morning she sprung a leak, being then fifteen miles from shore, to
> the northwest of this harbor. At one o'clock in the afternoon on Friday
> they made land nine miles north of here.
>
> In the report of the mate he says: "At one o'clock, she filled
> with water up to her decks. At this time we were away from land about
> fifteen miles. As the schooner **George L. Seaver** passed we hoisted the
> signal of distress. We got no assistance. At half past six in the evening
> of the next day after we started she rolled over. The men took to the
> rigging except the mate, who steered her until she rolled over. Three of
> the men got into the boat, the Captain and cook having before this
> washed off and drowned. The three men, including the mate, left the
> boat and got into the hull and made a line fast to the boat and let her
> hang to the hull; the line parted and the boat got away. The sea was
> running so high that the mate and the two men dared not trust the boat,
> and committed themselves to the wreck. The vessel began to break up
> and the three men were washed off of her. One was drowned and the
> other two got ashore on a piece of the wreck. The Captain's name was
> Robert McKee, and the cook's Michael Wade. The other man drowned
> was called Jim, his other name not being known."

The two survivors were Duncan McPherson, mate, and John Kisner, a sailor. The
body of the captain was found south of South Haven on October 24 and buried that
afternoon in the South Haven cemetery. The sum of $150 was found on the body and a
portion of this money was used to pay for the funeral. The cook who drowned the same
day met with less pleasant circumstances. His body was spotted off the shore in Casco
Township, Allegan County. According to a report in the October 25, 1873, issue of the
South Haven Sentinel:

> Last Friday afternoon word came to Capt. W. P. Bryan that
> another of the unfortunates from the Schooner **Lizzie Throop** had been
> found on the beach, three or four miles north of this village, and that
> gentleman immediately dispatched a team for the body. On arriving at
> the designated spot, the parties found an inquest had been held before
> Justice J. G. Potter of Casco and the body was then being taken to the
> cemetery. The procession was overtaken, the body turned over to our
> authorities and brought back here for shipment to Chicago, the
> unfortunate Michael Wade, having a family in that city. On opening the
> box it was found that the body was being buried just as it was discovered
> -- a sad looking sight in a country able to pay due respect to its living
> and its dead. A subscription of $32 was at once raised, a suitable coffin

and a suit of clothes purchased, the body dressed therein and forwarded to his friends in Chicago with a surplus of some $10 in money. It is not befitting for a newspaper to deal out words of censure and still we are pleased to know the body was given a christian burial at the hands of friends who cherished it. We refrain from publishing any of the communications offered us touching this case.

Captain John Murray of Chicago, the last owner of the **Lizzie Throop** traveled to South Haven and personally looked after the needs of the survivors and burial plans for the victims. He also worked to secure important pieces of the wreck and cargo.

Crew Abandons **Hamilton**

November 12, 1873
North of South Haven

The schooner **Hamilton** sprang a sudden leak November 12, 1873, forcing her crew into a yawl boat for battle against a raging storm. As the story was related in the *South Haven Sentinel* for November 15, 1873:

> The schooner **Hamilton**, owned by the Messrs. Donaldson of Chicago and Chas. LaMott of Pentwater and sailed by Capt. H. L. Burch of Chicago, left Muskegon Wednesday morning last at half past eight o'clock with a cargo of 117,000 feet of lumber bound for Chicago. After three or four hours sailing she was struck by heavy seas and sprung a leak, the men working the pumps until about three o'clock in the afternoon when they were obliged to take to the yawl, laying under the lee of the wreck until 12 at night, the schooner then rolling over and the seas driving the yawl from its position. From this time until 10 o'clock the next morning, Thursday, these men were at the mercy of the waves, in a 17-foot yawl, with nothing for nourishment but a basket of bread. They kept her head to, using the oars only to keep their boat in shape. They came ashore about a mile north of this harbor, being at their reckoning some forty miles from Chicago at the time they gave up the schooner.
>
> The names of the men are Capt. Harvey L. Burch, G. H. Hughes, mate; Samuel Martin, Steward, D. G. Holcomb, Thos. Williams, Richard Jones and Wm. Backus, seamen. The Captain and men desire to express their thanks to Messrs. Crosby Eaton and J. B. Starkey who assisted them to their houses and treated them with all the hospitality they could have shown to brothers; also to Mr. M. Strong of the Pacific [hotel] for the generosity in administering to their wants after getting able to come over into the village.
>
> As we go to press the men are still here but leave on the first boat for their homes. In all the instances of a wreck recorded in the *Sentinel* this is the most miraculous escape from death we have yet

known, and much is due to the bravery of Capt. Burch and men for holding out eighteen hours in a small yawl during such weather as we have had this past week, the boat being a mass of ice when she struck the beach.

All Hands Lost as **D. G. Wright** Capsizes

South of Saugatuck
May 11, 1875

The scow schooner **D. G. Wright** capsized north of South Haven, May, 1875, after leaving Saugatuck. The circumstances were described in the May 22, 1875, issue of the *Allegan Journal*:

Schooner Wrecked

On Tuesday, May 11, the schooner **D. G. Wright** from the harbor of Saugatuck for Chicago, laden with lath and fence pickets, in charge of Capt. Wm. Hansen and a crew of the three men, Frank Dye, Julius Macauley and James Emmett. Two persons took passage from Saugatuck for Chicago, Samuel Johnston of Milwaukee and Henry S. Blackman of Trowbridge in this county. The vessel scarcely made fifteen miles from Saugatuck where she was struck by a severe gale and driven ashore. She struck the beach a short distance from S. Mack's pier in Ganges. All on board perished and four bodies have been recovered at this date. These are those of Capt. Hansen, Mr. Johnston, J. Macauley and young Blackman. The vessel is a total wreck and there was no insurance on their boat or cargo. The beach is constantly watched in hope of finding the other bodies. The sails of the vessel were all set when she was wrecked, and a watch and some clothes were found lashed to the wreck. These things indicate that the vessel was struck suddenly and that the crew were aware of their danger before going overboard.

A later report in the Allegan newspaper corrected the crew member's name from James Emmett to Samuel Emmett and noted, "When she struck the beach near Mack's pier the bottom was entirely out. Considerable of her cargo has drifted ashore."

A brief story carried in the *South Haven Sentinel* for May 15, 1875, gave further evidence of the furor of her end. In reporting the discovery of the body of crew member Julius McCauley, son of Mrs. L. Bankson of Geneva it noted, "An indenture in the skull is evidence that he was struck by the load when the **Wright** capsized, thus rendering him unable to help himself in the least. Strict search is being kept up for the bodies of the remainder of the unfortunates, but up to the present writing no trace of them have been discovered. The wreck now lies on the bar one mile south of Mack's Pier."

Rosabella Capsizes in a Squall

August 6, 1875
Off Grand Haven

The crew of the **Rosabella** were imperiled and one lost his life when the . schooner capsized near Grand Haven on August 6, 1875. The *Grand Rapids Daily Morning Times* described the incident in a short story in the August 7 issue:

> The schooner "**Rosabella**," Capt. Peter Johnson, loaded with lumber and bound for Chicago from Muskegon, was struck by a squall about 4 o'clock this morning, when about two miles off Grand Haven and waterlogged and capsized. The steward was immediately drowned. The balance of the crew, five in number, clung to the rigging until almost 11 o'clock when they were rescued by parties from shore. The captain sustained serious injuries.

Other crew members recovered. The vessel was first recorded as a total wreck, but later returned to service.

Crew of the Hibbard Saved

October 31, 1875
North of South Haven

The schooner **J. Hibbard** was carrying lumber from Hamlin, a settlement on the shores of Hamlin Lake, near the mouth of the Big Sauble River north of Ludington when she sought shelter as the result of a serious leak. She came ashore at McDowell's Pier, in Casco Township, Allegan County, about three miles north of South Haven. According to the November 6, 1875, edition of the *South Haven Sentinel:*

> The schooner **J. Hibbard** of Chicago, left Hamlin Friday afternoon of last week bound for South Chicago with a crew of five men and a cargo of 93,300 feet of lumber. Soon after leaving port she sprang a leak, the men working constantly at the pumps until Saturday noon, when she filled, losing her entire stern. At this time she was off Saugatuck. Sunday morning about daylight she came ashore near Mack's Pier, and through the exertions of the people of that vicinity during the day the entire crew were saved, the **Hibbard** and her cargo proving a total loss. The boat was owned by the captain and had no insurance. The crew were Capt. P. Canovan, James Anderson, mate, Julius McLath, Jack Canovan and Tom, the name of the latter not being known. They were without food forty-eight hours, and during the severe storm raging their sufferings must have been dreadful. They express the heartiest of thanks to the citizens who so kindly aided them.

Schooner **Island Queen** Ashore in Gale

October 9, 1876
North of Grand Haven

If there was clear weather after a storm, often a beached boat could be salvaged. Continued storms and high waves could break the vessel beyond all hope of salvage in a few hours, or sometimes a few days. The **Island Queen**, a schooner, beached north of the north pier at Grand Haven on October 9, 1876. The 121 ton vessel was owned by Grand Haven interests and commanded by Captain Martin and was on her way from Grand Haven to Chicago with a load of timber. All six crew members aboard the schooner were saved. A contemporary report stated that the value of the boat was $3,000 and the value of the cargo was $2,500 and fittings and cargo worth $1,500 had been saved.

But the weather did nothing to help the situation. The *Holland City News* for Saturday, November 11, 1876, reported with finality: "The schooner **Island Queen** beached north of the north pier at Grand Haven during one of the severe gales of last month went to pieces on Friday last week. She is owned by Messrs Squires and White of Grand Haven. Uninsured."

Two Charlies Sinks Near Pier

October 9, 1876
South of Grand Haven Piers

The merchant schooner, **Two Charlies**, sank just south of the south pier at the Grand Haven harbor entrance October 9, 1876, as she was nearing her destination on a trip from Chicago to Grand Haven. The vessel had been launched in 1852 at Milwaukee. and was under the command of Captain Buiden. The crew was landed safely. The vessel valued at $3000, was a total loss.

Sloop **John Edward** Capsizes, Traps Passengers

November 9, 1876
North of Saugatuck

A strange and terrible accident occurred to the sloop **John Edward** shortly after they left on a long-contemplated trip to the south. The small sloop of 11 tons capsized just about five miles north of Saugatuck on November 9, 1876. According the *Holland City News* of Saturday, November 18, 1876:

> A sad accident occurred to the McCurdy family of Ferrysburg, on the morning of election day. This is the family who were announced as preparing to go to Florida in a sloop, built for the purpose, by way of Lake Michigan, Chicago, Illinois River, Mississippi and Gulf a short

time ago. They were struck with the same rough weather that beached the schooner **Kate Howard**. It broke one of her spars and became helpless, drifted to the beach and capsized on the outer bar, about half way between Holland and Saugatuck breaking up the rest of her spars and thereby fastening the old man down, rendering him entirely helpless and finally drowning him -- the water and sand washing continually over him. The rest of the family were in the cabin all this time, which appears to have been fastened down by the same process, and cut their way out after having been locked in there for twenty four hours, by way of boring and chopping through the sides of the boat whose name was **Edwards**. Capt. Brouwer of the towboat **Twilight** says he helped to bury the unfortunate old man and towed the sloop into this port on Friday last week.

The trip was abandoned and the small cargo of vinegar was a total loss.

The **L. Painter** Scuttled Again

October, 1877
South of South Haven

The sailing scow **L. Painter** can credit its long years of service to a captain and crew who knew when to fight the gale, and when to scuttle. The vessel went ashore in a fall storm in 1877 about seven miles north of St. Joseph. According to the October 13, 1877, issue of the *South Haven Sentinel*:

> The scow **L. Painter**, Capt. W. R. Johnson, now lies on the beach about seven miles to the north of St. Joseph. She is scuttled, and when the Captain left her Thursday morning, she was in about four feet of water, so she can probably be put afloat again. Monday night, at Union Pier, she was scuttled in four or five feet of water. Tuesday afternoon she was repaired, loaded and made away from the pier, but she was struck by the storm again in the evening and weathered it by using all the contrivances known to sailors until about five o'clock Wednesday afternoon when, with his canvas and deck load gone, and having lost all his chains and anchors, she went abeach, when the Captain again scuttled her. His men were so benumbed as to make work impossible, and his own hands from being cut and pounded are swollen to nearly twice their natural size. To Mr. Beech and family the Captain and boys desire to tender their heartfelt thanks for kindness shown.

One member of the crew returned to Chicago the following week on the propeller **Riverside.**

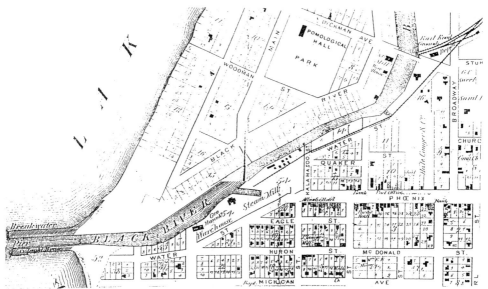

An 1873 map of South Haven harbor.

Saugatuck harbor from a 1935 map

Scow **Flora** Beached at Grand Haven

November 7, 1877
South of Grand Haven Harbor

The sailing scow **Flora** began work in Saugatuck in 1870 and was known for her speed and reliability. It was noted that she had sailed 2,576 miles in 54 days making 14 round trips from Saugatuck to Chicago carrying mostly lumber from Saugatuck mills. By 1877 most of her travel was under the tow of the steamer **Fanny Shriver** and in September it was noted in the Saugatuck newspapers that she had carried 187 cords of edgings from Saugatuck to Holland and brought back to Saugatuck 500 cords of bark for a local tannery in addition to her Chicago trips.

But in November of 1877 she succumbed, unexpectedly, to gale winds that drove her ashore despite the best efforts of those who tried to assist her. The November 16, 1877, issue of the *Lake Shore Commercial* reported:

> The steamer **Fanny Shriver** arrived at this port last Tuesday from Grand Haven where she has been engaged in securing a load of shingles from the scow **Flora** which went ashore at that place Nov. 2nd. Capt. Upham gives us the following particulars of the disaster: The **Fanny Shriver** with the scow **Flora** in tow, left Muskegon on Tuesday, Nov. 2d with a load of shingles for J. H. Eppink of Graafschap. When near Grand Haven the wind commenced blowing a gale and the sea made very rapidly. In attempting to enter the harbor at Grand Haven the tow line parted and the Shriver immediately whistled for help and Capt. Richard Connell of the tug **Warner** who also has charge of the life saving station at that place and who is always on hand for work of this kind came to the rescue with his tug. But she also parted her line and the **Flora** went on the beach south of the harbor. Capt. Upham succeeded in saving the cargo but the boat is a total wreck, loss about $300, no insurance.

The same gale disrupted shipping all around lower Lake Michigan. It was reported the next week in the *Holland City News* that the schooner **F. B. Gardner** was ashore at Lincoln Park, an "unknown schooner" was ashore at Hyde Park and the schooner **12th Ohio** was on the breakwater at Twelfth street, a total loss, but the crew escaped. Elsewhere around the lake, the schooner **Rob Roy** was reported ashore at Muskegon with all her forerigging gone, and the **W. H. Hinsdale** was beached at South Haven loaded with lumber from a Holland sawmill. The schooner **Selt** of Milwaukee had been beached south of Holland harbor in the same gale, but had been released Monday night "by the assistance of the sailors of four or five windbound vessels waiting for fair weather."

Rover Ashore, Crew of Two Saved

October 27, 1878
Near Saugatuck Piers

In addition to the larger steamers and schooners, that were well known throughout the lakes, there were many smaller vessels, some were so compact that they could be sailed with a single man on board. These small boats sailed up and down the coast, buying small cargos in one place and selling them for what they hoped would be a profit in the next port. The **Rover** which went ashore on the Kalamazoo River in October of 1878 was one of these. According to the *Lake Shore Commercial* for November 1, 1878:

> A little "hooker" the **Rover** of Holland capsized while attempting to enter this port last Sunday. One man and a boy were aboard of her but got safely ashore with a good ducking. The boat was loaded with groceries, provisions, etc., the most of which were saved. The boat is a total wreck.

According to the dictionary a "hooker" was originally either an English boat with one mast, or a Dutch boat with two masts. On American waters it came to mean any small sailing vessel (with semantical overtones that the boat was probably old and dilapidated). Later the word was sometimes applied to powered boats with the same qualities. Use of the word also implied that the boat was an independent operation, not part of a larger fleet.

Wm. Bates Upsidedown and Back Again

October 5, 1878
North of Holland

Leaking schooners were, at best, unpredictable. The crew of the **Wm. Bates** found this out in early October when their vessel sprang a leak. As the *Holland City News* for October 12, 1878, relates the story:

> A sad accident occurred on Lake Michigan on Sunday last, about 40 miles from our harbor. It was blowing hard, a high sea was running and the schooner **Wm. Bates**, Capt. John Thompson, was running under double reefed canvas when the schooner sprung a terrible leak under her bow, filled in a few minutes, capsized, rolled the mainmast overboard, lost her boat, dumped her deck load, and afterwards righted herself again. She laid with her nose so deep in the water, that it was necessary to let her anchors run out, which lightened her a little.
>
> They managed to set a piece of her forestay sail and were a long

while trying to get her before the winds; they finally succeeded in doing this and let her drift ashore, then that sail blew away, and the men took to the forerigging, where they remained until they neared the shore about a mile to northward of our harbor, when they were taken off by a little boat belonging to the schooner **Sandy Morrison** on Tuesday last. The men, three in number, were almost exhausted when taken off, and have suffered terrible while clinging to the rigging for so many hours. The schooner has gone to pieces and is a total wreck.

The oak lumber with which she was loaded belonged to Messrs. P. Pfanstiel and E. J. Harrington, and part of that will be saved. There was no insurance on the vessel and the loss falls heavy on the Thompson family.

Rescuing the Crew of the **Woodruff** and Others

November 1, 1878
At Grand Haven

The life saving station at Grand Haven was still very new when the crew was called on to render service in a variety of venues on November 1, 1878. The entry in the annual Life Saving Service report for that day notes:

> The crew of Station No. 9, Eleventh District, rendered extraordinary service, giving aid and succor to no less than five wrecks on this day. At eleven o'clock in the morning the district superintendent at Grand Haven received a telegram stating that the bark L. C. **Woodruff** of Cleveland, Ohio, was ashore at White Lake Harbor, 42 miles distant, sunk in 13 feet of water, with the crew all in the rigging. Keeper Connell started at 12 m by special train to the rescue, with the life car and apparatus and four of his men, the other four remaining for service at Grand Haven, and arrived abreast of the wreck in two hours, having to change cars once, and transfer the crew and apparatus again from the cars to a tug boat, which carried him six miles farther by inland water to the scene of the wreck. The vessel lay 150 yards from the shore with the sea making a clean breach over her, two of her masts gone, her crew of ten men in the fore rigging and hundreds of excited spectators looking on. Seven of the crew were saved, but three were unfortunately lost.
>
> During the preparations for the departure of part of the crew for the wreck of the **Woodruff**, the schooner, **Australia**, of Muskegon, Michigan, in attempting to make an entrance between the piers, which is about 400 feet wide, was swept aside by the heavy sea and strong current, and struck the end of the north pier staving in her starboard bow. One man jumped from her upon the pier, and another, in attempting to do so, was carried overboard by the heavy seas that now swept her decks and was lost. The vessel continued to thump the pier,

but finally worked nearly alongside and grounded, when the life saving men threw their heaving stick and line to her and getting her lines made them fast, thus preventing her from swinging broadside to the beach and becoming a total wreck. The remainder of her crew, six in number were taken off by noon.

The remnant of the volunteer life saving crew was now in charge of Surfman John de Young, the keeper having gone with the others to the **L. C. Woodruff**. Anticipating disaster from the heavy weather, Surfman De Young had the surfboat hauled down to the beach. Soon after, about twelve o'clock, the schooner **America** of Chicago, went ashore north of the piers and he and his men launched the life boat, and after a hard pull reached the vessel and brought her crew of eight men safely ashore.

At three o'clock the schooner **Elvina** of Oswego, New York, came ashore between the north pier and the **America**, her stern swinging against the latter's bow. The life boat crew waded out into the breakers as far as they could and succeeded in getting a line from her, which they made fast to the pier, thereby preventing the vessel from beating against the other schooner. They went out in the surf boat and brought the captain ashore at his request.

Shortly afterward the schooner **Montpelier**, of Detroit, in attempting to run into harbor, struck the outer bar, fell off to leeward and grounded on the abandoned wreck of the steamer **Orion**, knocking a hole in her bottom and filling immediately. The seas at once swept over her, and her men took to the rigging. The life saving crew launched the surfboat, and with great toil and difficulty succeeded in reaching the vessel from which they rescued seven men and a woman.

The exploits of the life saving crew at Grand Haven in effecting these rescues in the heavy sea that was that day running were the theme of general commendation in that region.

Career of **C. E. Bird** Cut Short by Fire

September 15, 1879
Kalamazoo River at Saugatuck

In the spring of 1879 Cal Heath of Saugatuck launched a small steamer designed to connect with larger boats during fruit season, and carry resorters to the beach in the summer. The vessel was named the **C. E. Bird**, after a local druggist, and officially enrolled at Grand Haven on September 5, 1879, rated at 22.94 gross tons, 14.45 net tons, 52 feet in length.

The September 19, 1879, *Saugatuck Commercial*, described the abrupt end to the vessel's promising new career:

Last Monday morning at three o'clock Cal Heath's boat the C.

E. Bird, was discovered to be on fire. Although every effort was put forth to save her, the fire had made such headway before seen all proved unavailing and she burned to the water's edge. The **Bird** was a new boat built last winter and as she was uninsured the loss falls heavily upon Mr. Heath who had invested his all in her, and had just got her in good running order. He estimates his loss at $2000.

Heath salvaged the machinery from the burned out hull and began work immediately on a new boat. This second vessel was launched near the end of June, 1880, and named the **Charles E. Bird**. This one remained in active service, mostly in the St. Joseph area, until 1891.

Gamecock Hits Piers, Goes Ashore

October 28, 1879
South of Saugatuck Piers

Running aground was often not nearly so important as what happened afterwards and how long a boat had to remain exposed to the action of wind and waves. The small fore and aft schooner **Gamecock** was running light, bound for Muskegon in October of 1879. It is unclear from contemporary accounts whether she was attempting to enter or leave the Saugatuck, or just got too close to the piers, but she struck the trestle work on the piers and carried away part of it, then went ashore just south of the south pier October 28, 1879.

The captain said that he felt it was only a temporary setback. According to the October 31, 1879, *Saugatuck Commercial*, "She is not damaged very much and her captain thinks can be got off as soon as the sea runs down."

However the weather did not cooperate and the same newspaper observed in the December 4, 1879, issue:

The **Gamecock** is in a bad place and will likely go to pieces before spring.

Part of the trouble may have been her captain's difficulty in paying for tugs and other salvage assistance. At the end of December the newspaper noted that the **Gamecock**, still described as "ashore south of the pier" had been sold at a marshal's sale for $180 to Captain R. C. Brittain of Saugatuck. If Captain Brittain got anything for his money it was just pieces, an August 10, 1883, issue of the Saugatuck newspaper in describing another near disaster noted:

The schooner **Wonder** had a very narrow escape from running on the beach near where the schr. **Gamecock** went to pieces, her bow sprit going over the wreck of the vessel, but by prompt work in letting go the mainsail she swung off just in time.

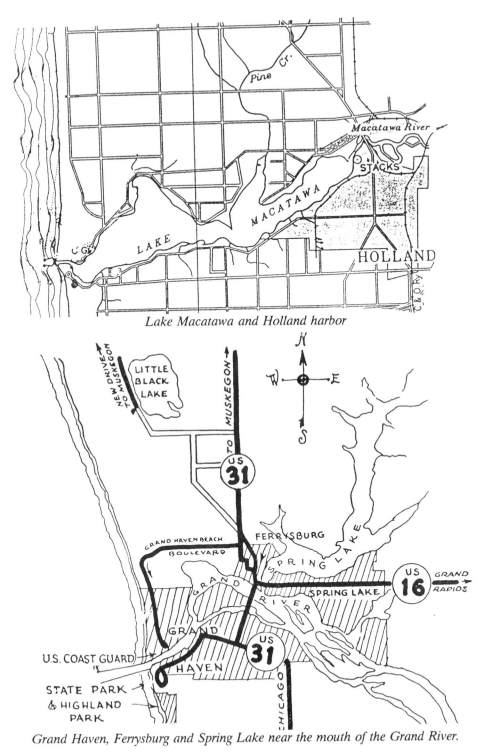

Lake Macatawa and Holland harbor

Grand Haven, Ferrysburg and Spring Lake near the mouth of the Grand River.

Amazon Survivors Rescued by Life Car

October 28, 1879
At Grand Haven Harbor

For sheer drama few disasters can top the 1879 sinking of the propeller freighter **Amazon**. The vessel was large for her time, being 1,406 gross tons, and 245 feet in length, and carried four masts. She was on her way from Milwaukee to Grand Haven with a cargo of flour and general merchandise on October 29, 1879, when a storm hit. The annual report of the Life Saving Service describes the day:

> The wreck of the **Amazon** of Detroit, Michigan, was the most notable of the season. She was a large and staunch four-masted twin screw steamer of 1,406 tons, 245 feet in length, and 40 feet beam, belonging to the Northwestern Transportation Company, and plying upon Lake Michigan, between Grand Haven, Michigan, and Milwaukee, Wisconsin, under the command of Captain James Fraser. On October 27, at 11 o'clock at night, laden with about 900 tons of flour, pork and sundries, and having 68 persons on board, her officers and crew being 32 in number and the remaining 36 being passengers, she left Milwaukee on her regular trip in a northwest blow, which was not, however, violent until toward morning, when the wind increased to a fierce gale, raising a very heavy sea and surf. The steamer arrived opposite Grand Haven at about 8 o'clock in the morning and attempted the passage between the piers which make out into the lake from the river at that place, forming the entrance to the harbor. The wind and sea were furiously driving in an oblique direction toward the end of the piers, over which the great waves were curling, and despite the best calculation, they swept the steamer aside from the entrance and carried her about 800 feet to leeward of the south pier and almost onto the bar. For a moment it seemed as if she were lost, but suddenly, to the astonishment of the spectators on the beach and piers, she backed, and with her powerful double engines and wheels tore her way out of the breakers. Fairly out in the lake again, she steamed away to the north for more than a mile, turned and again bore down upon the piers, laboring heavily through the water, the activity of her steam pumps indicating the leak that was already gaining upon her. The aim was to make in by hugging the north pier, and it was so well directed that she nearly effected the entrance, but at the very mouth of the piers, while she hung surging and staggering in the struggle to get in, the gale and the tremendous undertow slowly but irresistibly bore her past the southern pierhead and onto the bar below.
>
> From that moment all was over with her. She had struck the bar with her bow and gradually her stern swung around to the south, giving her broadside to the breakers, which now broke upon her whole length, streaming over her hurricane deck, while the spray flew in columns as

high as her cross trees. Although much enfeebled through the racking and straining to which her frame was subjected, her engines continued to work in the desperate effort to get her beyond the masses of water incessantly flung upon her, and which were battering her into a ruin, and by ten o'clock she had gradually worked up nearer to the south pier, without, however, getting beyond the destructive action of the breakers.

While this lamentable scene was going on, the crew of Life Saving Station No. 9, were not idle. The keeper being absent through illness, Mr. Loutit, the superintendent of the district, had had the surf boat brought across the river from the station on the north side, and had assembled the men upon the piers, and endeavored to throw lines to the steamer upon her successive attempts to make the harbor, with the view of aiding the entrance by holding her to the dock. These endeavors failing on account of the steamer not getting on either occasion sufficiently near, the crew, with the intention of setting up the hawser and hauling lines for rescue by the life car, embarked from the beach in the surf boat, carrying out a line, the slack of which was paid from the pier by a group of sailors. This dangerous expedition (which was undertaken because the wave swept condition of the piers made it impractical to employ the wreck gun) was finally so embarrassed by the line that the latter had to be cut, the boat being in danger of swamping and unable to make her way through the heavy seas. The crew, however, finally contributed to bring their boat alongside of the steamer, their object being to run back a line from the vessel to the shore, but it was found that unfortunately there was no line on board long enough for that purpose.

The passengers huddled together under the bulwark and pilot house to escape the seas incessantly breaking over the deck, shrank from the solicitations of the life saving crew, who wished to take back a boat load of them, and only three of the whole number who saw the daring surf boat half filled with water, which the men were bailing, could be persuaded to risk the return passage through the terrible sea. These three the boat soon landed on the beach in safety, though well drenched. Meanwhile, a lot of freight was discharged into the sea from the leeward gangway, somewhat lightening the vessel, which continued to work slowly under the stubborn though failing action of the machinery, until she was within about fifty yards of the pier, when by a bold cast of the heaving stick a line was thrown on board the wreck. By this the hawser and the hauling lines for the employment of the life car were now run out.

Meanwhile the breaking up of the vessel continued with increasing rapidity. A little after ten o'clock the first fragments of the hurricane deck had begun to strew the water. The hull was so heavily freighted and so imbedded in the sand that it did not pound much, but the gale and sea were smashing and splintering everything. The stanchions of the deck were giving way and the boats hanging on the windward side of the bulwarks were beating to pieces against the hull; one of them especially got loose and battered against the cabin with such force as to breach its walls. Captain Fraser, at the period of his life, got over the deck with an ax, and although several times actually buried in the flooding seas, succeeded in cutting the boat loose. The sea, however, still continued the destruction of the cabin, wrenching off piece after piece, until soon there was a large hole in the west side, through which the water swept without impediment. At the same time it was noticed from the shore that the ends of the steamer were lower than the middle, indicating that the vessel was broken in two and her wreck accomplished.

It was at this hour (eleven o'clock) that the life car made its first passage out to the steamer, the hawser and hauling lines having been set up to the foremast with their shore ends made fast to a timber of the pier. One of the life saving crew, John Vissel, went out in the life car to superintend operations, and from the moment that he was seen from the shore standing on the deck of the **Amazon**, it was generally felt that the people on board were safe. This confidence was not without warrant, for in an hour and a quarter every one on board was landed, being sixty-five persons, exclusive of the three persons landed by the boat. The first trip of the car brought ashore four ladies and a little girl; after which the hawser was doubled to prevent possible accident and the lines carried ten feet higher up the mast above the pilot house, so as to keep the car well away from the sea. The remaining six ladies on board came in the next car, followed in successive trips by the male passengers and the crew, the captain being the last to leave the vessel. The life car made fourteen trips in all, the last two or three being devoted to bringing ashore the United States mails and the baggage of the passengers. A dog was also brought ashore. The vessel was a total wreck.

Three years later, in 1882, the engine was recovered and given to M. M. Drake.

The life car was a metal capsule made of copper or iron, with a convex cover that had a hatchway in the top. The car held four to six persons. After the door was shut tight, it was conveyed to shore suspended by rings on a rope, often through the water, nearly always with the waves crashing over it. An 1880 life saving manual notes, "To be shut up in this manner in so dark and gloomy a receptacle for the purpose of being drawn, perhaps at midnight through a surf of such terrific violence that no boat can live in it, can not be a very agreeable alternative; but the emergencies in which the use of the life-car is called for, are such as do not admit of hesitation or delay."

Six Vessels Ashore

November 19, 1879
Near Grand Haven Harbor

When there was trouble at Grand Haven, there was often a whole lot of trouble. The harbor piers seemed to be more difficult than some to enter in a storm, and, like a chain collision on today's highways, one disaster often led to another. The night of November 19, 1879, the problems began at midnight. The story is chronicled in the Life Saving Station annual report:

> The schooner **Maple Leaf** of Milwaukee, Wisconsin, bound from White Hall, Michigan to Milwaukee, with a cargo of lumber and a crew of four men, encountered a heavy southwest storm and struck on the sunken cribs of the north pier at Grand Haven, Michigan. The accident occurred at midnight and was seen by the patrol of Station No. 9, Eleventh District. A line was thrown from the vessel to the pier and after securing it the patrol hastened to give the alarm at the station. The keeper and crew went immediately to the wreck which they found already full of water, lying with her jib boom over the pier, and the sea, which was very boisterous, breaking over her aft. The keeper and two of his men boarded her by the jib boom and assisted the crew to secure the sails and rigging and also to gather their personal effects and get them ashore. This done, they took them to the station and made them comfortable for the night.
>
> Three hours later (3 o'clock a.m.) while the keeper of the station was still on the pier after the disaster to the **Maple Leaf**, endeavoring to take measures for saving her, the schooner **J. A. Holmes** of Chicago, Illinois, crashed into her dismasting and almost cutting her in two so that she became a total wreck. As both vessels were being pounded to pieces by the furious collisions, the keeper directed the captain of the **J. A. Holmes** to scuttle her, which was done. The two vessels lay so as to form a breakwater and rendered it practicable for the keeper to get a boat to the **J. A. Holmes** and rescue the six men on board, who were taken to the station and housed with those before rescued.
>
> The keeper and crew of Station No. 9 had their hands full on this night of storm and disaster. An hour after the stranding of the **J. A. Holmes** (4 o'clock a.m.) the schooner **Margaret Dall** of Chicago, came ashore and stranded about 200 feet north of the north pier, where she was at once scuttled to prevent her from pounding to pieces. The life saving crew made two trips to her in a boat, and brought off her crew of seven persons and their effects and took them to the station where they remained until 8 a.m.
>
> Almost at the same moment that the **Margaret Dall** stranded the barge **C.O.D.** of Grand Haven, which had been cut away from her

tug on account of the violence of the wind and sea, was flung high upon the strand about 200 feet from the **Margaret Dall** The life saving crew, after landing the men from the latter, went to the **C. O. D.**, but her crew refused to leave her.

While the crew of No. 9 were still on duty at the scene of these disasters the steam tug **General H. E. Paine** of Grand Haven, Michigan, struck on the bar and began to leak. She went about 100 feet farther and struck again on the end of the north pier and sank immediately. The life saving crew went to her at once with the boat and in two trips brought off her two passengers and crew of thirteen persons. In thirty minutes from the time the vessel struck the pier she was in pieces and out of sight.

In the meantime, at 7:30 in the morning, the schooner **Mystic** of Grand Haven, from Racine, Wisconsin, with a crew of three men, when near the mouth of Grand Haven Harbor, broke her tiller, drifted to the lee shore, and stranded high and dry. The crew of No. 9 went to her, but found the men had walked ashore.

The bulk freighter **Maple Leaf**, 87 tons, was trying to deliver a load of lumber which she foundered, but after the collision was a total loss. The schooner **J. A. Holmes** 167 gross tons, was built in 1867 at Mears, Michigan, in Oceana county. She was raised and continued on the Lakes until at least 1890. The schooner **Margaret Dall**, 150 gross tons, had been built at Michigan City in 1867, she was raised and continued in service as did the **C.O.D.** The tug **Gen. H. E. Paine**, 48 tons, had been built in Boston in 1865 as the **Trefoil**, as described in the life saving station report she was declared a total loss.

The **Mystic** remained on the beach until December 10 when the captain and crew of the schooner were at work trying to get her off the beach. During the operation a violent storm arose, floated the vessel, and swept her away over 150 feet to the outer bar, where she began to pound so heavily that the men on board had to scuttle her to prevent her being battered to pieces. They then took to the rigging and showed signals of distress. The crew of Station No. 9 were unable to get the life boat out of the harbor because of the "violence of the sea" but finally succeeded in getting a smaller boat to the rescue by towing it along the shore until they were opposite the vessel and taking advantage of the larger boat's lee to get alongside and take off the imperiled sailors. The little schooner, 38 gross tons, had been built at Grand Haven in 1879. She was eventually raised and continued in service until 1891.

Stanton, King Collide in Lake Michigan

April 8, 1880
Off Grand Haven

According to the April 12, 1880 edition of the *Holland City News*:

A serious collision occurred about 60 miles off Grand Haven

last Thursday night between the schooners **E. M. Stanton** and **R. B. King**, the former bound for Manistee, light, and the latter for Chicago with slabs from Grand River. The accident happened in fair weather and the captains and crews of both vessels have their respective stories to tell as to the manner in which it took place, and both claim to be right. The crafts came together with terrific force, the **Stanton** striking the **King** on the bluff of the port bow and cutting clear into her, so badly in fact, that the latter became waterlogged, and subsequently required the former to remain along side of her so that she could be kept afloat.

The **R. B. King** eventually made it to port and was repaired. She was less lucky on November 7, 1885, when she sank in the harbor at Muskegon, Michigan. Two members of the crew died in the second accident.

Schooner **U. S. Grant** Misses Harbor in a Gale

November 11, 1880
Grand Haven Piers

The 87 ton schooner **U. S. Grant** was on her way from Michigan City to Grand Haven under Captain Ludwig which she wrecked at Grand Haven on November 11, 1880. The report of the Grand Haven Life Saving Station says:

> The schooner **U. S. Grant** of South Haven with a crew of four men was discovered by a patrolman of station 9 (Grand Haven) in danger as she was endeavoring to make the harbor at Grand Haven in a southwest gale. He made warning signals to her, but in the high sea and strong current she was unable to avoid the north pier, which she struck, then, falling off to leeward, stranded about 150 feet above. It was half past three o'clock in the morning, but the crew of the station were on hand immediately, and got her hawser ashore and made fast to windward, which kept the schooner from falling further to leeward and going to pieces on an old wreck. They kept watch over her all night, but nothing more could then be done. Much bad weather ensuing she became a total loss.

Schooners **Seaver** and **Wing** Collide

November 14-17, 1880
Saugatuck and South Haven

Two vessels involved in a midlake collision staggered afterwards into South Haven and Saugatuck. According to the November 20, 1880, *South Haven Sentinel*:

While the schooner **Winnie Wing** was on a voyage from Chicago to Pentwater, and when about thirty-five miles off Grand Haven, at five o'clock Sunday morning, she was struck by a three-master, supposed to have been the **George L. Seaver**, tearing away the stays of the foremast and letting that altogether with the sails, rigging, and all, but fifteen or twenty feet of the mainmast into the lake. The **Wing** drifted to within six or seven miles to the north of this port when Capt. Peter Peterson left her Wednesday and came here to have the **Groh** go and get her. She now lays in the harbor and will soon be towed to Pentwater, as she has some 6,000 bushels of oats and corn on board, the property of her owners. Whatever it was that struck her paid no attention to the blow or its consequences. Since then the **Seaver** went on the beach at Saugatuck and is reported a total wreck.

To the north in Saugatuck they also had only half of the story. The *Lake Shore Commercial* for November 19, 1880, reported:

> The schooner **Geo. L. Seavers**, C. Peterson, master, is ashore north of the piers. She collided with a schooner supposed to be the **Winnie Wing** forty miles southwest of Muskegon. The crew were all saved but the vessel and cargo will be a total loss.

Although both newspaper accounts mention in passing that the two schooners had collided no charges were brought by either owner and no more detailed account of the accident were published in any of the area newspapers. The *News and Reporter* of Muskegon noted in its Marine Notes for November 20:

> The Schooner **George L. Seaver**, ashore at Saugatuck, is a total loss. Jonathan Boyce the owner refused $4,000 for the vessel last spring. The cargo of lumber was valued $1,400 and is also a total loss. Mr. Boyce had no insurance on either.

The **George L. Seaver** was the first three masted schooner built at South Haven and bore the name of a local businessman. The vessel was launched in 1867 but spent only a few years, in the early 1870s, based at South Haven. In 1873 she incurred the displeasure of the local people by ignoring a signal of distress flown by the sinking schooner **Lizzie Throop.**

The captains of both schooners involved in the incident had the same last name. The *South Haven Sentinel* noted, November 27, "That is a rather peculiar coincidence, and the family strawberry mark on the left arm will undoubtedly be sought for and thus prove each to be the long lost brother."

On November 27 the tug **Messenger** arrived in South Haven to take the **Winnie Wing** to Pentwater for repairs. The **Winnie Wing** was 200.23 gross tons, 190.22 net tons and had been built in 1867 at Port Huron. She later returned to service. The **Seavers** was left to break up on the beach.

Alpena

Alpena Disappears during "Big Blow"

October 17, 1880
Wreckage Found Near Holland

One of the most famous wrecks on the east shore of Lake Michigan is that of the steamer **Alpena** which disappeared in October of 1880 during a storm that was so devastating to Great Lakes boats and shipping that it has been known ever afterward as the "Big Blow." The October 23, 1880, *Holland City News* described the events:

> The steamer **Alpena** of the Goodrich Line. . . left Grand Haven for Chicago on Friday evening last about 9:30 p.m. . . . while the weather was beautiful, the barometer predicted a violent storm, and the storm signals were out. She was met on her way by the steamer **Muskegon** at about one o'clock in the morning, all right, steering her course. All seem to agree that the worst gale that ever swept over Lake Michigan struck her at about 3 o'clock on Saturday morning, or a few minutes thereafter. Subsequent news from her shows that she, nor anything else, could keep her course in the face of such a hurricane. She was seen at six, seven and eight o'clock by the schooner **Irish** and by Capt. George Boomsluiter of the barge **City of Grand Haven** off Kenosha, at an estimated distance of about 35 miles from the west shore laboring heavy to crawl to the windward.

She was seen later in the same locality by other vessel captains one of whom reported that she was lying on one side, with one of her paddles out of the water. This would indicate that her cargo had shifted and thus she became unmanageable.

She must have drifted the rest of that day, and perhaps until Sunday morning at the mercy of the wind and waves well over to this shore -- say 15 or 20 miles -- when the wind shifted to the westward or nearly northwest and brought the debris of the wreck on our beach near our harbor.

Later reports named Captain Ludwig of the schooner **Challenger** as the last person to see the **Alpena** still afloat. He described the vessel as 30 miles east of Kenosha, wallowing badly in the troughs of high seas and blowing distress signals. Since the **Challenger** herself was then under bare poles fighting to remain afloat there was nothing Ludwig could do to assist the **Alpena**.

The Holland paper describes the debris that was coming ashore as that of a ship that was thoroughly broken up. "The wreck is complete," the report reads. "She is broken into small fragments. The stern part of her hull lies near the harbor. The whole coast for twenty miles is strewn with the debris, freight, etc." The largest piece to land near Holland was the piano. "it being barely able to float, our sailors concluded that she did not come very far. And the arrival of other heavy pieces of the wreck would seem to corroborate this idea."

The *Saugatuck Commercial* noted in the October 22 issue, "We were down on the shore last Wednesday afternoon and found the reports of the wreck strewn shore not exaggerated. Shingles, lath, lumber and pieces of the ill-fated **Alpena** were scattered thickly on the beach." The **Alpena** carried a deck load of apples, and many who visited the scene of the wreck reported thousands of bright right apples bobbing around in the surf.

The exact number of victims could not be determined with any certainty because the only passenger record was on board the boat itself, but it was estimated that there were about 45 passengers and a crew of 25. Other accounts insist that there were 80 or more. The crew included Captain Nelson W. Napier of St. Joseph; J. H. Kelley of Green Bay, Wisconsin, first mate; R. W. Johnson of Grand Haven, first engineer; Robert Patton of Chicago, second engineer; John Brown of Chicago, steward; and Arthur E. Haynes of Chicago, clerk. Passengers included W. S. Benham, the editor of the *Grand Haven Herald* and his wife; M. Crossman, foreman of the Stearns Manufacturing Co. of Grand Haven, and the Osborne family, parents and three children. Grand Haven hotel registries for the night preceding the sailing were scanned to gain additional possibilities. The Holland newspaper described the scene:

When the news became known throughout the surrounding county that the **Alpena** was actually gone under, the excitement rose higher and higher. A special train, loaded with anxious relatives and friends of the supposed lost ones, came from Grand Haven, and each day brings more and more of them.

Our livery stables are doing an immense business. But we are sorry to learn that some of them had the *gall* to overcharge.

Captain Thomas G. Butlin, superintendent of the Goodrich Line, arrived at Holland to help in the search for cargo, wreckage and bodies. The U. S. steam tug **Graham** was pressed into service to search for and secure floating bodies. Many wore life jackets that indicated that the boat went down after a long struggle.

A coroner's hearing was held in December of 1880 at Grand Haven, county seat of Ottawa County, and the verdict was that the persons aboard had come to their death by the foundering of the steamer **Alpena** and that the steamer "was in a bad condition and unseaworthy for a passenger boat." The charges stemmed from evidence that the life preservers were in bad condition, the lifeboats were rotten and unseaworthy, and that the steamer was manned by inexperienced sailors, except the Captain and Mates. The charges were actively opposed by A. E. Goodrich, president of the line.

The **Alpena** was a sidewheel steamer, 653 tons, built at Marine City in 1866. She was bought by Goodrich from Gardner, Ward & Gallagher in April of 1868, and had been completely overhauled in the winter of 1876. The vessel was valued at $80,000, partially covered by insurance.

Monsoon Founders in Storm

November, 1881
Lake Michigan, Location Uncertain

The **Monsoon**, a bulk freight schooner of 132 tons sailed from Muskegon in November of 1881. On her way to Chicago she was struck by a storm and foundered, losing all six hands aboard.

At least one newspaper editor thought he knew exactly what had happened. The November 26, 1881, issue of the *Muskegon Daily Chronicle* reprinted a paragraph from the *InterOcean*:

> The captain of the lost schooner **Monsoon** had great difficulty in securing a tug to clear the port. The vessel was so notoriously rotten that no tug captain cared to risk a collision no matter how slight. How long with this government permit such coffins to float?

Three Die as **Industry Misses Port**

June 3, 1882
Mouth of South Haven Harbor

The merchant schooner **Industry** capsized and sank trying on June 3, 1882, to enter the port of South Haven for a reason that has never been discovered. The captain and the two man crew were all lost.

The *South Haven Sentinel* for June 10, 1882, gives the following dramatic account:

One of the saddest accidents of a local nature we have ever been called upon to record happened at this port last Saturday evening. The schooner **Industry** left St. Joseph that morning, passed here about noon, and at 6 o'clock she was within less than a mile of this port coming back south. The fact of her trying to make port in such a storm showed that something unusual had occurred as an old sailor like Capt. King would have preferred an open sea and deep water to chancing the attempt unless he had extraordinary reasons for so doing.

She was carrying very little canvass forward, a jib and perhaps stay-sail, and in trying to hoist the foresail to give her sufficient headway to enter the harbor she careened and rolled over *against* the wind, which proved conclusively that she was waterlogged. She then drifted past the mouth of the harbor with her three men clinging to her bottom.

The alarm was instantly given and nearly our entire population rushed to the shore to give aid if possible. She drifted up under the bluff of R. Haigh, Jr., where her spars and anchors held her for a few moments. During her course to this point she was many times submerged each time re-appearing with her doomed crew clinging to her with hopeless tenacity. The feelings of the spectators may be conjectured when it is known that among them were many of the wives and relatives of the sailors of our home fleet, to which she was thought by many to belong.

L. A. Leighton, accompanied by George Williams, throwing off outerclothing, plunged into the surf in the vain hope of swimming out near enough to heave them a line, but the heavy breakers, the blinding and chilling wind and above all the treacherous and powerful "undertow" rendered every effort futile and the shouts of the multitude on the bank and those of the doomed men on the wreck were alike hushed in the voice of the storm. The fierce and chilling wind dashing the heavy seas over the unfortunates so frequently, often submerging them for so long a time that it seemed as if nothing but a miracle could save them from strangulation, at length completed its work. With her continued pounding her spars gave way and she rolled, returning to the surface to show her anxious watchers that she had rid herself of her living freight. L. A. Leighton thinks he was so near to them that had the men let go and been able to buffet the seas the force of two waves would have brought them within his reach, but it is probable that at that time they were too far gone from exhaustion to help themselves in the least. Brave and willing hearts and strong hands were there by the hundreds, and had our harbor contained a single surf-boat capable of standing such a sea the men would have been rescued long before the vessel rolled over, as our fleet contains as good and brave seamen as ever trod a deck.

As none of our steam craft were fired up no effort on their part could have been in time to prevent the catastrophe. With sad hearts the people returned to town, the wind whistling a sad requiem over the lonely grave of the lost men.

The **Industry** was owned by Capt. John King of St. Joseph, 59 years of age and for 31 years a sailor. He, his son Ebenezar and a young man named Callender were those lost. The son was 21 years old and Callender 18. Capt James King, another son, was here during the week with Capt. Jas. McDonald looking for the bodies, but without success. The **Industry** was found Sunday morning against Packard's Pier. As before said all was done by our people that could be done to save them. Imagine 500 or 600 people on a bluff 40 or 50 feet above the lake, with not an inch of beach below them, the wind blowing so a rope could hardly be lowered to the water's edge, those three men in plain sight on the brink of a watery grave, and the situation in which South Haven people were placed can be seen.

On June 16 the body of Ed Callender, was found floating near the shore seven miles south of South Haven, and the following day the body of Captain John King, was cast on the beach about a mile further south. The body of Ebenezar King washed up on the South Haven beach a week later. It was rumored that the disaster had been caused by the **Industry** coming in contact with pound nets set in the lake, when she attempted to hoist her sails, but the verdict at the coroner's inquest found no fault with the fishermen.

The Two Stage Disaster of the **Jesse Martin**

November 23 and 30, 1882
Grand Haven Harbor

A gale was raging when the Grand Haven Life Saving lookout noted a vessel trying to enter the harbor, November 23, 1882. The events were later described in the annual report of the Life Saving Service:

> . . . As the vessel could only carry a short sail, owing to the gale, she was swept too far to leeward by the strong southerly current setting along shore across the harbor mouth, and the result was that, despite the exertions of her crew to keep her up, she struck the south pier, and drove ashore just to the leeward of it. The alarm was at once given at the station, and the men, jumping into the surf boat, pulled across the river, and ran down the pier just in time to catch a line from the vessel to hold her there until they could assist the three men composing her crew on to the pier, whence they were taken across the river to the station for the night. She was the **Jessie Martin** from Milwaukee, Wisconsin, bound to Muskegon, Michigan, where she belonged, with a cargo of flour and oats.

After the gale it was determined that it was worthwhile to attempt to salvage the vessel. John Dibble of Muskegon was awarded the contract to float the schooner and have her towed into the harbor. She had two holes in the starboard bow. One hole was above water and was easily stopped from the outside. The other, about eight inches in diameter was below water level and could not be reached by the diver, so it was plugged from the inside with gunny bags held in place by wooden braces from the dock beams. The **Martin** was then pumped free of water. According to the life saving station report:

On the morning of November 30, the tug **W. Batcheller**, made fast to her by a line about 700 feet long. The weather was cloudy and freezing cold, a southwest gale was blowing at the rate of thirty miles an hour, and a stormy sea was running in great waves throwing showers of spray upon the schooner, which accumulated on her hull, spars and rigging in rough sheaths of ice. On board was Mr. Dibble, the contractor, a one-armed man, heavily dressed against the weather, and wearing long boots, and there were also six men whom he had employed to prepare the vessel for being pulled off, and who were also well swathed up in storm proof clothing.

About 10 o'clock the tug, then lying abreast of the south pier, steamed away, the tow line taut, and the schooner came off the beach with a plunge, and seemed to stand on end between the seas, the water meanwhile bursting upward and madly sheeting all over her. The next instant she plunged downward covered with foam and spray, then mounted again bow up, as though she were going to leave the sea, the breakers still scattering over her, and continued her progress in this way under the strain of the tow line, striking the bottom so heavily with each descent as to jar all her timbers, and make the men on board afraid that her masts would be unstepped and thrown out of her. Before long, as she got into deeper water, the pounding ceased, and she began to labor heavily, falling off sluggishly into the vast troughs of the sea, as though waterlogged. Probably the violent pounding with which she began her course displaced the gunny bag packing in the hole in her hull, letting the sea stream in, and it is also likely that with the torrents constantly bursting over her she took in water at her hatches, which were on but not fastened down as they should have been. She continued to move forward, wallowing more and more inertly, until the tug had gone about half a mile beyond the pier end and had swept around in a great circle to enter the piers. The schooner had now, following the same curve, swung around broadside to the sea, and as the tug made for the entrance began to feel the tow line pulling on her starboard bow to bring her head around. What ensued was as speedy as awful. The wretched vessel, lolling in the trough of the sea, so full of water as to be without buoyancy, pushed by the gale upon her port side and pulled by the tow line upon the other, instead of coming around under the strain, was simply dragged down and rolled over like a log to starboard, settling upon her bulwarks until her masts lay in the water. As she toppled, the sea burst all over her hull in a furious cascade, and her hatches fell off and floated away. The men on board as she capsized scattered out into her rigging in a wild scramble for their lives. Incumbered by their clothing, their struggles on an overturning ship, in the whirl of flying water, were of necessity terrible. Three reached the main shrouds, two got to the fore cross-trees and one to the main. The remaining man, Mr. Dibble, had been in the passageway alongside the cabin on the starboard side, and the men in the shrouds could see him, near the surface of the water in that region, vainly trying to climb on to the main boom. As he had but one arm, and was hampered by the abundance of his clothing, his efforts were ineffectual. For a short time he moaned and struggled in the water, but gradually the sounds and motions ceased and he slowly drowned. Meanwhile the prostrate wreck, with the men clinging to her shrouds and cross trees, was leaping and floundering, still sluggishly advancing in the tow of the tug, which was endeavoring to get her inside the piers where there was still water.

Keeper John De Young was at the Grand Haven Station, some distance away, watching from the doorway the operations of the tug from the beginning. His crew were in the house, with the exception of one man out on patrol on the north pier. The moment the schooner capsized he sprang back shouting to the crew to launch the boat. The station is on the edge of the pier, and with one rush the men poured out, shoved the boat into the water, and tumble in with alacrity. The tug **Johnson** was lying near the station, and at once took them in tow, giving them an opportunity to put on their cork jackets, which in their haste they had neglected to don. After towing them about half way down the piers the tug cast off, and the men seized the oars and pulled out, meeting the **W. Batcheller** outside the ends of the piers, still towing the wreck in, her steam whistle meanwhile screeching an alarm. They rowed on and soon reached the capsized schooner. A more exciting spectacle could hardly have been encountered. The vessel lay on her side, jumping about like a living thing in the huge wash of the seas, with her masts submerged. Two drenched and streaming figures, waist-deep in the water, clung to the fore cross trees, one horn of which bobbed around above the surface. Another similar figure was holding on at the main cross trees. Three others, limp and inert, were hanging in the main shrouds, dipped and thrashed about continually, and most of the time under water. The body of the contractor was in the sea, beneath the main sail, and not visible.

The keeper speedily made up his mind that the two men on the fore cross trees were in the most dangerous position, as a gaff or boom was flailing around them with every leap of the hull. Accordingly he steered the boat's bow up to them, the crew cautiously oaring in. The rigging of the wreck was beneath them, and every time the seas fell they could feel it press and scrape against the boat's bottom. As soon as they got within reach the forward men seized the two sufferers, one by one, and dragged them on board. The boat fell away.

The two men rescued, unmanned by fright and suffering, and fearful that the boat would be capsized in the raging sea, begged the keeper to put them on shore at once, but he told them that he would first save everyone on the wreck or perish, and bidding them stow close and keep still, ordered the boat pulled around the schooner's bow, which was under water, as well as the tow line, and dropping back on the windward side, abreast of the main rigging, took a momentary survey of the situation. In a moment he sang out to the man in the main cross trees that he was going to take off the three men in the main shrouds first as they were in the most danger, to which the man assented. A scene of terrible gallantry followed. The keeper ordered the men in the bow to throw the boat's painter to the three men in the shrouds, but as the rope fell upon one man inert and the other two apparently dead, it was drawn back, and the effort to attach the boat to the wreck was renewed with the small grapnel. The grapnel, however, could not be made to hold, and the bold surfmen now tried to attach the boat to the rigging by the boat hooks. Despite the convulsion tumbling of the water, they succeeded for a minute in keeping alongside, and dragged one of the three men aboard over the bow. The next instant a huge sea swept them on top of the wreck, the boat hooks scattering from the surfmen's hands and getting lost. Another high sea followed and swept them off, carrying them swiftly astern of the wreck a boat's length. In a second the oars were out and the men again pulled up alongside. The solitary man in the main cross trees had meanwhile worked his way along the rigging and was dragged aboard instantly. Then came a third enormous wave, which washed all over the wreck, and buried one of the two men clinging to the shrouds under water. The keeper could just see his head upon the surface, and, fearful that he was going to lose him, shouted to his men to jump and save him. Surfman Paul Vandenburg at once sprang into the flood, but caught his foot in the wreck as he went and pitched over to leeward, coming up again quickly, floated by his cork jacket. Surfmen Van Toll and Fisher followed him in the jump for the wreck, clutched the submerged man and hauled him by main strength above water, themselves holding by the rigging. They then helped their comrade, Vandenburg, to regain his place in the boat, which he effected with the loss of one rubber boot, his foot having been tangled up in the sunken shrouds.

The fearful excitement of the scene continued in the effort to get the two half-drowned and perishing men on board into the surf boat. Words can hardly describe the difficulties and perils involved in the task. Both of the men were unconscious, half sustained by being enmeshed in the rigging and half by Surfmen Van Toll and Fisher, who held by the shrouds, waist deep in the water, and buoyed up by their cork jackets, waiting their chance to heave the dead weight in their hands into the surf boat. This chance depended on the boat getting fairly alongside between the seas -- no safe or easy matter, as she followed a vessel steadily receding under tow toward the harbor and bounding from side to side like a wounded whale with every wash of the furious waves. It was only wary maneuvering that kept her from being at any moment flung into the air by collision with the wreck or stove to flinders. Every other minute the torn waters yawned in troughs, into which she dropped to rise the next instant, quivering and leaping on the summit of the curling ridges. The keeper and two surfmen worked her by the oars, while the two others on board were kept steadily bailing, the strong wind keeping her, nevertheless, half full with the spray it showered over her. So great was the peril that the rescued men on board, expecting every moment to be capsized thought they would be safer on the wreck and one man even wanted to get overboard himself to the half sunk rigging. It was under these conditions that the desperate toil of the rescue was conducted, and it was fully half an hour before the two drenched and inanimate figures were got into the boat. Surfmen Van Toll and Fisher than clambered in out of the water and the surf boat shoved off and made for the harbor.

Keeper De Young's greatest fear now was that the unconscious men might never revive, and the moment the station was reached they were taken upstairs and stripped and put to bed, as were all the others. The man who had been longest under water the keeper at once laid down and practiced on him the method of resuscitating the apparently drowned. It was half an hour before he showed any signs of life and about an hour before he came to. "He was just like a chunk of ice, he was so cold," said the keeper in his deposition. As soon as he became conscious brandy was given him, and for three hours he was swathed in hot flannels and vigorously rubbed with them by the keeper and his men. Finally he was left between hot blankets and in about five hours was himself again. Of the other men two were insensible but were revived without great effort by the rubbing of the life saving crew and the administration of cordials. There was not at the time any change of clothing at the station, and the six men were kept in bed until their clothes were dried. As for the life saving crew, they were drenched, and performed their ministrations in the wettest of wet habiliments.

The keeper did not learn of Mr. Dibble's death until after he had left the wreck, and as soon as he was assured of the revival of the man who had been so nearly drowned, or within an hour after the arrival at the station, he had an old metallic boat launched and rowed out with four men to the wreck, which was then lying in the still water abreast of the station. The body of the unfortunate man was found under water, beneath the mainsail, held by a turn of the peak halyards around one leg. He had been thus submerged for over two hours, and was of course lifeless. It is plain that under the circumstances of the catastrophe nothing could have been done to save him.

The **Jesse Martin** was salvaged, repaired and put back into service. Her career ended August 20, 1908. She was bound from Ludington to Manitowoc with a load of lumber when she was caught in a storm. At 7:30 p.m. the Ludington Life Saving Station lookout saw a distress signal on Lake Michigan, north of the station. The keeper and crew launched their power life boat and soon after leaving shore met two crewmen in the schooner's yawl who said that the vessel was leaking badly and beginning to list. The life savers returned to the station to secure the services of a tug but were unable to find the schooner. The following morning she was discovered stranded and broken up on the beach two miles north of the station. Only the spars and sails were salvaged.

Schooner **Thomas B. Skinner** Ashore

November 23, 1882
Grand Haven Harbor Entrance

The same night that the **Jessie Martin** went ashore at Grand Haven, the schooner **Thomas B. Skinner** suffered a similar fate. The **Skinner** was registered at Muskegon. She was 195 gross tons, 115.3 feet in length, 27.3 feet in beam and 8.9 feet in depth. She had been built at Port Huron, Michigan, in 1869 by Thomas Dunford. At the time of her loss she was owned by Henry W. Davis of Port Huron. The life saving station report describes the circumstances:

> On the same night that the **Jessie Martin** ran ashore in attempting to enter the harbor of Grand Haven, Michigan, the schooner **Thomas N. Skinner**, of and from Muskegon, Michigan, for Chicago, Illinois, with a cargo of lumber, which was also attempting to find shelter from the storm, met with a similar accident to that which befell the **Martin**, the current setting her so far out of her course that she struck the pier and afterwards drove onto the beach, where she subsequently became a wreck. She was discovered at 8 o'clock standing in for the harbor by the crew of the Grand Haven Station, who had just rescued the three men from the **Jessie Martin**. She struck the pier a quarter of an hour later, and the men, rushing to the spot, caught a line thrown by the sailors and made it fast. Two of the men at once jumped on to the pier, and the rest, six in number, were about to follow when the line parted under the strain brought to bear on it, and the schooner drove onto the beach to the southward of the harbor. The station crew sprang into the surf boat and pulled out and around the end of the pier to the stranded vessel, and in a short time took the six men off and safely landed them. The vessel was lost, but the sails and rigging and a portion of the cargo were recovered with the assistance of the life saving crew, who aided by every means in their power in saving the property.

During her attempt to make the harbor the **Skinner** ran square on to the south pier, carrying away her head-gear, and knocking off the red light on the end of the pier making it even more difficult for subsequent vessels to enter the harbor, until the storm subsided and it could be repaired. The loss incurred by the owners of the **Thomas S. Skinner** included: cargo, of lumber, $3,000; vessel $6,000.

Mary Nau Wrecks in Gale

October 30, 1883
Grand Haven Pier

Mary Nau, bulk freight schooner of 136 tons, sank at the harbor entrance at Grand Haven on October 30, 1883. The life saving station annual report states:

> At about 2 o'clock in the morning the schooner **Mary Nau** of Chicago, Illinois, from Whitehall, Michigan, bound to Chicago with a cargo of lumber and having a crew of six men, attempting to make the harbor of Grand Haven, Michigan, during a heavy westerly gale with a high sea, but, having lost some of her sails, and being in a waterlogged condition, she was swept by the strong current onto the beach about half a mile to the southward of the Grand Haven station.
>
> The station patrol discovered the vessel fifteen minutes after she struck and at once alarmed the keeper and crew. The surf boat was immediately manned and the crew pulled with all speed to the vessel. Upon arriving on the scene they were alarmed to find the vessel was rapidly breaking up. Watching their opportunity, they quickly dashed alongside and took the six men off in safety, and in less than an hour from the time they started all hands were safely housed at the station. The schooner was not long in going to pieces, and in twenty-four hours not a vestige of her was left to mark the spot where the wreck occurred.

The **Mary Nau** had been built in 1864 for Lambert Nau Sr., the father of George D. Nau, owner of the Nau Tug Line, in business in Green Bay 1890 to 1917.

Three Vessels Lost, 28 Saved

November 11-14, 1883
Holland and Saugatuck

The chain of events that occurred near the Michigan shore on November 28, 1883, actually began on October 31 when the schooner **Arab** of Milwaukee bound from Starkeville, Michigan, (later known as Arcadia) struck the bottom near the entrance to St. Joseph harbor and went on the beach south of the piers. The schooner was secured by the St. Joseph life saving crew and her men rescued by way of a makeshift gangway. When the storm cleared the **Arab** was towed into St. Joseph where part of her cargo of lumber was removed. She then left for Milwaukee on November 10 under tow of the steam tug **Protection** with two steam pumps on the schooner to keep her free of water. On board the schooner and tug were two engineers and two firemen to operate the steam pumps under Capt. Kelley; Capt. Starke and five men, the **Arab's** crew; the tug's crew comprising Capt. Anderson and six men, and Capt. Blackburn, wrecking master. The *Life-*

Saving Annual Report describes what happened next:

> At the time of starting there was bright moonlight, with light airs and an easy swell of the sea from the westward. The night continued calm and splendid, and the two vessels held their course west by north across the lake without incident until about 4 o'clock in the morning, when suddenly the people on the tug heard cries from the schooner, which was about five hundred feet in the rear and saw commotion on her decks. The next sight was her sailors rushing aft, while the schooner rolled over and plunged down by the head, sinking in a half perpendicular position and lying aslant in the water, with only about ten feet of her port quarter sticking up. To this part of the vessel the sailors were presently seen clinging, making the night echo with their cries. . . No time was lost aboard the tug in moving to the relief of the schooner's crew. The pilot instantly rang to stop and back the vessel; and now ensued another misfortune. In backing, the propeller caught the two line and twirled it up like a reel until it stopped and disabled the engine. . . A small boat was launched and rowed to the rescue. It was found on coming alongside the wreck that one of her men, William Kelly, an engineer of the pumps, had been drowned. He had been standing forward when the schooner made her lurch for the depths and (probably crushed by the overturning pumps) had gone down with her bows. Four of the men clinging to the unsubmerged port quarter, were at once taken to the tug in the boat, which presently returned and delivered the other five.

With two crews, a total of 17 men on board, the **Protection** was now adrift about midlake. It was later learned that the pumps were working so well aboard the **Arab** that only one was in active use. However it developed a mechanical problem and, although the workers began quickly to set the second pump in motion, the water increased rapidly before sufficient steam could be raised. The weight of the pumps forward aided in sending the bow of the vessel down.

All aboard the **Protection** began a concerted effort to free the propeller. As they worked the weather deteriorated and at the end of four hours when their efforts were abandoned the wind was approaching gale force.

Meanwhile, the steamer **H. C. Akeley** had left Chicago Sunday morning, November 11, for Buffalo, with a large cargo of corn. The life saving report continues:

> At about 11 o'clock (November 11) a large propeller, the **H. C. Akeley** of Grand Haven, Michigan. . . surged up on the horizon astern, and in response to the steam whistle of the **Protection** came plowing down the stormy waste and took her in tow, heading about north, or toward the Manitou Islands. The wind was constantly increasing. By the afternoon it had become a fearful gale, the records of the signal office at Grand Haven given its velocity at fifty-two miles an hour. The sea was also tremendous, and the **Akeley** began to make very bad weather. She

rolled heavily, and it was evident from her motions that she had shifted her cargo. With every roll the seas washed clean over her. At about 7 o'clock in the evening her steering gear became disabled, her engines stopped, and she fell off helplessly, broadside to the sea. Sail was made upon her, but the wind blew away her mainsail and mizzen, and she could only drift like her consort, the tug, which still continued in her tow. At 4 o'clock the next morning (November 12) one of her boats was swept overboard, and about 10 o'clock in the forenoon her smokestack toppled over and was lost. All this time the tug hung on to her tow line, but by swinging off to leeward, so as to keep her head to the wind, she rode the seas much better than the **Akeley**. The gale moderated somewhat during the afternoon and the vessels continued to drift. At about 6 o'clock in the evening the **Protection** found that the line was apparently unwound from her wheel and that her engines would work, and supposing that she was then about thirty miles from South Haven, cast off from her tow and started for Grand Haven, the intention being to coal up and then return to the relief of the **Akeley**. She ran about 10 minutes, when it was discovered that the rope still clogged the wheel and the engine would work only to back her. The only resource was to let her drift as before.

After the **Protection** let go, the **Akeley** began to drift and the captain ordered the anchor put down. By Tuesday morning the situation looked hopeless and the engineer was ordered to clear away the remaining lifeboat. Just as the boat was cast adrift, the **Akeley** gave a final plunge, going to the bottom stern first, about nine miles off shore near Holland. Just in time the schooner **Driver** under Captain David Miller arrived. The captain's brother, Daniel, later described the scene for the *InterOcean*:

> We left Chicago Tuesday morning at 6 o'clock with the wind southwest. At 12:30 o'clock we made land at Holland and sighted the steamer ahead. I went in the rigging and said to my brother it was the steamer **Akeley**. I said: "Good God, Dave! She is foundering." We bore down on the wreck and sighted a small boat with twelve men in her.
>
> We three times tried to pick them up, but couldn't on account of the high sea. I called for a volunteer to man the lower boat. A young man we called Paddy -- I never knew any other name for him -- offered to go.
>
> I bid my brother goodbye; we got into our small boat and started for the other. We pulled down toward them, and then dropped toward them stern first. We picked three men out of their boat into ours, to lighten her up; then gave them a line and pulled to windward as far as possible, till the schooner came up on the other tack, when we got them on board. Then our boat capsized and myself and Paddy climbed up on the schooner by the boat tackle falls. All of the twelve men were saved.

*A painting of the sinking of the **H. C. Akeley***

The captain of the **Akeley**, Edward Stetch, and four of the crew, including the steward, remained with the vessel and were lost. Unwilling to risk a landfall on the coast of Michigan the **Driver** took the men rescued from the **Akeley** back to Chicago. The **Akeley** was owned by Captain T. W. Kirby and the man for whom she was named Healey C. Akeley, both of Grand Haven. She had been launched at Grand Haven in 1881.

No one had heard from the **Protection**, nor yet did anyone on land know what had happened to the **Arab**. Back in Chicago families of the crews knew only that the tug had left with a schooner of questionable seaworthiness and would have been midlake when the storm hit. The *InterOcean* reported:

> Crowds of people visited the Vessel Owner's Tug office yesterday morning to learn if any word had been received from the missing tug **Protection** and the schooner **Arab** . . . The officers of the company could give no encouragement for hope, as no tidings had been received.

So matters stood until 11 o'clock when the following dispatch was received:

> SAUGATUCK, Mich., Nov. 13 -- J. L. Higgie, V. O. T. Line, Chicago: One of your tugs is anchored outside, disabled and dragging anchor. Very heavy sea.
>
> C. M. COOK
> Deputy Collector

The dispatch was read aloud to the crowd in the office and a hearty cheer went up. There was at least some hope. Someone with an excellent bass voice broke out in song and the whole assemblage joined in:

Bright star of hope
Shed your beams on me.
And send a loving message
From far across the sea.

The VOT office sent to St. Joseph asking the tug **Lew Wallace** to go to the assistance of the **Protection** but received a return telegram from the captain stating "it is impossible for me to go out now."

After she left the **Akeley**, the **Protection** had drifted all night, and about 9 o'clock the next morning, November 13, she dropped anchor about half a mile off shore north of the piers of Saugatuck harbor on the Kalamazoo River. The tug blew her whistle constantly and carried a piece of awning fasted to an oar stuck upright in her bow as a signal of distress. But the sea was running so high that she could not enter the piers, and no vessel could get out to assist her. Citizens of Saugatuck gathered on the beach and decided to send for the nearest life saving crew. A dispatch to Grand Haven soon brought the news that the crew from that station was elsewhere, engaged in a rescue and not available. (See below) A dispatch to the station at St. Joseph, brought a more positive reply. While the **Protection** tossed in the waves Keeper Stevens of the St. Joseph station made arrangements with the Chicago and West Michigan Railroad for transportation of his crew and life saving apparatus about sixty miles north to the Kalamazoo River. The equipment was rowed across the river and taken apart to get it into a baggage car as there was no flat car available. The train left the depot at St. Joseph at 12:55.

Because one man was lost the story of the rescue was included in the *Life Saving Service Annual Report*:

By 3 o'clock in the lowering afternoon, the life-saving party reached Richmond, on the banks of the Kalamazoo River, having run a distance of 51 miles. The tug **Ganges** was awaiting them, sent by the people of Saugatuck to transport them thither. In a few minutes the apparatus was lugged on board and the boat steamed off. The distance was 13 miles down a bending river, so shallow that several times during the voyage the tug rubbed bottom hard. By 5 o'clock in the afternoon the life-saving party arrived, and landed near the light-house, proceeding thence with the mortar-cart and its load to the beach abreast of the wreck. The latter was still riding at anchor. Two attempts had been made during the afternoon by fishermen and sailors to get out to her in a large Mackinac fishing boat, but were baffled by the violence of the wind and sea. She was beyond shot-range, and nothing could be done for the present except to keep the apparatus ready for immediately use in case she should part her hawser and drift nearer shore. It was considered that so long as her anchor held she was safe.

At 6 o'clock the wind hauled to the northwest; flurries of snow thickened the air, and there were signs of deepening tempest. The growing force of the storm sharpened the vigilance of the watchers on the beach, and the time passed until 9 o'clock, when all at once the whistles on the tug broke out with shrill continuity in the distress signal. It was the token that the vessel had begun to drag her anchor. To the men on board this was a supreme moment. . . It was now evident that the hull beneath them would soon be in the rending and shattering breakers, and giving themselves up for lost they shook hands all round and bade each other good bye.

On the beach it went like wild fire that the tug had begun to move. The keeper and his men saw that her drift was to the southward, and that she would fetch up, if anywhere, south of the south pier. It was therefore necessary to cross the river, and the apparatus was at once hauled to the bank, where Captain Kendrick, of the Government tug **Graham**, received it on board and transported it to the other side. There a force of excited citizens aided the life-saving crew to land and drag it to the beach, abreast of which the drifting vessel was expected to strand. Their aid was of great service, for the way was of the roughest description. . . The distance from the south pier to the locality at which it was foreseen the wreck would come in was about half a mile, and the best part of an hour was consumed in reaching it. . . .

Meanwhile the tug had passed the piers and continued to drift on her southward course, gradually working in nearer the excited congregation the fire-lit beach revealed to those on board. She drifted quartering, or half stern foremost, and her whole company were clustered at her bows, watching the shore. They had not known until now of the presence of the life-saving crew, and the first hope they had felt since the dragging of the anchor reanimated them as they saw in the vast fluctuations of light from the beach-fires the files of the life-savers and their allied plunging forward down the sands with the mortar-cart behind them. They were thus braced as they entered their worst danger with the consciousness that organized effort was on foot for their assistance. The storm appeared to augment as they approached the surf. It is certain that the snow fell and whirled around them in increased profusion. The tug lifted and dropped like a dead hulk on the surge of an awful sea, staggering and quivering as she drifted under the shocks of the battering wind. Presently, when about two hundred yards from the beach, she struck the outer bar with a great crash. The sea at once made a clean sweep over her. She continued to rise and fall, striking the bar with shivering shocks, while the floods burst across her from end to end, smashing and rending. In a few moments the pilot house was broken in, the doors of the engine-room and the cabin were beaten down, and the hull was half full of water. One of the firemen, William Grace, who was standing aft, near the fantail, was swept overboard and instantly perished. The tug continued to pound upon the bar, slowly working over, sea after sea sheeting across her. In the midst of all the hurly-burly, the spectators on shore were astonished to see a young fellow get up quietly out of the surf, and walk coolly streaming with water to a neighboring fire. It was one of the sailors from the tug. He had put on a life-preserver, plunged overboard, and, by one chance in a million, reach the shore.

Before long the vessel had pounded over the bar into deeper water, and at length brought up with her stern solid in the sand. The men on board then slackened away the line which had been bent to her cable to give her scope to ride by, and she swung around with her stern to the sea, which continued now and then to shoot over her. The wreck gun was soon trained upon her, and the shot flew, carrying the line across her stern. The line, however, parted near the shot, and before the men on board could seize it, a sea washed it overboard. A second shot was immediately fired, and the line fell directly amidships, where it was caught. It was now about 10 o'clock. By half past 10 the hawser and hauling lines had been drawn out and set up between the vessel and the shore; the breeches-buoy had been rigged on, and the hauling home of the men from the wreck began. . . Despite incessant exertion the hawser could not be wholly kept from sagging, the convulsive roll of the hull alone being sufficient to keep it from being made taut, it followed that the men in the breeches buoy were more or less dragged home through the water, though with such rapidity that, as the keeper testified, they left a streak of foam behind them. . . the weather was bitterly cold. The men landed from the wreck, and the men nearest the water landing them had their clothing freeze upon them at once at the first contact with the air.

It was half past 10 when the first man was hauled ashore. At half past 11 the last one of the fifteen on board was safely landed. Each man as soon as rescued was taken to the fire and stimulants given him. As soon as they were all landed, twelve of them were taken in the tug **Graham** up to the hotel at Saugatuck, where they were sheltered and provided with dry clothing and food. The cook of the vessel got ashore in the worst condition of any, being so exhausted that he was helpless. he was taken, with two others, by the keeper and surfman Lysaght up to the neighboring light-house, where they stripped and rubbed him, and he was supplied with warm clothes by the kind light keeper. These ministrations ended, the keeper and his man walked through the wintry night, with their clothes frozen stiff as buckram up to the hotel at Saugatuck, where they arrived at 2 o'clock in the morning. The next afternoon the life-saving crew returned to the Saint Joseph Station by the way they came, arriving early in the morning of November 15.

Salvage rights to the **Protection** were bought by Saugatuck's Captain R. C. Brittain and most of the Kalamazoo River boats spent their spare time in the spring of

1884 trying to pull the tug off the bar. Finally on June 3, 1884, the Kalamazoo river steamer **Alice Purdy**, with the assistance of the fishing tug **Clara Elliott** and the passenger steamer **A. B. Taylor** completed the task and, with pumps working, what was left of the **Protection** was brought up the river to Saugatuck.

Parker's Crew Rescued from Rigging

November 13, 1883
Near the Pigeon River

The St. Joseph life-saving crew rushed by train to the scene of the **Protection** grounding (see above) near Saugatuck because the closer Grand Haven life-saving crew was engaged in a breeches buoy rescue of the crew of the schooner **Clara Parker** which had sunk south of Grand Haven about 5 o'clock Tuesday morning. She was discovered at daylight by the small son of Dan O'Connel who rode (barefoot according to tradition) to Johnsville (later called Agnew) to have a wire sent to the life saving station at Grand Haven requesting assistance. The life saving report describes the day:

> At 8 o'clock in the morning, during a terrific southwesterly gale, with frequent snow-squalls, and extremely cold weather, the keeper received a dispatch informing him that there was a vessel ashore about ten miles south of Grand Haven. the report also stating that the crew had taken to the rigging for safety. The roads were in fearful condition, and the district superintendent (Captain Robbins), who was present, advised the procurement of two teams in order to get the life-saving apparatus to the scene of the wreck as quickly as possible. This was accordingly done, and the men started off at a lively gait. When they were within a mile of the vessel they met Superintendent Robbins, who had driven on in advance, and he ordered all the gear loaded onto one wagon and the other team sent back for the surf-boat in case the lines should fail, as the wreck lay so far out from the shore and dead to the windward.
>
> He had found that it was even as the report had stated; the people were in the rigging and in the greatest peril. The vessel, a three masted schooner, was completely submerged with the immense waves dashing over her, and rolling her from side to side in a manner that made the shore-folk shudder with fear that she might go to pieces before the rescue of her crew could be effected. It was indeed an appalling sight. Nine men could be counted, three being in the fore-rigging and six in the mizzen, the latter being in by far the greatest danger as the mast threatened by its swaying to topple over into the surf at any moment.

Captain Andrew Lewis, later described the coming of the life saving crew from his point of view:

It was a blessed sight for us to see them come. Six of us were in the mizzen-rigging, with the head of the mast gone and nothing for the shot-line to rest on. After one trial, the second shot made us shudder to see the pieces of steel coming directly for us, but above us, and thank God, the line fell in our arms. We were fully four hundred yards from the shore, and had been in the rigging eight long hours and in our weakened condition it was hard work for us to haul the whip-line off, as there was a strong current setting northward alongshore . . .

The life saving report continues:

[The line] was set up on shore as taut as they dared, short of pulling the mast down, six men being stationed at the tackle-fall to veer and haul with the motion of the vessel. The breeches-buoy then went spinning out, and in a short time the six men were landed. . . A fire had been kindled on the beach, and while some were attending to the wants of these men the rest were taking active steps to rescue those in the fore-rigging. The hawser was slacked up and tracked along the shore to the southward, to throw the bight within reach of the three men. As soon as they caught it, it was again set up as before and one by one they were all brought safe to terra firma. The beach apparatus was then unrigged and reloaded into the cart, and the entire party set out for Grand Haven, where they arrived after 3 o'clock. The vessel and cargo being a total loss.

The **Clara Parker** was bound for Collingwood, Ontario, with a cargo of wheat when she sprung a leak off Sheboygan, Wisconsin, the wind sending her to the eastern shore. She had been built at Detroit in 1865 and was owned by Captain John Lindgren of Evanston, Illinois. Although there was no insurance on the vessel her $29,500 bushels of corn were insured for $6,000. In addition to Captain Lewis the men rescued included mate William Peterson and sailors John and William Oleson, Henry Gunville, Andrew Nelson, Robert Zindre, Henry Francis and Charles Stewart.

Grummond Up in Flames

November 4, 1884
South Haven Harbor

The small steamer **Grace Grummond** was a former government boat that had been rebuilt to serve as a small passenger and freight steamer between South Haven and Detroit. She had been extensively rebuilt in the winter of 1881-82, by Captain Welcome, her owner at the time, with ten new staterooms added to accommodate passengers. The boat ran two more seasons then burned at her dock at South Haven. According to the November 7, 1884, issue of the *South Haven Messenger*:

GONE UP IN FLAMES!

The steamboat **Grace Grummond**, while lying at Prouty's dock was discovered to be on fire about half past one o'clock on Tuesday night, and so rapidly did the flames spread that very little was saved. The fire was first discovered in the coal bunker by the night watch, who immediately proceeded to arouse those who were asleep on board who had no extra time to prepare for their exit. A large number of people who were awaiting telegraphic dispatches bringing election returns, were quickly on the ground, but nothing could be done, but haul the boat to the opposite side of the river and watch the fire fiend do his work. The boat was built about twenty years ago, for Government use, was subsequently purchased by Mr. Grummond of Detroit, and for the past four or five years has been mainly employed between this port and Chicago. She was well built with an iron hull, which now floats the boiler and engine together with the paddle-boxes and paddles, in a very fair state of preservation, which is a wonder to very many but probably owing to their being so thoroughly water-soaked. The boat was partly loaded for Chicago, where she was owned by Peter O'Conner. There was some insurance on her but we have not been able to learn the amount. Some expressions of relief are heard from those who entertained the idea that she was not a safe boat, on account of her age; how that may be we do not know, and do not care to know; we are thankful that no lives were lost with her, which would probably have been true if she had burned while out from port, and been wrecked by a furious storm.

What will be done with the hull and machinery, is an unsolved problem.

Michigan Founders in Ice

March 20, 1885
Near Holland

The steel steamer **Michigan** was a ship wreck in slow motion in the winter of 1885. She left Grand Haven in late February with extra provisions for the steamer **Oneida** which was struggling in the frozen lake. However, even with a metal hull she had trouble maneuvering in the ice and became ice bound opposite South Haven. At that point 17 of her crew left her and walked ashore, at least partly to leave more adequate rations to the remaining men. About the first of March the steamer was driven into an ice field and was stuck there, flowing slowly north. The *Saugatuck Commercial* reports that the steamer was clearly visible from the top of Mount Baldhead, a tall sand dune near Saugatuck, for nearly a month. The editor wrote in the March 6, 1885, issue:

The steamer **Michigan** was seen Sunday noon about opposite M. Chase's farm, some seven miles further north than when she was first noticed. No water was at that time visible and she must have moved right with the ice. She was opposite this harbor on Wednesday evening. She will get to Grand Haven after awhile.

The tug **Arctic** carried provision and fuel to the steamer, while she was still south of Saugatuck, but could not free the 209 foot **Michigan**. On Monday March 17 the tug **Arctic** was again sent to help the **Michigan** but the ice was so thick she couldn't get within six miles of her. After she moved past Saugatuck and Holland the **Michigan** was not so easily visible and her fate was not known until March 23 when the **Michigan's** captain arrived by train at the vessel's home port of Grand Haven. According to a March 23 dispatch from Grand Haven to the *InterOcean*:

> This evening Captain Prindiville of the steamer **Michigan**, arrived here on the Chicago and West Michigan Railroad from Holland. He reports his steamer to be at the bottom of Lake Michigan, about twenty-five miles southwest of this port. . .
>
> Last Thursday morning at 10 o'clock the ice crushed against the ship and made a hole in her port side. The pumps were worked to their utmost capacity until 4 o'clock in the afternoon, but with no success. She rapidly began sinking, stern first, and at 4 o'clock went down. The captain and crew of twelve men took to the ice with a life boat, and walked over the almost impassable ice, dragging the lifeboat, to the tug **Arctic**, where they arrived at night almost frozen and thoroughly exhausted. Had not the tug been sent to their assistance, or been farther away, all the retreating party must have perished.
>
> After recuperating until Sunday morning the Captain led the crew ashore, reaching land seven miles from Holland after a terrible experience on the ice. This morning all walked to Holland and came here on the 4 o'clock train. The steamer had been out in the ice forty-two days and on the day she foundered she saw the only chance to escape. Captain Prindiville exerted himself to the utmost to save the steamer, and did all that an experienced captain could do.
>
> A man named Robinson gave up on the ice, in the walk yesterday, and George Sheldon, the brave porter of the **Michigan**, went back after him. By great exertions he rescued the unfortunate man and arrived here late this evening.

The iron steamer **Michigan** was built at Wyandotte by the Detroit Drydock Company in 1882 and was owned by the Grand Haven and Milwaukee Transportation Company. She was rated at 1,183 tons and classed A-1. Insurance records described her as an iron passenger steamer costing $150,000. She was an exact mate to the **Wisconsin** and was built at the same time and place.

Schooner **Annie Tomine** Capsizes

October 4, 1885
Off Grand Haven

The lumber schooner **Annie Tomine**, 128 tons with a cargo of lumber and lath was six miles off Grand Haven on October 4, 1885, when the weather began to overwhelm her. The annual Life-Saving Service report states:

> Shortly before eight o'clock in the morning a schooner was sighted about six miles west of the Grand Haven Station standing toward the harbor with a signal hoisted for a tug. There was a high sea running with a fresh northwesterly breeze, and, as the vessel labored heavily and was erratic in her movements -- first hauling on the wind and then going off before it -- she was carefully watched by the lookout. Not many minutes elapsed before her ensign was half masted and her distressed condition made manifest. The alarm was given and almost immediately the life saving crew were proceeding to the scene in the surf boat. In the meantime a messenger had been dispatched for a steam tug, with directions to follow and lend whatever assistance was possible. The surfmen had pulled out about four miles when to their horror, the tottering craft lurched heavily and went over. She partly righted, but a furious onrushing wave struck her down the second time, where she remained on her beam ends swept by the foaming seas. With redoubled energy the men urged their boat on to the rescue. At about fifteen minutes to 11 they succeeded, after much hard pulling, in reaching the vessel, and found the imperilled crew of six men clinging to her weather side. As opportunity offered they were taken off, one by one, in a benumbed and perishing condition, the captain being the last to leave the wreck. The tug **Arctic** had by this time arrived, but the heavy weather precluded any attempts being made to save the vessel. The castaways were taken as quickly as possible to the station, provided with dry clothing, and otherwise comfortably cared for.

It was only afterwards that they determined that the vessel was the schooner **Annie Tomine** of Chicago, Illinois, bound from Muskegon, Michigan, to Michigan City, Indiana, with a cargo of lumber. Captain John Disbrow later explained that he had left Muskegon early in the morning and only a few hours out discovered that his vessel was leaking badly. He tried to make a harbor, but she continued to rapidly fill, despite the efforts of the crew to keep her free with the pumps. Within fifteen minutes of the discovery of the leak she was completely waterlogged. Rolling heavily she became unmanageable and getting into the dangerous trough of the sea, the force of the waves capsized her just as the rescuers were approaching. He also stated that when rescued he was so numbed with cold and exposure that he had lost the use of his lower limbs and he felt certain that none of his men could have held on an hour longer.

After a hot lunch the life saving crew went out in tow of the tug, hoping to be able to bring the **Annie Tomine** into port, but she had drifted about six miles to the south and was found to be fast going to pieces. The sea was so high that the lines which were run to her parted and the attempt had to be abandoned. The next morning the schooner had finally stranded on the beach seven miles south of the harbor and was a total wreck but a portion of her cargo was recovered. The shipwrecked crew were sheltered at the station for 24 hours, when they departed for their homes.

The following week Captain Disbrow wrote a letter to the life saving station which he also had published in the *Grand Haven Venture*. It read in part: "To you we owe a debt of gratitude which mere thanks are incompetent to repay. Your timely arrival at the wreck of the schooner **Annie Tomine** was the means of saving the lives of all on board. . . The rapidity with which you performed your duty was proof positive to us that commander and men were well fitted to fill the responsible positions you occupy. Your pull of five miles against a northwest sea and fresh breeze inside of sixty minutes was something that required the nerve and muscle of just such men as you have proven yourself to be." In gratitude the owner gave the life saving crew $108 reward money. The **Annie Tomine** was officially 127.71 gross tons and had been launched in 1867 at Green Bay, Wisconsin.

Leak Strands **S. P. Wilson** on Beach

October 20, 1885
South of Grand Haven

The **S. P. Wilson**, a merchant schooner, 142 tons, was lost south of Grand Haven, October 20, 1885. The story of the stranding of the vessel and the rescue of her crew is recounted in the annual Life Saving Service report:

In the evening of the 19th the schooner **S. P. Wilson** of Chicago, Illinois, left Grand Haven, Michigan, bound home with a cargo of pine slabs, and a crew of six men. Near midnight the wind veered and freshened and soon afterwards blew a gale from the west-southwest, making up a heavy head sea. The vessel had proceeded about 30 miles on her course when the increasing violence of the storm decided the captain to put back into port. At 8 o'clock in the morning of the 20th, some fifteen miles from the harbor entrance, the schooner sprang a leak. She at once began to fill and, in spite of the efforts of the crew at the pumps, became completely waterlogged. The canvas had been gradually taken in, and when the accident occurred the craft was running under bare poles. Laboring heavily she became unmanageable and the tremendous seas that broke over her from all sides threatened every minute to capsize her. The crew, by tying themselves to the masts with long lines, to save themselves from being washed away, succeeded in throwing a part of the deck load overboard, but the situation still grew more alarming and signals of distress were hoisted. The lookout at the Grand Haven Station, observed the vessel acting strangely as she approached from the distance, and when the colors were half-masted the life saving crew at once launched the surf boat but the heavy weather made it impossible to get out between the piers and so another boat, kept on the south side of the harbor, had to be used instead. It was with difficulty got off the beach and worked through the surf, which was tumbling in with terrific force. Three times the boat was nearly swamped, but two of the crew, constantly bailing with buckets, kept it afloat, and while the oarsmen were exhausting themselves in a vain attempt to make headway the keeper had to quickly elect between alternatives -- whether to take the chances and give battle to the surging breakers with all hands on the oars, or be driven back on the beach. He chose the former, and by a bold dash, with every muscle strained to its utmost tension, the boat was sent through the foam-lashed waters and reached the less dangerous sea beyond. In its perilous passage it half filled and had to be bailed out ere the life savers could press forward again. The propeller **Wisconsin**, in the meantime, had made several attempts to get a line to the distressed vessel, but failed, and as the latter drifted near the shore, the steamer was obliged to abandon her. The waves were sweeping the decks of the schooner and the crew had taken to the rigging. Shortly past noon she struck on the outer bar, a short distance south of the piers. The station men managed to beach their boat to leeward of the stranded craft and then jumped out into the surf up to their armpits, and dragged it, amid the floating slabs, as close as possible to the wreck, from which point it was pulled under the lee of the starboard fore rigging, where the sailors had taken refuge. The imperiled men were speedily taken off, safely landed, and conducted to the station, where their wants were cared for and they were sheltered over night. The surfmen were nearly all more or less bruised after their gallant work, and it was said by old seamen, who witnessed the events described that they had never seen greater courage displayed or a boat handled in better shape.

The captain of the **S. P. Wilson** issued a statement which said in part, "The life saving crew with great difficulty reached us and succeeded in rescuing myself and crew from what would have been certain death but for their heroic efforts. The vessel was a strong and staunch one, but nevertheless she was entirely broken to pieces by 5 o'clock P.M. of the same day."

E. R. Blake Saved by Accident

October, 1885
At South Haven

The miraculous story of the schooner E. R. Blake in the fall of 1885 was as remarkable a tale as many of the wrecks. It was told in the October 30, 1885, issue of the *Lake Shore Commercial*, reprinted from an earlier *South Haven Messenger*. The South

Haven reporter wrote:

A GREAT FORGETTER

The Schooner **E. R. Blake** of Chicago loaded with 200,000 feet of lumber from Muskegon, sprang a leak Tuesday and at 2 o'clock Wednesday morning in a waterlogged condition made our port. She missed her reckoning, supposing she was off Saugatuck light, and feeling that she could not enter the harbor the Captain decided to beach the boat north of the pier, and not remembering that the light had been changed to the south side of the harbor, steered accordingly and was surprised to find himself in our harbor.

Milwaukee Goes Down After Collision

July 8, 1886
Off Grand Haven

The wooden steamer **Milwaukee**, 277 tons, sank following collision a few miles off Grand Haven with the **C. Hickox** on Lake Michigan. The steam barge **Hickox** was on her way from Muskegon to Chicago with a load of lumber when she drove her bow deep into the port side of the **Milwaukee** which was traveling empty. Both masters Captain "Black" Bill Alexander of the **Milwaukee** and Simon O'Day of the **Hickox** had their licenses revoked.

One theory is that Captain Alexander turned the wrong way, because it was his custom to turn the ship to starboard in order to make a left hand turn. The **Milwaukee** was not a new vessel and the hull was warped and the starboard quarter had sagged several inches. Some seamen have theorized that in the fog, when watchmen spotted the light of the **Hickox** dead ahead he may have ordered the ship turned to port, but the wheel might have actually began a starboard turn.

The **Hickox** turned to port and the two vessels continued on a collision course until the **Hickox** hit **Milwaukee** so hard amidships that she nearly turned her over. The **Hickox** backed away and was already lost in fog by the time Captain Alexander had manned the pumps and used the remaining steam to sound the boat's whistle. Captain O'Day traced the sound of the whistle and found the sinking ship once again and took off crew. One man was thrown overboard and died at impact.

O'Day said at a later inquest that he had heard the whistles, "I worked the boat carefully in the direction from which they seemed to come from, but, strange to say, fully three-quarters of an hour elapsed before I sighted her masthead light." About the same time the **Hickox** pulled alongside the **City of New York** arrived at the scene. After the **Hickox** took the crew off the sinking ship the **City of New York** tried to take the **Milwaukee** in tow, but she settled rapidly. The tow line was cut free and the ship sank by the stern about nine miles west of Grand Haven.

Rescued **Emma Thompson** Sinks at Pier

If it was not tipped over by wind or waves a waterlogged boat, one full of water but kept afloat by the wood of her structure and the lumber in her holds, could remain in that condition for many hours, making slow progress. A calm sea was the salvation of the **Emma E. Thompson**. Her story was told in the August 20, 1886, issue of the *Lake Shore Commercial*:

> The steamer **Emma Thompson** waterlogged last Tuesday night. The steamer left Muskegon at 5 o'clock on Tuesday bound for Chicago, loaded with hemlock timber; at 7:30 two feet of water was discovered in her hold. The pumps were immediately manned, but the water continued to gain at the rate of a foot an hour. At 7:40 she was headed for Grand Haven and half an hour later the steamer **Annie Laurie** was sighted and took the **Thompson** in tow and reached Grand Haven with her at 12 o'clock. The disabled steamer was made fast to the south pier and an hour later she sank in 16 feet of water where she now lies, her stern and part of her deck load under water.

The **Emma Thompson** had been launched in 1875 at Saginaw, Michigan, at 238.82 gross tons, 157.44 net tons. In 1887, following her sinking in the summer of 1886, she was rebuilt and increased to 260.62 gross tons, 176.23 net tons and a length of 126.1 feet.

Telegraph Used to Save **Lady McDonald**

Wireless in the pilothouse was still several decades away when the land-based telegraph was used to summon the Holland life-saving service to the rescue of the schooner **Lady McDonald** in the summer of 1887. The work is described in the annual life saving report for that year:

> August 23 -- Shortly after dark a telegram was received at the Holland Station, that a vessel was in distress off Saugatuck, eight miles to the southward. The life-saving crew at once manned the surf-boat, and reaching the scene found an abandoned schooner lying at anchor, half a mile off shore. The crew of eight men, with their personal effects, had landed safely in their own boat, and from the captain it was learned that the craft was the **Lady McDonald**, of Port Burwell, Ontario, bound to Kingston, in that Province, from Chicago, Illinois, with a valuable

cargo of wheat. From his statement it appeared that the vessel had sprung a leak when off Big Point Sable on the 21st, and he had then headed her back for Chicago, but finding that the crew were unable to keep the water from gaining he had hauled her in for the east shore, and after coming to an anchor hoisted a signal of distress. She was leaking so badly that the crew, not receiving any assistance, left her on the 23rd during the early part of the night. The life-saving men took the captain and mate, who were anxious to save the vessel if possible, off on board, and on examination it was ascertained that there was six feet of water in the hold, with the decks amidships already below the surface. The surfmen at once manned the pumps and after an hour's hard work discovered that they had made a slight gain. This encouraged them to renewed efforts, and by pumping steadily until 2 o'clock in the morning they succeeded in reducing the water two feet. As the labor was very trying the keeper then deemed it advisable to obtain additional aid, and so went ashore in the surf-boat and obtained the services of four fishermen and the schooner's crew, besides sending word to Saugatuck for a tug. By half past 6 in the morning the life-savers, with the aid they had secured, had pumped the water down to a foot and a half, to the surprise and great joy of the captain, who several hours before had been obliged through sheer exhaustion to seek a needed rest. He could scarcely believe his eyes on seeing the progress that had been made, and ascribed the saving of his vessel to the persevering efforts of the station men, as in her previous condition he said that she must certainly have soon gone to the bottom. The good work was kept up until 3 in the afternoon, when the tug that had been sent for arrived and the life-saving crew were relieved. After the anchors had been weighed the schooner was taken into Grand Haven, the surf boat towing astern until opposite Holland, when there being no further cause for apprehension, it was cast off and returned to the station.

Purdy Burns Afloat on the Kalamazoo

September 5, 1887
Kalamazoo River at Saugatuck

The Kalamazoo River was always a tricky highway. Some years the water was so shallow that even floating logs had problems. Some years sudden spring floods made navigation impossible. The **Alice Purdy**, was a typical side wheel river boat, 77.5 feet long, 24.4 feet in beam, built with the shallowest draft that the ship's carpenter could manage. She was launched at Saugatuck in 1881, built to provide a connection with the railroad at New Richmond, six miles upstream and as a way for inland fruit growers to send their produce to Chicago-bound vessels at Saugatuck.

The **Purdy** was one of the more successful boats to attempt the upriver run, but most of the time even she had a hard time of it. Her short career ended abruptly

September 5, 1887. The *Saugatuck Commercial* reported:

About 2 o'clock last Monday morning the river steamer **Alice Purdy** took fire in some unaccountable manner and burned to the water's edge. The fire was first discovered by the night watchman at Griffin & Henry's mill, who immediately rang the fire alarm. Will Rode, the assistant engineer of the steamer was awakened about the same time by the light of the burning boat, and sans hat and shoes he ran to the Moore dock where she lay. When he arrived the upper works and deck of the steamer were burning and the stern line had parted. He threw off the head line to allow the boat to drift away from the dock as the flames had already communicated to the waterhouse. A crowd quickly gathered and the fire on the building was extinguished by the means of buckets. As soon as a sufficient number could be induced to go to the engine house the fire engine was brought out and the warehouse given a good soaking. Meantime the flaming steamer had drifted across the river to the old sawdust piles where the work of destruction was going bravely on. It took Lew Smith about five minutes to get steam on the little yacht **Homer Reeves** and Capt. George Crawford took command and soon had the **Purdy** towed back across the river where streams of water from the fire engine soon extinguished the flames, leaving little of the boat however, but a gutted hull. She was owned by Capt. George Crawford of Saugatuck, Philetus Purdy of Douglas and George T. Arnold of Mackinac Island and was insured for $3,000.

Alice Purdy

The End of the schooner **Australia**

September 30, 1888
Near Holland

On September 30, 1888, the 159 ton schooner **Australia**, 109 feet in length, was wrecked near the Holland piers. She was owned at Chicago and was under Captain Edwards. The *Annual Report of the Operations of the United States Life-Saving Service* reports:

> At 7 o'clock in the evening the schooner **Australia** of Milwaukee, Wisconsin, being full of water, attempted to stand into Holland, Michigan, for a harbor. When entering between the piers, however, the channel being too shoal for her in her waterlogged condition, she went aground about 150 yards west of the Holland station, the crew of which at once hastened to her assistance. There was a fresh south west wind and a heavy surf and the vessel was in great danger of breaking up. The station men made her lines fast to the pier, helped her crew of seven men to get ashore and saved her papers and other moveable articles, besides unbending and landing the foresail. This was all that could be done at the time, and the keeper took the men to the station where they were made comfortable. One of the number left on the following day; the others remained until the 3rd of October. The vessel was from Beaver Island, Michigan, bound for Chicago, Illinois, with a cargo of posts. She went to pieces within 24 hours from the time she struck. The station crew subsequently saved a very small portion of her cargo.

Life saving station records show that the Holland Station supplied 25 days of accommodations to her crew and officers, this figures out to be one man for one day, and six for four days. The October 5, 1888, issue of Saugatuck's *Lake Shore Commercial* tried to put the tragedy in perspective:

> The schooner **Australia** loaded with about 5,000 cedar posts, attempted to enter Holland harbor last Monday night, but being waterlogged, struck the bar repeatedly, as the sea ran high, and went down between the piers. She is a total loss, with no insurance. She was loaded at Sand Bay, Beaver Island, bound for Chicago, and with about thirty others lay behind the Manitous until Thursday. Friday while off Racine Point, she sprung a leak, and with her crew at the pumps for three days and nights became waterlogged. She then ran before the wind until she reached Holland, where the crew were all taken off safely by the lifesaving crew. The **Australia** was built in 1853, and has been in continuous service, most of the time trading to Chicago, for thirty-five years. In her day she was considered a great vessel, as she had the then magnificent dimensions of 109 feet long and 22 feet beam. For a decade,

however, she has been a floating coffin, and has changed hands repeatedly. She was not worth much, and her extinction without loss of life is some crew's good fortune.

The hulk of the **Australia** came to rest about 150 yards offshore of the Holland pier. One notable previous grounding occurred in a storm in 1855 when the **Australia** was washed ashore with the **Orient** and the **C. P. Williams**.

Barge **R. N. Rice** Goes Ashore

October 1, 1888
4 Miles North of Holland

The big problems that would eventually bring about the end of the freight barge **R. N. Rice** began September 29, 1888, as she was bound, lumber-laden, up Lake Michigan in tow of a steam barge. The **Rice** began leaking badly and when she and her escort were just off Ludington the steamer sounded four blasts on her whistle to summon help from the Ludington Life Saving Station. The crew rowed out and found a crew worn out by continuous pumping. They relieved the tired sailors at their pumps and after an hour and a half succeeding in emptying the vessel of water, allowing her to proceed.

No more was heard from the steam barge until October 1, 1888, when the man on watch at the Holland station noticed a lumber-laden barge, apparently in distress, eight miles northwest of the station. The *Life Saving Service Annual Report* continues the story:

> He reported her to the keeper who at once roused the crew, manned the surf boat and set out for her. There was at the time a fresh northwest breeze, with a heavy surf and the pull to windward was long and difficult; but the station men reached the craft after nearly three hours of hard work, and found that she was the barge **R. N. Rice** of Buffalo, New York, which had received assistance at the hands of the crew of the Ludington Station two days before. She was water-logged, had lost her foremast and steering gear, and no one was on board. The station crew could do nothing for her, and they returned to the harbor. An hour before noon the vessel went upon the beach four miles north of the station and the keeper immediately sent a surfman to take charge of her. On the 3rd the owner and the underwriters agent arrived and the keeper turned the craft and cargo over to them, receiving their grateful acknowledgments for his services. The vessel proved a total loss; but about one-sixth of the cargo was saved in good condition. It was learned during the storm of 30th of September the barge had filled and become unmanageable, compelling her crew to abandon her.

The vessel that became the freight barge **R. N. Rice** was launched in 1866 as an elegant and popular sidewheel passenger steamer, 1,096 tons, 247 feet in length, that ran mainly on Lake Erie until sustaining a major fire in 1877. She was then reduced to a

94

barge of 622 tons and used to carry lumber. At the time of her beaching she was under the command of Captain Stubbs, and was on her way from Ashland, Wisconsin, to Chicago with a load of lumber. Some of her deck load of lumber washed ashore in several areas including a quantity discovered at Saugatuck on October 5.

Steamer **Farnam** Sinks after Fire

July 20, 1889
20 Miles south of South Haven

The steam barge **Joseph P. Farnam**, 410 tons, bound from St. Joseph to Escanaba, light, burned and sank off South Haven in July of 1889. According to a description in the *South Haven Sentinel* for July 27, 1889:

> Between two and three o'clock last Saturday afternoon William Kibbe, watchman in the tower of the life saving station, noticed the smoke of a steamer almost due west of this post and about 20 miles distant, steaming along on a course generally taken by northern bound vessels. He noticed she was a three master but nothing about her particularly attracted his attention. Walter Boardman relieved Kibbe in the tower at four o'clock. Occasionally he had her in his vision, when about a quarter of five he was surprised to see that she had changed her course and was heading for this port. Watching her more closely he soon saw her again change her course, this time to the south, and when she came broadside to view at a quarter past five he saw that the two masts which he had a first seen were gone, the mizzen mast having been carried about the time he relieved Kibbe, and then he could see that the smoke which had shown as coming from her stack all right, was really enveloping her nearly from stem to stern and that she was on fire. He at once gave the alarm to Capt. McKenzie and that officer went at once to the dock of the **Glenn** to get Captain John Boyne to tow the life saving crew out to the burning steamer in their surf boat.

While the two watchmen were trying to decide whether there was any problem aboard the boat near the horizon of their vision, the captain and crew of the **Farnam** had their hands full. Their captain, L. B. Vosburgh later testified, in a letter addressed to the Life Saving District Superintendent:

> I left St. Joseph at 8 a.m. Saturday, July 20, bound for Escanaba, and shaped a course for Deaths Door Passage. My vessel was the steam barge **Joseph P. Farnam**, of Cleveland, 346 tons register. She carried a crew of eleven man all told. Mrs. Vosburgh was with me, making twelve people on board.
> The wind had been fresh from N.N.W. all the previous night, and there was considerable sea running. The steamer had small power

for her size, and being light, made very slow headway against the sea. At 2 P.M. I concluded we were seventeen miles N. by W. from St. Joseph. My watch had turned in. Mrs. Vosburgh, who remained awake, aroused me by asking what made it so smoky. I went on deck at once and found flames bursting from the skylight over the engine room. The mate was on the main deck dropping the fire hose, which is always kept connected to the fire plug. But the donkey pump was in the midst of a mass of fire, and it was impossible to start it. With the failure of this pump it became evident that the steamer must be abandoned. I carried one excellent boat, sufficient for the safety of all hands, but it was slung abreast the engine room hatch and was enveloped by the flames within three minutes from the time the fire broke out.

The crew behaved well, and at once set to work making rafts by lashing together hatch covers and planks. All hands were hardly afloat on these hastily constructed rafts before the steamer was afire forward and aft. The last raft launched, carrying eight persons, hung to the steamer until the hawser burned off. The vessel drifted for two hours S. by E., or directly back on the course she had come. In this time she must have drifted five miles. As nearly as I can tell at about 5 P.M. the wind shifted into the N.E., and the burning hulk, assisted by wind and current, went up the lake at a rate which astonished us on the rafts.

At that time life saving stations had no motive power for their boats. They counted on wrecks that the crew could row to, or for distant disasters, the boat was towed by privately owned tug boats or other small steamers that were handy. The government paid a set amount for the this kind of assistance and there were several small tug boats in the Chicago area that made a big portion of their livelihood in this manner. The **Glenn** was a small steamer that had been built at South Haven by Philip Hancock for H. W. Williams. She was less than three months having been launched in May of 1889. On the day of the fire aboard the **Joseph P. Farnam** the captain of the **Glenn** was willing to help, but the ship had reached port some time ago and had no fire under the boilers. The South Haven newspaper takes up the story:

The **Glenn** had no steam, but engineer Sam Johns went to work as every true sailor does when another is in trouble, and at ten minutes after six the **Glenn** winded around under twenty pounds of steam, and ten minutes later left the mouth of the harbor with the life saving crew in tow, and with eighty-five pounds of steam. After a run of a few minutes everything came into working trim and the **Glenn** shot ahead at what must have been a speed of near or quite fifteen miles an hour, proving herself a boat of which her owner, H. W. Williams, and her captain and crew may well feel proud. After a run of about an hour the hull of the burning steamer could be plainly seen, afire from end to end and of course deserted. The eager eyes on the **Glenn** scanned the horizon for a sight of those who had been on the burning steamer. . .

Although the water was summertime warm, Lake Michigan never gets above 80 degrees for very long, and is usually between 60 and 70 degrees even in the middle of summer. The crew of the **Farnam** had been on the rafts, most of the time waist deep in water for more than three hours and had seen no hint of rescuers on the horizon. The captain continued his narrative:

> When we abandoned the vessel it seemed as if we might expect assistance from South Haven; but the wind and current set us so rapidly to the S.E. that we soon lost sight of that port and picked up St. Joseph. We were able at sundown, and while the burning hulk was still afloat, to see Plank's new hotel and the pier light house at that place; but no assistance came from that quarter. As darkness set in we made out a steamer coming from the direction of South Haven and steering for the wreck. She proved to be the **Glenn** of South Haven, towing the lifeboat, with crew, from that place. With the last light of day we managed to attract her attention to the raft, and at 8:30 all my crew were safe aboard the **Glenn**.

The local editor must have been aboard the steamer, he described the efforts to get up steam and finding the wreck and the strain of all aboard to find the crew:

> . . . and finally by the aid of a ray of the setting sun, and two or three miles to the north and west of the wreck, a spot was seen and towards it the **Glenn** steamed. A realization of what that speck proved to be will never be erased from the minds of those who saw it. It was a fragile raft, constructed of the fenders, hatchways, doors, and other light stuff from the steamer, held together only with chafing ropes insecurely fastened, entirely submerged with almost every sea, and still in its fragile grasp holding the lives of eight persons, who, had the **Glenn** been twenty minutes later could not have been seen half a mile from her decks and some of whom would undoubtedly been drowned before morning had their frail raft gone to pieces which it certainly would have done.

By 8 p.m. all were aboard the **Glenn** which returned them to South Haven and gave them dry clothes and accommodations for the night. The burned out hulk eventually sank, some accounts say near Benton Harbor, and was declared a total loss.

Squall Strikes the **Phantom**

August 12, 1891
Off Glenn

Short-handed to begin with, the **Phantom** was in real trouble after its only crew fell from the rigging and left the captain to deal single-handedly with a sudden squall. The August 21, 1891, *South Haven Messenger* tells the story:

Last week Thursday afternoon when the squall struck the lake, the lookout at the life saving station saw a signal of distress on a vessel some distance this side and off Glenn and as soon as possible got the **Myrtle McCluer** to tow the surf boat to its relief. It was found to be the scow **Phantom**, Capt. D. Morey. When the squall struck the vessel, only the Captain and Wm. Slater, of Saugatuck, were aboard, and the latter losing his hold when just below the cross trees fell to the deck and lay there insensible. The captain ran to him but had only time to turn him over upon his back, and run back to the wheel, where he had his hands full. When the rain began to fall Slater revived and was just able to crawl into the cabin. Meantime the wind had blown away the topsail and torn the other sails, and the boat was in a bad way. She was towed in all right by the tug. Slater was not badly injured and was around again the next day.

Capsizing of the **Little Harry**

August, 1891
Off South Haven

Yacht owners, often with little experience in the handling of small craft, were frequently in trouble in the changeable waters of Lake Michigan. The August 28, 1891, edition of the *South Haven Sentinel* describes one summertime tragedy:

Found: Little Harry -- Dismasted, drifted ashore nine miles from station. Hauled up on the beach by the life saving crew. This yacht had sailed from Holland the preceding day, having on board a man and his young son. It is supposed she was wrecked in the heavy squall that swept over the lake on this day and the man was washed overboard. The boy's body was found in the cabin.

Rockaway Fills and Sinks

November 18, 1891
Off South Haven

The 164 ton schooner-scow **Rockaway** was too waterlogged to maneuver when she arrived off South Haven in November of 1891. According to an account in the November 21, 1891, issue of the *South Haven Sentinel*:

The scow **Rockaway** was sighted to the northwest of this harbor Tuesday in a waterlogged condition, she remaining at anchor through the night and the crew of Capt. Ole Oleson [it was later discovered his last name was Thompson] and his four men being brought to port by our own life-saving people. Friday morning the boat was gone and the sight of the top of her mainmast is proof that she sunk where she had been at anchor. She was loaded with lumber and bound from the north to St. Joseph.

The South Haven Life-Saving station reported:

> November 18, 1892 -- **Rockaway,** a schooner, was waterlogged and sunk eight miles from the station. Rescued a crew of 5 men, worn out and almost overcome by long exposure to the cold. Procured medical attention for one whose hands were frozen and cared for all at station until they were able to leave for their homes.

The December 5, 1891, issue of the *South Haven Sentinel* published an account that had been printed in the *St. Joseph Herald* which claimed that the captain had stood at the wheel for nineteen hours prior to the rescue, and that when he was taken off by the lifesaving crew his feet had to be pried off the ice, which held them to the deck. The South Haven paper commented:

> Just how that story first got afloat is more than we know. . . The Captain and his crew were very much chilled and would undoubtedly have frozen to death had relief not been afforded by Capt. McKenzie with the life-saving crew, but no one was frozen tight to the deck nor to anything else.

The 104 foot **Rockaway,** owned by Muskegon interests, was a total loss, along with most of the cargo. The life-saving service reported that they had furnished 20 days of accommodations (probably five men for four days). The captain and four of the crew then moved on to the life saving station at St. Joseph until the arrival of a steamer that could take them to Chicago.

The exact whereabouts of the wreck was not known until September of 1983 when she was located two and a half miles off South Haven. Although the major part of the wreck is broken up over a large area the centerboard trunk and stern sections stand erect on the bottom.

A State of Michigan grant was obtained to study the wreck and procure and preserve some of the artifacts. An outgrowth of the project was *The Conservation of Archeological Artifacts From Freshwater Environments* by Katherine Singley which was published by the Michigan Maritime Museum in South Haven in cooperation with the Michigan Department of Natural Resources Coastal Management program in 1988.

Crew of **Stevenson** Rescued

November 18, 1891
Near Grand Haven

The schooner **Ellen Stevenson** struck the pier near Grand Haven and was so disabled that the life saving station was alerted and sent a boat to take off the crew. According to the November 19, 1891, issue of the *Grand Haven Evening Tribune*:

> The schooner **Ellen Stevenson** with a crew of three, Capt. Nicholson, Emet Bouring and Carol Talpo, bound homeward from St. Joe to Ludington, struck head on to the pier at 12 o'clock last night while trying to make this harbor and was dismasted and totally disabled. The life saving crew went at once to the rescue and did as fine a piece of work as ever a life saving crew did. Lines were thrown over her first, but they parted and the crew went to her. The sea was a terrible one, but they reached the wreck in safety but came along side several times before the men could be gotten off, and once, their boat struck with such force as to split her bow and before the station could be reached got half full of water. The men were in the water an hour and a half and got severely chilled, but at the station were worked over, thoroughly warmed and cared for and warmly clad and today are as well as ever.
>
> The **Stevenson** is owned by Swanson & Nicholson of Ludington and valued at $1,000, not insured. Just before leaving her the crew threw out the anchor and she is now anchored 50 feet from the north pier and about 100 feet from shore. Unless the wind goes down she will probably go to pieces before night.

The **Ellen Stevenson** had left St. Joseph in the company of the schooner **Tenie, Laura** and **Tallahassee**. The newspaper reports that the **Tenie** and **Laura** had come inside the harbor at Grand Haven during the storm that had damaged the **Stevenson**, but the **Tallahassee** had not been heard from. The **Stevenson** was salvaged and put back in service until October of 1897 when she foundered midlake.

Dog Only Fatality as **Wanderer** Blows Ashore

November 22, 1893
At Two Sisters, South of Grand Haven

The crew of the schooner **Wanderer** spent anxious moments in the rigging until lakeshore residents came to their rescue in November of 1893. According to an account in the November 23, 1893, issue of the *Grand Haven Evening Tribune*:

> Tuesday night the schooner **Wanderer**, Capt. J. Woltman, loaded with staves left Holland for Milwaukee. Before morning the northwest gale increased in force until it reached a velocity, at one time. of 42 miles an hour, blowing away some of the **Wanderer's** rigging, and at 2 o'clock yesterday morning drove her on the beach at the Two Sisters, about five miles south of this city. When the boat first struck her yawl was washed away so that the crew were obliged to take to the rigging until rescued by Chas. Weaver, Fred Behm and John Renwick

at 10 a.m. in an exhausted condition. The sufferers were taken to the house of John Renwick where everything was done to make them comfortable, so much so that they were soon themselves again. They feel thankful for their narrow escape and grateful to those who have so kindly cared for them. The schooner was allright at last accounts. Capt. Woltman, who is a cousin of Jurrien Ball of this city, was here today and left for the beach where his ship lies this forenoon, in company with Mr. Woltman. A pet dog belonging to the Captain froze to death on deck before the rescuing party reached him.

Dreadnaught Goes to Pieces

December 8, 1893
Mouth of the Kalamazoo River

Some of the wrecks that landed on the Michigan shore represent accidents that happened in other places. On Friday, December 8, 1893, the small tug **Harvey Watson** was on her usual run taking freight and passengers from Holland to Saugatuck when she ran across the waterlogged small scow **Dreadnaught** near the mouth of the Kalamazoo River. The scow had been deserted by her crew December 4, near Milwaukee on the other side of the lake and was driven to the eastern shore by wind and currents. The **Watson** took the small scow in tow, with a plan toward salvage of the cargo, and possibly the vessel itself.

According to the December 15, 1893, edition of the *Saugatuck Commercial*:

> Owing to the **Dreadnaught's** being waterlogged it was impossible to bring her inside over the bar and she was left outside. During the night, however, she was driven in by the sea and went to pieces well inside the piers, the wreckage afterwards being carried out by the current. She had about thirty cords of hard maple wood in her hold, much of which was picked up next day.

Four Die in Fire on the Myrtie M. Ross

July 10, 1894
South Haven Harbor

In the summer of 1894 the South Haven-built steam barge **Myrtie M. Ross** obtained a charter to carry lumber from Manistee to St. Joseph for the Graves Lumber Company. This meant frequent trips past South Haven where the captain and most of the crew resided. The temptation to stop was hard to resist. On the trip which began July 9 there was an additional reason, a dock strike in Chicago made it risky to try to bring cargo into the city. The captain had decided to hang back a day or so in the hope that the strike would be settled "so the lumber traffic was not interfered with," according to the South Haven newspaper. Instead of being a pleasant interlude at home the pause ended in disaster and death for four members of the crew.

According to the U. S. Life-Saving Service report:

> The **Ross** sailed from White Lake in the afternoon of July 9, under the command of Captain Joseph F. Smith, and after calling at Muskegon for the purpose of taking on wood, proceeded on her way to South Haven, where it was the master's intention to make a stop, and where she arrived just before 1 o'clock A. M., Tuesday, July 10. Besides the master, there was a crew of eight men, and after attending to various matters pertaining to the vessel, the captain, leaving the crew on board and placing two of them on watch, departed for his home in the village, where he purposed to spend the remainder of the night. It would appear, however, that two of the men subsequently left the barge to visit their own homes, and some time afterward one of the two on watch also went ashore, while the other, to escape the heat of the engine room which adjoined the cabin, betook himself with some reading matter to the pilot house on the forward part of the barge. Four went into the cabin to sleep.

Sailor John Henderson was left as watchman and later testified that he was reading a newspaper in the pilot house about 3:45 a.m. when he heard an explosion on the after part of the vessel. He rushed aft and discovered a flame "like that of burning oil" which he later decided it was, despite the fact that to the best of his recollection he had extinguished the lamp in the engine room when he went forward. The life saving report continues:

> At this moment the four men in the little cabin were fast asleep. The sudden flame spread like wildfire, and it is not quite certain how soon they became aware of their horrible predicament. However it was not soon enough to enable any of them to escape. The watchman testifies that the life saving crew reached the barge in four minutes after the explosion. . . the surfmen, who discovered the fire the instant it burst forth, had hastily placed their force pump and hose, with three or four axes, in the surfboat, pulled straight to the barge, which lay only a few hundred feet from the station. At the moment of their arrival the cabin was all ablaze, the narrow companions way, leading out by way of the engine room, enveloped in raging fire and the men inside were frantically shouting for aid.
>
> There was no means of egress that the life-savers knew of except the door, which was wrapped in flame, and they therefore instantly fell to work with axes cutting a hole in the side of the cabin, and had just succeeded in making a trifling opening when somebody informed them that there was a small escape scuttle aft, in the top of the cabin, concealed under a huge pile of wood. Upon this information they quickly turned their attention to the work of pitching overboard a sufficient quantity of the wood to clear the scuttle, and under the spur

of the heartrending cries from within, threw over the necessary two or three cords, in about as many minutes, snatched off the scuttle cover and pulled out of the stifling heat and smoke, William Smith, a fireman who was so terribly scorched and frenzied that he would have jumped overboard had not the surfmen prevented him. As soon as he could speak he said, "There is one more in there," probably supposing and meaning that only one was alive.

Myrtie M. Ross

Smith was the son of Jack Smith of South Haven and a nephew of Captain Smith. He was helped ashore by the surfmen and walked unaided to the home of the captain nearby. He died ten days later.

A stream of water from the station force pump was promptly turned on, and in a moment or two Surfman Curran descended for an instant a little way into the smoldering death trap and drew out from close to the scuttle Charles Connell, the first engineer, fearfully burned and for the time being a raving maniac. Four men were required to restrain him and get him to the life-saving station . . .

No other persons were near the scuttle and the heat and smoke were still so intense as to preclude the possibility of searching the place until the fire could be much further subdued. Meantime the village fire department for which the keeper had promptly rung an alarm, appeared upon the scene, and with their efficient cooperation the flames were speedily so far extinguished that a thorough search of the cabin was possible. Members of the fire department then went in, and soon brought to light the bodies of two men, one of whom was dead and the other with barely a spark of life remaining. The former was Frank Smith, mate of the barge, and son of the captain. His body was found alongside the engine, its location being such as to indicate that he perished while engaged in a desperate effort to escape through the blazing doorway of the cabin. The other was William Leroy. . .

All of the burned men died despite prompt attention by such medical men as were available in South Haven. In the investigation that followed the lost of life was attributed to two circumstances. First, the desertion by the second engineer of the post on watch which had been ordered by the captain. Second, the closed escape scuttle that was so encumbered by a pile of wood that the men could not force their way out.

The **Myrtie M. Ross** had been built at South Haven in 1880, and, after less than a year of service, was rebuilt and lengthened. Following the fire of 1894 she was rebuilt and plied the lakes until 1913 when she sank near Gull Island.

Schooner **Antelope** Capsizes, Three Lost

November 15, 1894
Off Grand Haven Harbor

The **Antelope** was a merchant schooner, 32 tons, 56 feet, that could carry a maximum of non-perishable cargo with a minimum of crew. She was on her way to White Lake to lay up for the winter when she went on the beach at Grand Haven November 15, 1894. All three aboard perished. The event was chronicled by the November 15, *Grand Haven Evening Tribune*:

> Three sailors met a watery grave off Grand Haven piers early this morning. They were the entire crew of the little schooner **Antelope**. All were strong young men in the prime of life. As for the vessel, the beach north of the piers is strewn for miles with the wreckage. Another schooner, the **Alert** is high and dry on the beach near the north pier and just back of the life saving station. Her crew were rescued without trouble.
>
> About two o'clock this morning just at the change of watch in the life saving station, a light was noticed and a small vessel made out making for the piers. Some minutes later the vessel disappeared in the twinkling of an eye. She had capsized and went down instantly. The watch in the station notified the crew and in a short space of time they had the surf boat on the beach. No sooner had they got there than the sailing scow **Alert** came jumping along for the harbor. The great swells at the mouth of the river hurled her north of the pier and she soon struck bottom. The life saving crew went out and rescued her men, Capt. Chas Boomsluiter and Henry Schippers of this city. Gradually the **Alert**

worked in towards shore and now she is practically high and dry on the beach. She does not appear to be damaged badly.

Nothing could be seen of the schooner that capsized but it was not long before wreckage began coming ashore and her signboard with the name "**Antelope.**" Then the crew of the **Alert** thought of the schooner of that name they had been lying very near to in South Chicago. It was the same craft. The **Alert** left South Chicago yesterday morning, light, bound for Grand Haven to lay up. When she went out, the **Antelope** was still tied at her dock. It is believed that the **Antelope** went out shortly after the **Alert**. Both vessels must have been close together but Capt. Boomsluiter says that he did not see the **Antelope** while in the lake. The latter was ten minutes in advance of the **Alert** when she met her fate in the jaws of the harbor.

A terrible sea was piling up at the time and the roar of the surf was indescribable. The **Antelope** bravely tried to make the harbor. She was within 200 feet of safety when she suddenly careened and went clear over. Her crew probably attempted to save themselves by hanging onto wreckage, but no man could live in that sea. All went down and their bodies have not yet been recovered. It is believed that the action of the wind and waves will carry the bodies far to the north of us. If found at all, Capt. Lysaght thinks they will come ashore near Muskegon.

From Little Black Lake to the north pier the beach is strewn with the wreckage of the **Antelope**. Most of it came ashore near what is termed the "Point of the Woods" two miles north. The strange thing about the parts of the vessel coming ashore are their wrecked appearance. Everything seems to have been smashed by the surf into small pieces. A quantity of onions must have been on the wrecked vessel as the beach is covered with them. Some of the rigging was found three miles north of the pier.

The life saving crew at the mouth of the river did all that was in their power to do. So suddenly did the **Antelope** founder that no assistance could have been rendered her crew. The life savers did good work in bringing ashore the men from the **Alert**.

Capt. Lysaght of the life saving station says that there was a terrible sea on last night. It was at its height when the two vessels were wrecked. The capsizing of the **Antelope** cannot be laid to poor seamanship by her sailors for in the gale that was prevailing, it could hardly have been prevented. . .

The lost schooner **Antelope** was built in Muskegon in 1878 and launched as the **Ellen G. Cochran.** Her hailing port was Chicago. She was 55.7 feet long, 16.1 feet beam, 5.4 feet depth of hold, with a gross tonnage of 32.02. The **Alert** was built in Grand Haven in 1879. She hailed from Grand Haven and was owned by Captain Charles Boomsluiter. Her dimensions were 40 feet in length, 12.6 feet beam, and 4.2 feet depth of hold, gross tonnage 17.75.

There was some difficulty ascertaining just how many sailors had been aboard the

Antelope and who they were. Captain Boomsluiter of the **Alert** said he thought there were three men but could not recall their names. "They were Norwegians and unmarried. All were comparatively young men." The next day the captain of the schooner **Nellie Hammond** that had been lying at the pier in Grand Haven, supplied the information that the men on the **Antelope** were "Capt. John Larson, and a relative of his also named Larson and another Norwegian sailor known only as Chris, all the men hailed from Whitehall. None of them were married men."

Captain John Larson had been sailing on the schooner **Monitor** all summer in the general coasting trade, but had accompanied the **Antelope** on this trip to get to his home in Whitehall. The other two were the owners of the **Antelope**. The life saving crew continued to patrol the beach in search of bodies, but had found none.

The November 16 newspaper reported that further head scratching aboard the **Nellie Hammond** had brought about a consensus that they had given Captain Larson's name correctly, but that the other two were named Hanson and Johnson. "The latter two owned the vessel but Capt. Larson was with them this trip. Larson and Johnson hailed from Whitehall, but Hanson made his home in Chicago a good deal of the time."

To add to the mystery a piece of a trunk had been found on the beach with the address: Hennig A. Petterson, Englewood Jct., North Amerika, stamped inside. "It is possible," the newspaper speculated, "that some one of this name was also on board. A dog which was roaming about town yesterday is said to be off the wreck, but the crew of the **Hammond** do not know of a dog on the boat."

Three days later there were still no bodies. A sailor speaking of the loss of the schooner **Antelope** said that it was his opinion that the men had been washed from the boat before she reached the piers and that the **Antelope** was a rotten and unseaworthy craft and probably became waterlogged out in the lake. Being full of water she rolled over in the breakers at the harbor and broke up.

Several of the participants in the drama near Grand Haven during the storm of November 15 were strangers to trouble. It didn't take residents of the city long to remember that Captain Charles Boomsluiter and Henry Schippers of the scow **Alert** were on the schooner **Presto** when she had beached in almost the same place some years before.

Chicora Missing on Crosslake Run

January 21, 1895
Somewhere Between St. Joseph and Saugatuck

The Graham & Morton company steamer **Chicora** was the **Titanic** of her day and lake. She had been especially built for winter traffic on the Great Lakes at her launch from the Detroit Drydock yards in 1893, and had later had portions of her hull ironed over for additional strength. She had in command Captain Edward G. Stines who had sailed on Lake Michigan for more than two decades. Thus, when the vessel failed to make St. Joseph during a winter storm, January 21, 1895, many people waited for several days confident that she would turn up somewhere, in the lee of an island, or locked in an ice field.

The **Chicora** left Milwaukee very early Monday morning, January 21, laden with 632 tons of flour from midwestern mills. After two days of silence on Wednesday morning wreckage, which was later identified as the **Chicora** began to wash up on the beach near South Haven. Two days later more wreckage was discovered at Douglas and Saugatuck.

No bodies were ever found. The hull of the vessel was never found. Twenty-two members of the crew and one passenger were lost when the boat went down, apparently a victim of the ice, which blocked the entrance to west Michigan ports, and the raging winds and subzero cold of the storm.

(For a more detailed account of the loss of the **Chicora** read *Chicora: Lost on Lake Michigan*, Book 3 of the Saugatuck Maritime Series.)

Three Die as **Artist** Capsizes

July 14, 1895
Off South Haven

Three west Michigan men died when the **Artist**, a new yacht on her trial run, capsized off South Haven, July 14, 1895. According to the July 19, 1895, issue of the *Lake Shore Commercial*, a weekly newspaper published in Saugatuck:

> By the capsizing of a small sail boat off South Haven last Sunday three men lost their lives, two of whom, Wm. Stillson and A. L. Coates were formerly residents of this place. These two have been engaged in building small boats at South Haven for a year past. They had just completed a sailing yacht for U. S. Tisworth of that place and last Sunday was fixed upon as the date for the trial trip. In the afternoon the three started in the boat for this place. There was only a fresh breeze blowing and an easy enjoyable trip was expected. All went well until the boat was about two miles out from South Haven. At that time there was a sudden but severe squall on the lake and observers on shore say they saw the yacht suddenly roll over, keel up and sink before any of the victims on board had a chance to escape. The life-saving crew was at once notified of the disaster and pulled their boat with all speed to the scene. They were too late to pick up anything except a cap belonging to one of the drowned men. Relatives of the unfortunate men, who live here, heard nothing of the disaster until Monday morning. J. L. Coates, father of one of the drowned men and J. C. Stillson, brother of another, immediately started for South Haven where they found the citizens of that place had already provided for a search for the bodies which was made by means of tugs dragging the lake. The search proved unavailing.

The bodies were found the following week. There is no record of what happened to the sailboat.

107

Ferry **Watson** Burns in Morning Fire

August 30, 1896
Black Lake near Holland

The small steamer **Harvey Watson** had been launched at Saugatuck in 1893 and operated for most of her early years in various capacities on Black Lake near Holland. On August 30, 1896, while she was filling in for the ferry boat **Music**, the **Watson** was destroyed in an early morning fire. The September 5, 1896, issue of the *Holland City News* reported:

> Early Sunday morning our citizens were awakened from their slumbers by an alarm of fire. The ferry steamer **Harvey Watson**, which was lying at the Bradshaw dock, was the scene of the conflagration and upon the arrival of the fire department was enveloped in flames, which soon spread to a quantity of lumber piled upon the dock and owned by the Scott-Lugers Lumber Co. Engineer Baker, sleeping in the cabin, was awakened by a sense of suffocation caused by the dense volumes of smoke and with difficulty forced his way out of the burning steamer. The firemen succeeded in saving the hull and machinery. The damage to the steamer is estimated at about $600, with no insurance. The Scott-Lugers Lumber Co. place their loss at about $150, and Engineer Baker mourns the loss of two suits of clothes, and a watch. The steamer will be rebuilt for next season's business and the steamer **Greyhound** of Saugatuck succeeds her for the remainder of the season.

The steamer which was 27.74 gross tons, 56.6 feet in length was rebuilt for service in 1897. In 1906 she was sold to Chicago interests and ran on the Calumet River where she was a victim of fire in 1908 and again in 1911. She ended her days operating out of the port of Milwaukee as a fishing tug. The **Watson** was recorded as abandoned in 1926.

Three Die as **City of Kalamazoo** Burns

November 30, 1896
South Haven Harbor

The steamer **City of Kalamazoo** had been built at South Haven and was one of their newest and finest vessels when she burned while in port, November 30, 1896. Three of her crew died as a result of the flames. According to story in the South Haven newspaper:

> The steamer **City of Kalamazoo** came into port a week ago last Sunday and since then her crew have been stripping her and getting her

ready for winter quarters. Last Monday morning about four o'clock "Doon" Dimock, a cabin boy occupying one of the staterooms, was awakened by the smell of smoke and with some difficulty awakened his companion, Will Flanders. They found the steamer was on fire and at once tried to wake the others -- the engineer, Geo Jones, Will. Sherwood, Sam Wellerman, Joseph Lang, Robbie Van Ostrand and Miss Rose Goins, the latter in charge of the cabin and with the **Kalamazoo** since it went into service three years ago.

*The **City of Kalamazoo** after the fire.*

As soon as possible the firemen were at work, and the remains of the wreck shows good work was done in the face of the heavy wind. . . It soon became evident that Joseph Lang and Robbie Van Ostrand had not escaped from the burning mass, and a search followed up the driving back of the flames. The bodies of the two unfortunates were found at the foot of the ladder leading to the upper deck in the stern of the steamer, burned to death, they having escaped from their room and gained some ten feet toward safety. . .

Doon Dimock says he saw Miss Rose Goins on the guard of the boat, partially dressed and with the skirt of her dress over her arm. He

109

told her to jump to the dock and until 8 o'clock it was supposed she had done so and gone to the Center street home of her friend, Mrs. John A. Dungill. After his breakfast Mr. Dungill reported she had not been at his house. . . .

Friday morning her body was found in the river near where she must have fallen overboard while in a stupefied condition from the effects of inhaling smoke.

For two days there had been no fire in the engine room. The engineer made the rounds of the steamer at midnight and everything seemed all right. From these two facts the opinion is a fair one that the fire was caused by the bursting of a lamp.

The **City of Kalamazoo** was built for the H. W. Williams Transportation Co. by John B. Martel at South Haven and launched in 1893. She was 728.19 gross tons, 529.05 net tons and 161.7 feet in length. In 1896 she had spent the summer running from Chicago to South Haven, and had been chartered for fall, running mostly from Grand Haven and Manistee to Milwaukee. The newspaper reported after the fire that her original cost was $48,000 and since her building an additional $5,000 had been spent on improvements increasing her value to $53,000. "An insurance of $25,000 was held in her favor, placed in small amounts in ten or twelve companies. The settling of this is awaited before any decision can be made as to what will be done about replacing her."

The **City of Kalamazoo** was eventually completely rebuilt at South Haven, but this was not to be her last experience with fire.

Historic **Porcupine** Asleep in the Mud

1896
Spring Lake on the Grand River

In 1896 work was begun on raising and rebuilding the historic **Niagara**, the vessel that had been the flagship for Commodore Oliver Hazard Perry at the climax of the Battle of Lake Erie, considered the turning point in the naval engagements that were part of the War of 1812. This set western Michigan to remembering that their waters too housed an historic ship that was part of that event. The May 1, 1896, *Saugatuck Commercial* reported:

It is probably not generally known, but lying in the waters of Spring Lake, near Ferrysburg is the lower portion of the hull of the schooner **Porcupine**, one of the nine vessels that Commodore Perry commanded in the memorable battle on lake Erie when the British were vanquished. The **Porcupine** was taken to Detroit in 1830 and her name changed to the **Caroline**. In 1855 after long years of service, she was allowed to sink off Johnston's boiler works.

110

The **Porcupine** was one of the smaller vessels commanded by Perry during the most important naval battle which took place off Put-In-Bay on Lake Erie, September 10, 1813. The vessel is described in some histories as 83 tons with a crew of 25. She carried only one gun, a long 32. Under the ritualized battle of the day the two fleets approached and engaged each other in single file. On the American side was the schooner **Scorpion** the schooner **Ariel,** the **Lawrence,** the **Caledonia,** the **Niagara,** the schooner **Somers,** the schooner **Porcupine,** the **Tigris** and the sloop **Trippe.** In the British line were the sloop **Little Belt,** the ship **Detroit,** the brig **Hunter,** the **Queen Charlotte,** the schooner **Lady Prevost** and the schooner **Chippewa.** In the original battle plan it was the task of the **Porcupine** to engage the **Lady Prevost** in action. However, official reports of the battle mention only that she had some role in hemming in the **Lady Prevost,** cutting off her retreat astern, but saw no close action during the battle. She was the only one of the American ships to have no men wounded or killed in the battle, but was permitted to share in the prize money. Her acting sailing master during the battle was Midshipman George Senat, a native of New Orleans of French extraction, who was later killed in a duel.

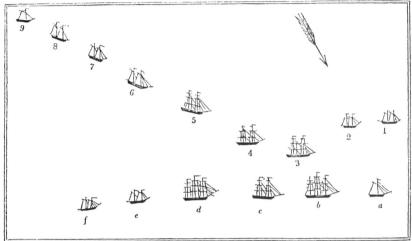

On this map of the Battle of Lake Erie the **Porcupine** *(7) is set to engage the* **Lady Prevost** *(e). The original flag ship, the* **Lawrence,** *is designated as 3, the* **Niagara** *is 5.*

After the war the **Porcupine** was repaired and used as a naval ship. In 1817 and 1818 she was under the command of Captain Steven Champlain who had commanded the **Scorpion** during the Battle of Lake Erie and claimed to have fired the first and the last shot in that battle. Her first assignment was to assist in determining international boundary lines, in 1820 she was assigned to the revenue service.

In 1830 her upper works were rebuilt, and she became a trading vessel under the name **Caroline.** Some accounts list Thomas W. Ferry of Ferrysburg, who afterwards became a U. S. Senator, as her first civilian owner. Other accounts show that she was run by pioneer lumbermen Barber & Mason first, and later the property of Ferry & Sons. She was commanded for several years by Captain Harry Miller and used in the lumber trade carrying lumber and other wood products from the Grand River in Ottawa County to Chicago, until she became unseaworthy.

Legend has it that the vessel was then set adrift near the mouth of the Grand River and the current carried her out into Lake Michigan, but a west wind blew her back a day or two later. The **Caroline** was claimed, refitted and put back in use for another season, then was sailed up into Spring Lake and allowed to sink in the mud near the Johnston shops about 1855. According to old histories, during her last year on the lakes her condition was such that Capt. Pat Mahoney was obliged to hire a new crew at every point, as it was a case of "pump ship" in order to keep afloat.

In 1896 most of what remained of the old vessel was removed from the water and put under the apple trees near the Johnston Boilerworks. The only recognizable parts left were weather-blackened oak ribs and keel. That year she was raised by E. C. Richards, principal of the Fruitport schools. In June of 1913, with plans for the Perry Centennial well underway, Charles C. Bolthouse a Johnston employee, and B. J. Reenders, a relative who was a former Cleveland school teacher, but a native of Ferrysburg, and Klauss Katt, supervised the packaging of the remains, the keel, some ribs, and a little planking. The boxes containing the remains were shipped to Detroit where they were placed aboard the steamer **Frank E. Kirby** to be taken to the exhibit at Put-in-Bay, although no mention of the ship is made in the official program of the event.

There is one account of a ceremony that was held somewhere on Lake Erie. A piece of **Porcupine's** stem was attached to an anchor and thrown overboard with the words:

> In honor of Commodore Oliver Hazard Perry and his brave sailors, I consecrate the old relics of the schooner **Porcupine** to the waters of Lake Erie. May his memory be ever cherished by patriotic and liberty loving American people.

Smaller and less recognizable pieces were crafted into yardsticks and rulers and the hand forged iron spikes converted into paper weights. These were offered for sale at the centennial with cards that said, "This is a souvenir of the old Porcupine." Other salvaged portions of the ship were put on display at the Perry Victory Centennial Celebration. Afterwards they were stored in basement of the City Hall in Cleveland. Eventually "a bundle and a couple of boxes" were taken over by the Western Reserve Historical Society and remain in their vaults. A few fragments were left in Grand Haven and eventually became part of the Tri-Cities Museum collection.

There was a precedent for this kind of treatment of historic battleships. The **Lawrence**, Perry's original flagship during the battle of Put-in-Bay, had been raised from its watery grave during the celebration of the national centennial in 1876, and the good portions made into souvenirs.

The **Niagara**, the ship to which Perry transferred in mid battle, was raised as part of the 1913 centennial celebration of the battle and was rebuilt using the original keel and some ribbing and sailed around the lakes after being the focal point of the anniversary festivities. She was rebuilt again 1933 to 1943 and completely overhauled and rebuilt for a third time, 1988 to 1990 and is again enrolled as an active sailing ship, based in Erie, Pennsylvania.

Stevenson Sinks, Crew Saved by Long Row

October 6, 1897
Lake Michigan 40 Miles off Holland

The sinking of the **Ellen Stevenson** on Lake Michigan, October 15, 1897, left the crew with no choice but to row to safety. The incident was described in the October 9, 1897, issue of the *Holland City News*:

> The **Ellen Stevenson** foundered in mid-lake Wednesday. Capt. Schippers and crew of three men escaped from the sinking craft in their yawl boat and reached this port. The **Stevenson** was bound from Grand Haven to Kenosha with a cargo of fruit. Forty miles west of this harbor, in a strong breeze from the northwest and a considerable sea, she sprung a leak which soon grew too large for the pumps, and the crew were compelled to abandon the ship. Rather than head against the wind for the west shore, they turned back to this port and arrived in the afternoon. They were sighted two miles out and the life-savers went out to help them in. They reached the dock in safety. The schooner is owned by Capt. J. DeYoung of Grand Haven,

The **Ellen Stevenson** (on some papers referred to as the **Stephenson**) was 43.92 gross tons, 41.73 net tons, and 61 feet in length.

Florence M. Smith Strikes Pier

July 10, 1897
South Haven Pier

The merchant schooner **Florence M. Smith** struck the north pier at South Haven, trying to get into the port during a storm, and became a total loss in the waves. According to the *South Haven Sentinel* for July 17, 1897:

> Last Saturday evening about eight o'clock the schooner **Florence M. Smith** passed this port, light, on her way from Chicago to Ludington. On account of the heavy seas she was put about when opposite Glenn and made for this port. In endeavoring to enter the harbor at three o'clock in the morning she made a miss of it, struck against the outer side of the north pier, and at once commenced going to pieces as a total wreck, everything being taken from her that could be moved. She was owned by Mrs. Frank Reddy of St. James and sailed by Capt. Richard Lick. From her general appearance it is fortunate she found a watery grave beside a pier, where her crew of four people could escape with their lives, the rapidity with which the seas tore her to pieces showing her hardly worthy of battling with rough weather. The Captain estimates

the loss as about $800 with no insurance.

The **Florence M. Smith** was a merchant schooner of 60 tons, 71 feet in length. She had been launched in 1884 at Charlevoix.

Whole Crew Lost as **Doty** Founders

October 25, 1898
On Lake Michigan

Beers, in his classic *History of the Great Lakes*, made the sinking of the steamer **L. R. Doty** the headline event for 1898. He wrote: "The most disastrous event of the season, in loss of life, was the foundering of the steamer **L. R. Doty** on Lake Michigan with her entire crew of 17. The **Doty** left Chicago, Monday, October 24 with the **Olive Jeanette** in tow, both loaded with corn, for Midland, Georgian Bay. They encountered a furious gale the following day. The towline parted and the manner of her loss remains unknown. Indications were that she drifted a considerable distance before she went down in mid lake. Her wreckage was picked up 25 miles off Kenosha. The **Jeanette** was sighted on the 27th and towed to Chicago in a crippled condition. The **Doty** was a stanch wooden propeller, built at West Bay City in 1893. She was in command of Capt. Christopher Smith. The crew of the **Jeanette** could throw no light on the fate of the **Doty**. The vessels were struck by the northeast gale on Monday, when below Milwaukee. Tuesday afternoon the steamer parted from her consort.

The **Jeannette** was left on her own about 5 p.m. and in the midst of a northerly gale. She formerly sailed the lakes as a four masted schooner and Captain David B. Cadotte ordered some canvas spread and headed before the wind to Racinc. She missed Racine in thc gale about 11 p.m. because of a faulty steering rudder, and headed for Chicago. As the storm died down the schooner was found adrift by a steamer a few miles off Chicago and towed in port.

The **L. R. Doty** had been built in 1893 at West Bay City, Michigan. She was a propeller vessel, 2,056 gross tons, 1,709 net tons, 291 feet in length, and 41 feet in beam. She had experienced a serious fire at Chicago in 1896 and been thoroughly rebuilt. At the time of her foundering she was owned by Cuyahoga Transit Co. of Chicago. The **Doty** was declared lost October 27 after the tug **Prodigy** found wreckage from the steamer about 25 miles off Kenosha including pieces of deck, a pole mast, cabin doors, stanchions, and a part of the steering pole from the bow.

Shortly afterwards pieces of boat and bodies began to show up on the Lake Michigan shore. The Holland newspaper reported in the November 5 issue that a lifeboat from the **Doty** had been found at Macatawa near Holland. The *Grand Haven Tribune* for November 8, 1898, reported:

> Two bodies of the **Doty** victims were found at South Haven and Ganges yesterday. While John Luikens and Harry Oakes were patrolling the south beach this morning about six miles south of the pier they came across an oar upon which was inscribed the name **Doty**. It was a

fine oar and a new one and will be highly prized as a valuable relic. From what wreckage that has come ashore the **Doty** must have been an exceedingly fine boat. All the way between here and Holland beach combers are at work securing lumber and wreckage.

A farmer living back of the sag in Ferrysburg yesterday found on the beach a bottle containing an insurance policy. The *Tribune* has been unable to learn the name of the man whose name was on the policy, but it is believed was one of the victims of the **Doty**. The policy was in favor of his wife. This act on his part was one of the last of his life and goes to show that the sailors of our lakes are made of splendid stuff and of heroic mold. With the seas beating down his ship this sailor thought of his own little fireside and associates at home.

The **Olive Jeannette** was repaired and put back into service. Four years later, on September 3, 1905, she was lost with the steamer **Iosaco** off the Huron Islands on Lake Superior.

Schooner **Aberdeen** Rescued, Twice

November 7, 1898
Grand Haven Harbor

The schooner **Aberdeen** was bound from Chicago to Buffalo under the tow of bulk freight steamer **Horace A. Tuttle** on October 26, 1898, when the **Tuttle**, heavily loaded with corn, was overwhelmed by a fall gale. The steamer cut loose the **Aberdeen** and struggled to save herself, but was driven ashore near Michigan City and became a total loss, her wreckage blocking the entrance to the Michigan City harbor for several days.

The **Aberdeen**, adrift on Lake Michigan, blew northward and was finally approached by the tug **Miller** and the captain offered the tug captain $100 if he would tow the schooner into Grand Haven. This was done and the schooner remained at Grand Haven, making repairs and waiting for motive power to continue her trip. The November 7, 1898, *Grand Haven Daily Tribune* tells the next chapter:

ABERDEEN ON BEACH

This is a windy exciting day at the pier, the most exciting since the loss of the **Amazon** many years ago. Shortly after noon the big barge **Aberdeen**, in tow of the Crosby liner **Nyack** bound for out in the lake to meet the tug steamer **Philip Minch** which was to take her to Buffalo, had the misfortune to break her tow and line. The result was that the **Aberdeen** drifted on the beach about 600 yards from the north pier, and is still there hard aground. The prospects are that she will be totally wrecked. The life saving crew took off the crew of the **Aberdeen**.

The loss of the **Aberdeen** was really too bad and in some respects unaccountable. This morning the tug barge **Philip Minch** of the

Nicholas Transit Co. appeared off the harbor and made known the fact that she was waiting for the **Aberdeen** to tow her down to Buffalo. At once the Captain of the **Aberdeen** bargained with the **Nyack** to tow him out into Lake Michigan to the **Minch**. The **Minch** was heavily laden with grain and drawing eighteen feet of water and did not attempt to come in. She could have done it, but her captain claimed was not insured for this port.

Consequently the **Nyack** started to tow out the **Aberdeen** and had just about started when she ran onto a sand bar in the river near the fish shanties. After working for two hours the **Nyack** released the **Aberdeen** about 11:30 a.m. and started out. Near the harbor mouth Capt. Cartwright went aloft to see if he could see the **Minch** but she was not in sight and the **Nyack** continued on her way with the intent on of dropping the **Aberdeen** when out in the lake. The captain of the **Aberdeen** however concluded to remain at the pier until his big consort came in sight. It was too late to tie up however and while working away the frail tow line parted. The **Aberdeen** narrowly missed the north pier and swiftly went on the beach. She is hard aground in about twelve feet of water, broadside to the lake. If the wind comes up strong from the southwest nothing will save her. Some of her crew have about given her up now, and think she broke in two when she struck the beach. If she is leaking and there is every reason to believe she is, the barley in her will swell and she will split open. As soon as she struck the crew made all preparation to leave and took their clothing ashore in safety. The sea was not heavy at the time but a high wind was blowing. Her yawl boat was lost and when last seen was heading toward Muskegon.

From what can be learned the **Nyack** was in no wise to blame. The line used in towing belonged to the schooner. The **Aberdeen** as is now well known, was towed in here about ten days ago after a terrible experience. She was lost by her consort, the **Tuttle** and the latter is now a wreck at Michigan City. It seems that the **Aberdeen** will follow her to Davy Jones' locker unless some big tug can be secured at once to haul her off. The odds are against the **Aberdeen**, however. She is fully insured.

Strangely enough four boats whose names begin with the letter A have been lost at this harbor, or in going from here. The big **Amazon** went to pieces here, the **Alpena** left here on her last trip, the little **Antelope** was lost here a few years ago, and now comes the **Aberdeen**. It is said that the **Aberdeen** rests on the hulk of the old **Antelope**. She foundered there a few falls back and her crew of three Norwegians drowned.

Work continued on assessing the damage to the schooner and pulling it off the beach before the weather changed. It was reported that the **Minch**, tired of waiting for the **Aberdeen** to be freed in her early difficulties, had gone on to Chicago. The November 8 Grand Haven paper reported:

116

*The schooner **Aberdeen***

The insurance men interested in the **Aberdeen** are again inspecting the boat this afternoon. It is understood that they have sent for the big wrecker **Favorite**. She is now in Cheboygan and if she can get here before a blow sets in the barge may yet be saved. This noon the big barge **Philip Minch** again appeared off the harbor and after seeing the predicament her would-be consort was in, turned about and put towards Chicago.

About 8 o'clock the crew of the life saving station accompanied by several insurance men went over to the vessel and boarded her. Several of the **Aberdeen's** crew were also along. It did not take long to find that the "boat's back" was not broken. The crew of the **Aberdeen** thought she broke in two when she struck the sand, but her staunch timbers stood her true. There was considerable water found in her, however, and the least sea from the southwest or northwest will completely wreck her. The seas had washed over her and carried away her hatches. Considerable grain had been swept out and barley was found on the beach just opposite the ship. This is believed to come from the open hatches. Her seams were also found to be parting in many places, caused by the sea and heavy strain she is subject to. Amidships was one particularly dangerous break. The **Aberdeen** is in a serious predicament and unless a powerful tug and pumps can be put at work at once nothing will save her. The weather is so uncertain at this time of the year that a heavy blow can be expected any time. Her grain, if wet, will complete the work of cracking her open. Capt. Cartwright says that the rope used as a tow line yesterday was a new eight-inch line, fifty or sixty fathoms long. It was considered strong enough to pull any boat.

But the winds remained calm and the big wrecking tug **Favorite** arrived November 9 to rescue the grounded **Aberdeen**. The work began to lighten the stricken vessel by removing her cargo of 5000 to 6000 bushels of barley. At first the grain was simply pumped out into the lake but by the second day, "A large number of small boats hover about the **Aberdeen** and their enterprising owners are filling them with grain as it is pumped from the deck of the vessel. Some of these amateur wreckers secured barley enough to last them a lifetime."

The schooner was found "in better shape than supposed" and just less than half of the barley was still in the hold when she was pulled off the beach at two o'clock the afternoon of November 12 and taken inside the harbor. "She is leaking quite badly and a sailor can detect the fact by looking over her hull that her timbers have stood a terrible strain. The pump is kept working continually but what barley is now in her hold will be kept." She left Grand Haven early in the morning of November 15 and the **Nyack** met the **Favorite** with the **Aberdeen** in tow at midlake. At Milwaukee the wet barley was delivered to the American Malting Co. and subjected to drying in malting drums and the vessel placed in the stationary drydock at the west yard for examination and repair.

The **Aberdeen** was a merchant schooner about 1045 tons, 211 feet in length. She had been launched at West Bay City, Michigan, in 1892. In 1906 she was sold into British registry. Later the schooner was enrolled in Canada under the name **Gladys H.** Records show that she was abandoned in 1932.

Barge **Rand** Disabled and Drifting

November 8, 1898
Off Grand Haven

The same Grand Haven newspaper that carried the account of the beaching of the **Aberdeen** had additional information and a secondary headline:

Barge Rand in Distress

About the time that the **Aberdeen** went ashore, four men, part of the crew of the barge **Rand** loaded with lumber bound from Ludington to St. Joe came into the harbor in a yawl boat. They left the barge because she was disabled in an endeavor to get a tug to go out to her assistance. These four men, Mate F. W. Crossaint and three of the **Rand's** sailors were drenched to the skin. The engine of the **Rand** was wrecked when about 15 miles off Holland. The wind carried her to within about eight miles of the harbor and the four men mentioned volunteered to go ashore after assistance. There was a heavy sea outside of the land, and the wind blew hard from the south. But the men went at their task bravely and arrived in safety. There were warmed and given a change of clothing at the life saving station. When they left the **Rand** no other boat was in sight but when the men reached here a glass revealed the fact that some unknown barge had taken her in tow. Later the **Rand** and the unknown barge seemed to separate and it is believed the tow line parted. The **Rand** is commanded by Capt. Kelly of Milwaukee.

A later story carried the news that the vessel had come into view from the south about 2:30 under tow of the little steamer **J. S. Crouse** but even as people on the beach watched the tow line parted twice. About that time the steam barge **Edward Buckley**, laden with shingles, arrived at Grand Haven seeking shelter from the storm. Seeing the problems of the **Rand** she at once put back into the lake with the four men who had come ashore in the yawl boat. Two hours later, the **Buckley** returned with the **Rand** in tow. Details of the harrowing day and rescue were reported in the Grand Haven newspaper for November 8:

> The little steamer **Rand** had a terribly exciting time in the lake yesterday. While bound from Ludington to St. Joe yesterday morning and about ten miles south of Grand Haven and ten miles in the lake her engine broke down. The injury to the engine was caused by the piston rod breaking. There was no other craft in sight and four of the crew volunteered to come to Grand Haven in the boat's yawl. The sea was heavy, but the volunteers were brave and plowed ahead. They were able to hoist a piece of canvas and sailed most of the distance. Several times they were in imminent danger of being capsized and very often they shipped water. But good fortune was with them and they made the harbor about the time the **Aberdeen** struck the beach. Their's was a brave act and Mate Croissant and his three sailors are heroes if ever there were any. It was the intention of these men to get a tug to go out to the **Rand**. None of our tugs are powerful enough, however, to be effectual in towing. Some time after the four members of the crew left the Rand the little steamer **Crouse** hove in sight. She was signalled and went to the **Rand's** assistance. The **Crouse** got the **Rand** about 11 o'clock and towed her fully ten miles. The tow line parted twice and the **Crouse** at last concluded to come to Grand Haven and get a new line and start out again. The mate of the **Rand** had, however, already bargained with the captain of the barge **Edward Buckley** and he it was who towed the **Rand** into port. The **Buckley** went out at the risk of her cargo of shingles.
>
> When the **Buckley** and **Rand** were in the harbor, the bit in the **Rand** to which the tow line was fastened was pulled out by the great strain, and for a time the little barge was in great danger of going on the

beach. She was caught in the trough of the sea and the lurches she made pitched off about 15,000 feet of lumber. Happily the line was soon made fast again and the **Rand** was brought into the harbor in safety. A big crowd witnessed the sight and for a few seconds held their breath, for fear the **Rand** would join the **Aberdeen** on the beach. Other than the injury to her engine and the partial loss of her deck load, the Rand was all right. She is a trim little boat and has a brave crew.

Strangely enough two vessels named the **Rand** are in port. One is the schooner **Rand** which has been here nearly two weeks waiting for favorable winds and the other is the barge of that name. The little steamer **Rand** was built in Manitowoc in 1886. For a number of years she carried the garbage and refuse out of Milwaukee and is a well known boat.

Another story in the local news notes that although the crowd held their breath when the little barge hit the trough of the wave, they swung into action shortly afterwards. "Immediately after the **Rand** tipped off part of her deck load at the harbor mouth yesterday every boat and ship procurable was brought into requisition to secure the lumber. The life savers got several thousand feet and every other beach comber in tow made more or less of a haul. Skiffs were on the river last night picking up lumber

Yacht **Starlight** Saved After 8 Hours in Waves

September 3, 1899
Off South Haven

The yacht **Starlight** of Chicago was eventually rescued September 3, 1899, but forced to wait eight hours in high waves because of repairs underway on the rescue craft. The story was related in the September 8, 1899, issue of the *South Haven Weekly Tribune*:

With spars gone and the sails and rigging in the water the sailing yacht **Starlight** was tossed about at the mercy of the waves for eight hours Sunday but was finally towed into port by the steamer **Glenn** of the Williams Trans. Co. There were four people aboard Capt. R. E. Smethell, Miss Lillie Smethell, Geo. Darling and Harry Davis and they all escaped with nothing worse than a thorough drenching.

The **Starlight** left South Haven Sunday morning at 8 o'clock with all sails set and started across the lake for Chicago. There was quite a sea running and a stiff breeze was blowing from the north with indications for more wind and it was thought strange that the boat should start across the lake in the face of it.

About 8:30 o'clock the lookout at the life saving station saw the yacht give a lunge and a moment later the spars of the yacht snapped off halfway between the cross trees and the deck and when they fell took the sails and rigging with them to the deck and into the water. The signal was given by the lookout and immediately the crew launched the surf boat and Capt. Mathews with surfmen Curran, Robinson, Jempson, Klock and Allers started through the sea for the disabled craft. Soon after the crew had started for the yacht a signal of distress was run up on the piece of the after mast which was left standing. The crew reached the yacht which was then about four miles to the southard and about three miles in the lake and found that no one was hurt and that they were in no immediate danger but wanted a tug to tow their disabled craft to shore.

The life saving crew returned to shore and went to the Williams dock to have them send the steamer **Glenn** out to the disabled boat but upon arriving there they found that the boilers of the **Glenn** were being cleaned and that she would not be able to get out before one o'clock. With this information the life savers launched their big life boat and returned to the yacht to assist in picking up the rigging so that she could be towed into port. The topmasts and sails all went overboard and it was with difficulty that they were picked up, as the sea by this time had increased so that the waves were washing up over the deck.

About 11 o'clock the steamer **City of Louisville** which was coming from St. Joe with an excursion saw the signal of distress and ran alongside the yacht. Capt. Boswell enquired of Capt. Mathews whether they were in immediate danger and on being told that they were not he steamed away and came into port as he did not care to take the risk of towing the boat in through the waves which were breaking over the piers at the entrance of the harbor, unless it was necessary to save lives. The yacht lay in the trough of the sea rolling heavily and shortly after noon it was getting so rough that Capt. Mathews thought it would be best to bring Miss Smethell ashore and accordingly took her into the life boat and started for shore. When about half way in they were met by the steamer **Glenn** which was then going out to tow the yacht in. A line was thrown from the **Glenn** and the lifeboat was towed back in order that they could assist in getting a line to the yacht.

After considerable difficulty a line was made fast and the disabled boat was towed into port. The trip in was quite an exciting one as every wave washed the deck of the yacht and broke over the life boat which was being towed behind the yacht. The life saving crew and Miss Smethell all donned life preservers and one of the crew stood in the bow of the boat with a hatchet in his hand prepared to sever the tow line in case the life boat was tipped over. Fortunately it came in all right. The life saving crew as well as those aboard the yacht were thoroughly drenched and chilled through as the wind in the afternoon was quite chilly. . . .

The accident was a peculiar one and no one aboard had the least warning of it until the spars and rigging came down with a crash. The captain and his sister were sitting aft steering when the crash came and it was almost a miracle they were uninjured. . .

121

The **Starlight** had been built by Saugatuck boatbuilder John Martel about 1893. She was repaired and returned to Chicago, her new owner B. C. Lindley of the Park Yacht Club, Chicago. The yacht was later taken north to Pentwater.

A. B. Taylor

A. B. Taylor Burns at Dock

November 6, 1901
Grand Haven Harbor

The steamer **A. B. Taylor** was nearly destroyed in a fire that swiftly consumed her wooden superstructure as she lay at her dock three-quarters of a mile northeast of the north side entrance of Grand Haven harbor. The event was chronicled by the November 7, 1901, issue of the *Grand Haven Daily Tribune*:

> The steamer **A. B. Taylor** was burned to the water's edge at her mooring place this noon, and was totally destroyed. Yesterday afternoon fire was discovered in the **Taylor** and the blaze was extinguished by the fire department after several hundred dollars damage had been inflicted. Probably an ember of fire was left undiscovered by the firemen and smoldered all night between the timbers, until this forenoon's heavy gale fanned it into a blaze. At any rate, the crew of the **America** discovered that the **Taylor** was burning again at about 11:40 this forenoon and an alarm was turned to.
> It took some time to get across the river to notify the fire

department and when the department reached the scene, the **Taylor** was ablaze from stem to stern. Her light upperworks furnished excellent fuel and the northwest gale made it a roaring blaze. Sparks were carried over the city by the wind, and the new O T & M warehouse, which stood not over 50 yards away was in imminent danger of burning. In fact the elevator and the city's entire water front was in danger for a time as great brands of fire were carried by the wind across the south channel.

But the fire department by close vigilance saved the warehouse and put out a number of embryo fires which started under that structure. It was useless to attempt to save the **Taylor**, but the department, the crew of the steamer **America** and the life saving crew, with a hand pump kept several streams on the hulk. Water for the fire department was secured at the hydrant on the corner of Elliott and Fulton streets about a quarter of a mile away. The fire engine was also brought into use, but too late for any actual good.

The handsome steamer **America** is moored within a few feet of the **Taylor**, but still has steam up, and was in no danger. The fire was an unusually hot one and within twenty minutes after the firebell rang the boat was practically burned. The boats in the harbor and a factory whistle added to the din in giving the alarm.

The **A. B. Taylor** was owned by E. C. Dunbar of the city, and was valued at $8,000; insured for $5,000. Her loss is total. The **Taylor's** last regular route was on the Chicago drainage canal in the excursion business. Previous to that the **Taylor** plied between Chicago and Michigan City. For over a year she has been idle and was tied near the D. T. & M. dock on the "island."

The **A. B. Taylor** was built in Saugatuck in 1884. She was named after a well known Saugatuck resident, a son of a former Episcopalian rector of this city. The boat measured 103 tons and 106 feet long, 20 feet beam, with 7.8 feet depth of hold. Mr. Dunbar has owned the boat about six years.

Despite the gloomy forecast in the newspaper, the **Taylor** was rebuilt at Grand Haven and came out in 1903 as the **Ottawa**. She worked first on Lake Michigan, then on the eastern Great Lakes ending her service in a final fire December 14, 1910, at her dock at Clayton, New York.

Hattie B. Pereue on the Pier

October 15, 1902
Holland Harbor

The wooden lumber hooker **Hattie B. Pereue** had left St. Joseph with a partial load of salt about 4 p.m. on Tuesday afternoon, October 14, under Captain John Kemming, riding high in the water, bound for Chicago to secure fuel. According to the

Ottawa County Times, a Holland newspaper:

When about two hours out of St. Joseph the sea began laboring and an hour later the boat was laboring in one of the fiercest gales that ever swept Lake Michigan. Capt. Kemming left the Chicago course and started toward Grand Haven.

At midnight he sighted the Saugatuck lights and the coal supply was then so greatly reduced that he gave up hope of reaching Grand Haven and made for Holland harbor. At 3 p.m. (Wednesday) the boat reached the piers here. The sea was running mountain high, the waves dashing completely over the piers.

Hattie Pereue

The *Holland City News* takes up the story:

Just as the steamer was about to enter the pier a terrific wave struck her and threw her broadside into the trough of the sea. She fell off to the northward and struck the third bar where for a brief space she lay helpless, the waves washing her decks.

As soon as the lookout of the life saving station saw that the steamer missed the harbor he gave the alarm. It looked as if the boat would break to pieces in a short time and Capt. Jensen (of the lifesaving service) decided to get the beach apparatus ready for business. Such a heavy sea was running in the harbor that it was impossible to cross from the station to the pier with the apparatus. Therefore the surfboat was launched and taken around the winged pier to the shore on the south side. Then the surfmen hauled the cart to the surfboat, loaded it aboard, and in a remarkably short time transported it to the scene of danger and were ready to send the shot line to the imperiled crew.

But aid of this kind was not needed. A huge wave washed the steamer off the bar, her captain took advantage of the chance, gave the signal to go ahead and ran the boat against the pier on the Lake Michigan side. Her crew of thirteen men watched their chance, and, assisted by the lifesavers, reached the pier in safety. By rare luck all escaped without injury.

The **Pereue** had been built at South Haven in 1881 and was a strictly freight vessel. She was 193 tons and 123 feet long, used chiefly in the lumber trade having delivered a cargo at St. Joseph the Monday before her disaster.

The *Manistee Daily News* of October 16, 1902, reported the incident and commented, "Capt. John Kemming has sailed out of this port for many years and always with good luck until this season. A few weeks ago he had a remarkable escape from founder off Pt. Sauble. His steamer was picked up in sinking condition and towed to Ludington, finally settling on the bottom just outside of the harbor. She was taken inside, pumped out, and towed to Milwaukee where repairs to the extent of $2,000 were made." The **Pereue** was just a few trips out of drydock when the wave sent her onto the bar at Holland."

The tug **Barnes** was sent from Manistee and an attempt was made to raise her, but the seams of her hull had opened when she struck the beach. The old wooden hull of the **Pereue** had filled with water and the vessel broke in two. The machinery, the ship's cabin, and other salvageable portions were removed with the assistance of the tug **Carrie Ryerson** of Montague in charge of Captain Skeels and her owner David Wilson. The remaining hull was left to break to pieces on the beach north of the piers where she eventually went ashore.

According to the Life Saving Service Annual Report of 1903 the 13 shipwrecked men were fed and given shelter by the Women's Relief Association of Holland until October 19 when all either left for home, or managed to obtain some other employment.

The **Indian Bill** Abandoned

South Haven Harbor
1902

Captain "Indian Bill" Bean of Muskegon was a well-known character of the Lake Michigan shore. His little vessel also known as **Indian Bill** which he usually singlehanded around the coast is variously described as a small hooker, a tramp schooner, and a three n' aft. From time to time improvements added to her uniqueness. The October 25, 1895, *Saugatuck Commercial* noted: "Everybody along the east shore of Lake Michigan knows the odd looking tramp schooner **Indian Bill**. She has made several visits to this port, but none since the addition of a third spar which increases her oddity if such a thing is possible. Everybody does not know the history of her name. When Capt. Bean, the present owner, got control of her, he proposed to name her in honor of Chas. H. Hackley of Muskegon. Mr. Hackley heard of it and offered Capt. Bean $100 if he would name her anything else. The offer was accepted and thus her present name."

*The **Indian Bill**, with Indian Bill himself aboard, tied up at South Haven*

In the fall of 1902, Captain Bean elected to abandon the **Indian Bill** and left her in South Haven. The little vessel was towed to the south beach where the waves demolished what the souvenir hunters left behind. The October 10, 1902, *Commercial* reported: "The **Indian Bill**, the flatiron shaped schooner sailed by Capt. Bean of Muskegon will be relegated to the scrap heap this fall. His strange experience on the **Indian Bill** would fill a volume. He has run her on the beach, run it against nearly every pier on the lake and more than once it has reposed on the bottom with the water to the top rail."

As a replacement he chose the **H. M. Avery** a small sailing vessel that had been built at South Haven in 1887. It sounded like his kind of boat. In April of 1897 the **Avery** was reported "injured beyond all possibility of repair" in Holland harbor after her rudder unshipped as she tried to enter the harbor in a high sea and ended by driving against the south pier. Two years earlier, in May of 1895, the Saugatuck editor reported that the

126

schooner **Avery** was on the beach near South Haven, then commented: "She was noticed passing this harbor in the afternoon, scudding before the gale, and from the weather she was making of it looked doubtful that she would live to reach South Haven."

But the **Avery** weathered all of these problems and Captain Bean seemed genuinely happy to be aboard such a handsome and well appointed vessel, until his death in June of 1903, when he was crushed between the boat and the pier at St. Joseph.

Mechanical Trouble Grounds Joe

September 17, 1903
South of Holland

The small steamer **Joe**, 38 tons, 80 feet in length was one of those utility boats that ran up and down the coast doing whatever formed a paying job for the moment. She was bought in 1901 by Captain L. B. Upham and E. E. Weed of Saugatuck to carry fruit and fruit baskets between Holland, Saugatuck and South Haven. In 1903 she spent the summer season at Manistee carrying resorters between Manistee and Portage Lake. The **Joe** returned to the Kalamazoo River the second week in September and had just begun a series of trips for E. E. Weed & Co., running in connection with the Graham & Morton boats at Holland. According to the *Holland City News* for September 18, 1903:

> The **Joe** cleared Saugatuck harbor yesterday forenoon loaded with peaches and apples for the Graham & Morton steamer at Holland. There was nothing to face but a fresh northwest wind and all would have gone free and easy, like a drunken sailor's money, if, when near Holland harbor the gasket of the handhold plate had not given way and allowed water and consequently steam to escape from the boiler. The accident rendered the tug helpless and Capt. L. B. Upham who was in command, gave the order to drop anchor and to bellow forth to the life saving crew at the harbor distress signals.
>
> Captain Poole [of the life saving service] sent word to Captain Harrington of the **Harvey Watson** to report, hoping that the tug could be towed ashore, and then set out for the steamer with his crew. Captain and crew tried hard to keep the **Joe** from shore but about 2 o'clock the tug struck the bar and it was "all off." Nothing remained but to rescue the crew and this was accomplished without difficulty. The **Harvey Watson** steamed to the scene of the wreck but Captain Harrington saw that it was useless to assist. It was simply impossible to approach the bar without making it two wrecks instead of one.
>
> The **Joe** pounded on the bar all night and today there is no **Joe** worthy of mention in Lloyds marine records.

A lifeboat from the **Joe** was brought back to the E. E. Weed Basket Co., possibly in partially payment for their lost cargo of fruit, and turned into a river towing vessel called the **Big Joe**, 7 gross tons, 27.5 feet in length. She was used for more than 20 years

127

delivering scows of baskets on the river.

The **Joe** had been launched at Grand Haven 1888 for T. W. Kirby.

The steamer Joe at a Manistee dock.

Condor Crushed by Spring Ice

April 1, 1904
Near the Mouth of the Kalamazoo River

The schooner **Condor** had lived a long and eventful life from her launch in 1871 at the Olson-Roth Shipyards of Sheboygan, Wisconsin, until her final encounter with spring river ice April 1, 1904, near the mouth of the Kalamazoo River. Her name occurs frequently in the Life Saving station logs of the day. On May 14, 1883, she was driven hard ashore north of Sheboygan, Wisconsin; on October 22, 1881, she lost a man overboard near Milwaukee during a fall storm; on July 29, 1901, she struck the pier at Holland.

Her end was less dramatic. On the first day of April, 1904, the 30 ton, 58 foot schooner was moored to a dock on the Kalamazoo River just upstream from the mouth of the river at a collection of homes and docks called Fishtown, where many of the area's commercial fishermen lived so that their boats could slip easily into Lake Michigan. She was about to make her first trip of the season and carried a deck load of cord wood, when an avalanche of ice from upriver swept lakeward and the ice breached her old hull. Rube Sewers, who later spent 60 years on the lake was then just a youngster. He said that he got up one morning and discovered the boat nearly submerged near the dock. It was Rube's job to split and gather firewood and he was delighted that morning to make his collection by boat, gathering in much of the **Condor's** deckload that was floating in the river.

Owner of the **Condor** at that time was Benson A. Ingraham of South Haven. Shortly after the accident, on April 8, 1904, the submerged vessel was sold to Captain Ben Randall of South Haven who had plans to make repairs, but she never sailed again. Her final enrollment papers were surrendered March 13, 1905, with the notation "sunk and abandoned."

The portion of river where the **Condor** sank became part of a land-locked lagoon when the new river mouth was built to the north. Although she started out tied to the dock, over the years the schooner slipped into deeper water until there was nothing left above the waterline but the tip of the mast. In 1938 yachtsmen from the Jackson Park Yacht Club of Chicago, assisted by Saugatuck diver William Green, used a homemade diving helmet to reach the hull and succeeded in sawing off the ship's wheel and anchor chain. They were later presented to the Netherlands Museum in nearby Holland. Portions of the hull remain yet, in the quiet sand of the lagoon.

Annie F. Morse Capsizes in Storm

May 19, 1904
Off Glenn

The **Annie F. Morse**, a merchant schooner of 32 tons, capsized off the Casco settlement of Glenn, May 19, 1904, as she tried to wait out a storm. Only two of her three man crew made it safely to the beach. According to the Monday, May 23, 1904, *South Haven Tribune Messenger*:

> After an all-night battle with the fierce gale that was churning Lake Michigan into one mass of foam and amidst billows that tossed her as a child would toss a plaything, the little schooner **Annie F. Morse** went to pieces at an early hour and today her wreckage is scattered for two miles along the beach, one of her men drowned in the lake and the other two reached land in an exhausted condition.

> The **Annie F. Morse** left South Haven one week ago yesterday for Pentwater, manned by Capt. W. J. Minter and two young sailors, Marcus Tyler and Walter Craft. On the trip north she was windbound at White Lake and also at Grand Haven, but she reached Pentwater all right and was loaded with about sixty solid cords of stove wood.

> Thursday noon she set sail on her return trip but encountering headwinds made slow progress. The storm struck them the heaviest about 9 o'clock just off Saugatuck coming directly out of the north. Sails were close reefed and they stood out in the lake. All night the three men worked and watched and waited and hoped and at 3:30 a.m. they

were about four or five miles off Glenn Pier and there was no water in the hold as the captain was keeping it pumped out. And then without warning the boat seemed suddenly to sink, soon after she careened and then the spars snapped off and the captain called to the men to take to the yawl. They endeavored to do so but Tyler was washed overboard.

The others helped him aboard again and again he was washed overboard. Three or four times he was assisted aboard the schooner and then the yawl was adrift with the captain in it and the deck of the vessel broke in two with young Craft on the forward part and Tyler back by the cabin. From this time and even to some extent before, the memory of both survivors seems confused and they only know they were both thrown upon the beach at the same time and only a quarter of a mile apart. Both were well nigh exhausted, the boy especially so since in hanging to the wreckage, he had been in the water for a full hour. They reached the residence of G. Benson about 5:30 and were put to bed and Mr. Benson telephoned the news of the wreck to the Life Saving Station.

*The picture of the wreck of the **Annie F. Morse** was taken on the beach in November of 1904 by Nanna Louise Brown and won third prize in 1906 in a contest conducted by the Burr McIntosh Monthly magazine.*

Captain Jensen of the Life Saving Service did not send a boat, but the captain walked up the beach to see the wreck and search for the body of the missing crewman. It was determined that he had probably drowned when the after part of the deck which he had been clinging to was thrown up on shore near Sleepy Hollow, north of South Haven. The hull of the schooner came shore near the forward deck, with the hull split open from stem to stern and no braces or stays left to hold it together. The cargo was strewn along the beach for about two miles.

The drowned crewman was Marcus F. Tyler, known as Frank, a 23-year-old man from South Haven whose wife was a cook in a South Haven restaurant.

The **Annie F. Morse** was 32 tons and 61 feet in length and had been launched at Muskegon 1881. She had been brought to South Haven about 1902 by Capt. G. O. Ingraham who sold her April 29, 1904, to Captain W. J. Minter and John Overheul of South Haven.

Ferry **Post Boy** Burns in Morning Fire

August 7, 1905
Macatawa Park Dock

The little steamer **Post Boy**, used to ferry resorters around Macatawa Lake near Holland, was destroyed by fire after a busy weekend as she sat at her Macatawa Park dock in 1905. According to the *Holland City News* for August 10, 1905:

> Burned to the waters edge in a conflagration that damaged the machinery almost beyond repair, was the fate that befell the ferry steamer **Post Boy**, owned by the Macatawa Park company, early Monday morning.
>
> Barney McDonald and Joe Kelley were the only members of the crew on board and they were glad to escape minus shoes, minus hats and minus other articles of clothing.
>
> Evidently the fire started in the boiler room and the flames had a good start when first seen. The **Post Boy** was lying along side the big scow south of the boat houses near Macatawa Park dock and near to her was the ferry steamer **Harvey Watson**. It looked for a time as if the **Watson** too was doomed by Captains Beckman and Young cast off her lines and took her out of danger. From then until the flames were subdued the **Watson** played an important part in saving the boat houses, yachts and launches. Captain Austin Harrington and Captains Beckman and Young were busy every minute. When it looked as if the flames would be communicated to nearby floating property a line was run to the **Post Boy** and the **Watson** towed her out of the danger zone.
>
> In spite of their efforts however, the sailboat **Kid** owned by Idema Bros. of Grand Rapids was destroyed and the sailboat **Siren**, owned by J. M. Baker was damaged. . .

The great loss is the **Post Boy**. She was valued at $8,000 and insured for $5,000. But this does not measure the loss. It is the height of the season now. Just the time when the money should flow at high tide into the coffers of the **Post Boy**. The first part of the season was simply a preparation for the ferry and excursion trade that prevails now.

The **Post Boy** was repaired this spring at a stiff cost, and 500 new life preservers were added. The **Post Boy** has been here for three years. She was bought in Chicago. She was 80 feet long, 21 foot beam and was licensed to carry 300 passengers.

The **Post Boy** saw strenuous days before she came to Holland. She was built in 1888 and traded for a time on the Saginaw river. During the World's Fair at Chicago she furnished a good shipwreck story by stranding on Park reef in a heavy storm, with a lot of passengers on board. . . .

The resorters will not be inconvenienced by the burning of the **Post Boy** as Judge Everett's steamer **Mary** will handle the business.

Phylida Sinks after Collision with **Eastland**

August 12, 1905
South Haven Harbor

Quick action by both the life savers and spectators kept a 1905 accident by the cross harbor ferry **Phylida** from becoming a major tragedy. As the incident was later reported:

At about 7 p.m. while crossing the harbor with 14 persons on board (12 of them passengers) the **Phylida** ran under the stern of steamer **Eastland** and had her bow crushed and sunk. In the collision the fuel tank of the launch was demolished, the gasoline igniting and spreading the flames in all directions. The life saving station crew went to rescue in the Whitehall boat, skiff and three other small boats. Running into the flames, they picked up six of the imperiled persons, the others being rescued from the pier by persons on shore. Some of these rescued were painfully burned and were treated at the station. Two of them were given a change of clothing from the store of the Women's National Relief Association. The life saving crew recovered from the water two pocketbooks and other personal property belonging to the rescued persons.

Ten years later the steamer **Eastland** capsized in Chicago harbor with a loss of over 800 lives.

Bird Disappears, Two Lost

August 25, 1905
Off Saugatuck

The **Bird** was a small sailboat, the kind sometimes called a Mackinaw, that was popular with Saugatuck fishermen. In August of 1905 she disappeared on a routine net-lifting expedition. Saugatuck's *Commercial Record* for September 1, 1905, reported:

> Early last Friday morning Chas. Shriver went out to lift his nets as usual, Julius Lense of Chicago, who had been spending his vacation at Mr. Shriver's hotel, being his only companion and neither of the men have returned. No fear was felt regarding their safety until night although they were expected back by noon. When the sailboat, the "Bird" did not return by dark search was begun and it was found that no one had seen it since about noon and as she was an old craft it was thought she might have sunk or become disabled. Most all of the boats in Saugatuck harbor joined in the search going far out into the lake as it was thought that if the craft had not sunk and only been disabled the wind which was blowing from off the land would have taken her far out.
>
> Nothing could be found of the ill-fated craft that night but the next day the **Joseph H** picked up eight well-boards and two fish boxes twelve miles out of South Haven which were known to have been aboard her. A few days after the tiller was found on the shore near Pier Cove.
>
> The boat was an old one having been bought by Captains Wm. Edgecomb and Jack Roda in Milwaukee over ten years ago and sold to Will Shriver eight years ago when she was named the **Bird**. Mr. Lense was a building inspector in Chicago and one of the men who made a favorable report on the Iroquois Theatre shortly before the disaster to that building.

Will Shriver, the owner of the **Bird**, was the nephew of Charles Shriver who was lost. The following week there was a rumor that the body of a dog had come ashore near South Haven. Will investigated and found where a boy had buried the dog. The body was dug up and identified as Charles Shriver's dog, Spot, who was often aboard the fishing boats. Neither the bodies of the men nor the remains of the boat were ever found.

Struggle to Free the **Argo**

November 20, 1905
North of Holland Pier

It started out as a routine trip for the Graham & Morton steamer **Argo**. When she left Chicago, November 19, the weather was fair with clear skies. As she went north toward Holland a storm accompanied by dropping temperatures and intermittent showers began. When the vessel arrived at the entrance to Holland harbor between 4 and 5 a.m., Captain John Stewart decided to lay by until it was light. About 5:30 he headed for the entrance.　　　　As the November 30, 1905, *Holland City News* reported:

> Ordinarily the trial would have been successful, but in this instance a bar had formed in front of the piers and the **Argo** struck this bar and lost steerage way.
>
> Before she again gained headway a couple of heavy breakers battered her and threw her against the piers. Another breaker struck her a little forward of midship and drove her to the north of the north pier where she struck the bar fairly hard, and although the engines were kept working she could not again be brought under control and lodged on the bottom about 500 feet north of the pier.

Surfman William Woldering was on watch at the Holland Life Saving Station lookout tower and summoned the crew to go to the assistance of the steamer. They attempted to approach in the surfboat but could not get near enough to take off the passengers because of the shallow water and the surf so they returned to the station for the beach apparatus.

> They took the beach apparatus and transferred it to the north side of the harbor and made ready to shoot out the shotline. In the meantime the steamer had been pounded along to the northward until it reached a point about 1,500 feet from the north pier and about 500 feet from shore.
>
> The first shot went too far south, but the second went over the bow and the line fell in a little tangle over a fender forward. Mate Crawford climbed down the side of the steamer and brought it to the deck when all heaved away and drew the whipline to the steamer. Those aboard the steamer did not seem to understand the intricacies of the whipblock and whiplines well enough to work rapidly, and to hasten the obtaining of communication between shore and steamer Capt. Pool decided to put one of the surfmen aboard.
>
> The surfboat was manned, and after a severe buffeting was rowed near enough to the lee of the steamer to get a line. One end of this line was fastened around Surfman William Smith, the other was aboard the steamer. When a point of vantage was reached, Smith jumped overboard and struck out for the steamer. He was hidden from sight by a huge wave but soon reappeared and was hauled to the upper deck scrambling up the sides in good shape.

He helped secure the line around the steamer's spar, but that proved insecure so it was tied to the lee bow. The boat was still being pounded northward and while the line was being made ready the sand anchor at the landward end of the breeches buoy line had to be moved three times. A line was shot to the steamer and a breeches buoy set up to rescue the passengers. Finally Smith wigwagged to the life saving crew to send the buoy out. The *Grand Rapids Press* reported:

> Mrs. C. E. Johnson of Big Rapids was first. She is a pleasant faced little elderly woman who won the hearts of all on board. She took her place in the buoy with a smile and a blush at the cut of the big oil skin breeches of the buoy and was hauled away through mist and surf to the shore. She never dipped into the surf and her journey inspired confidence in those who were to follow. . . .
>
> Mrs. W. P. Canaan (of Grand Rapids) who with her husband and little 10 year old daughter, Juliette, were on board was next. An unlucky movement of the stranded vessel slacked the life line and Mrs. Canaan was dragged out of the surf half drowned and terribly frightened. Of the women passengers, she fared much the worse. She was taken to the home of Mrs. Calvin Ainsworth, almost in a state of collapse, but recovered in a few minutes and greeted her laughing little daughter, who came across high and dry in the buoy and looked upon the whole affair as an immense joke. . . .
>
> Perhaps the most thrilling experience among the men passengers was that of W. P. Canaan, well known in Grand Rapids, where he has the agency for several big outside newspapers. His wife and child had gone safely before and he was jubilantly happy when he stepped into the buoy. The cold dip he got almost immediately after he swung clear of the steamer did not put a damper on his spirits. Another sag shoreward by the stranded steamer and Canaan dropped ten feet into the water and disappeared. The crowd frantically hauled the tackle taut again and Canaan emerged from the water like a catapult. Down he went into the water again. He was enveloped in a great roller and came clear again. Another sag of the steamer and a great cry went up. The line had parted and Canaan had dropped into the surf. He struck just as a roller was receding and was in only two feet of water. Before the next sea came roaring in a dozen men had rushed out and brought him, still smiling, to dry sand. Canaan convulsed those about him with his first words. He shook the water from his ears and, looking at Captain Pool said: "It isn't so cold in there as I thought, but you fellows ought to heat it up before you give anyone else such a dip."

The hawser had broken where it was constantly chafed by the surging of the steamer. The spare hawser was across the channel at the station, and the wind and sea were increasing, so Captain Pool decided to make another trial with the life boat, which at this time was on the beach about 800 feet north of and therefore to the lee of the steamer.

The *Holland City News* continues the narrative:

> The life boat was manned, and, assisted by a willing crowd, the

life savers headed her into the breakers. Twice the life boat was dashed back upon the beach and then part of the crowd got a hold of the bow painter and others assisted the crew in keeping her away while she was towed and pulled to a point nearly opposite the steamer. Then the boys bent to the oars and Capt. Pool swung her into the breakers for another trial. They forced her to within about 100 feet of the steamer's bow when the wind and waves struck her flush and gradually beat her back. . . Inch by inch the boat was beaten back, but captain and crew kept at it struggling against the elements with all their might until they were beaten down the shore about a quarter of a mile and reluctantly beached the surfboat.

By this time a new line had arrived and was shot to the **Argo** and the breeches buoy was reestablished. The rest of the passengers and the purser were brought ashore.

Later in the day, when all of the simple things to remove the steamer from the sandbar failed, most of the crew were taken off the vessel, with the remainder spending the night on the stranded steamer. The beach apparatus was left in place and two life savers remained on duty throughout the night.

On Sunday the Graham & Morton tug **Bonita** arrived from Benton Harbor to try to help the **Argo** off the bar, and remove the freight, but the water was too shallow for her to get near the **Argo**. Captain Boswell, captain of the tug, remained in Holland to take charge of the **Argo** while Captain Stewart left for Benton Harbor to take command of the steamer **Holland** which took the **Argo's** place on the Holland to Chicago run.

John Graham, president of Graham & Morton, released a statement that no blame for the tragedy was attached to Captain Stewart:

> "It was one of those unaccountable things," he said. "The sea was not dangerously high and the boat could have made the harbor a thousand times in safety. Something went a little wrong and the control of the ship was lost. No one was to blame, Being a steamboat captain is not an easy place. Had Captain Stewart made no effort to enter the harbor that morning it would have been said that he and his men were cowards."

The **Argo** was 1,089 gross tons, 173.5 feet in length, and powered by a steam-run screw propeller. She was built in 1901 by the Craig Shipbuilding Co. of Toledo, and ran for the Booth Line from Duluth to Port Arthur, Ontario, for a year before being sold to Graham & Morton in 1902.

While J. S. Morton, secretary of Graham & Morton, arrived by special train to talk with the insurance underwriters, the tug **Pup** from Saugatuck, with a much shallower draft than the **Bonita**, was hired to remove the freight. On the main deck there was a large dappled gray horse consigned to the Grand Rapids Fire Department. The animal was backed out on a gangplank thrust through the side hatch. As he cleared the hatchway the board tipped, dropping him into the water which was about four feet deep. After a moment of confusion men standing on shore and holding firmly to ropes tied about the animal's neck succeeded in bringing him in.

*A tug tries vainly to free the stuck **Argo**, this scene was probably photographed in November before it was realized how firmly she was grounded. (See cover for a wintertime view.)*

Then work began on the rescue of the **Argo**. On Monday following the Friday grounding the big tug **Favorite** arrived from Chicago. This rescue effort was delayed by high seas, but even after the lake calmed the **Favorite** was not equal to the task.

The first week in December, more than two months after the grounding, the tugs **Rita McDonald** and **Tomlinson** of the Great Lakes Dredge and Dock Co. started work, but to no avail. The *Commercial Record* of Saugatuck reported:

> The Great Lakes Towing & Dredge Co. has given up the task of getting the **Argo** off the beach. . . They have worked to save the steamer from further disaster. At one time she was hauled 100 feet from the shore but a squall came up making it necessary to quit the job for a while and the steamer again settled back in her old position and a 12 inch hawser valued at $800 was lost. The tug **Rita McDonald** was disabled at a critical moment which helped in making the job a failure.

The Marine Underwriters company which held the insurance on the boat opened the project to bids. A combined crew from Saugatuck and Holland bid on the job but the contract was awarded to the Reid Wrecking Co. of Sarnia, Ontario, owned and run by Captain Tom Reid of Port Huron, the largest and most active wrecking company on the Great Lakes for $9,000. The big tug **Salvor** was sent to Holland along with the **Aldrich**, a lighter vessel of shallow draft to help with the dredging, and an "immense steam pump."

137

The last week in January, 1906, after a wait for good weather, Captain Reid placed two steam pumps aboard the **Argo** and pumped her out until she floated. The Holland newspaper reported:

> On Sunday afternoon the boat was pumped nearly dry, her engines started and all was in readiness for the trial. The tug . . . churned her way close to the steamer and the towline was stretched from tug to steamer. When all was ready the tug strained on the towline and the machinery of the **Argo** was set in motion. Little by little the wheel of the steamer churned out a channel and little by little, with the help of her own propeller and of the strain on the towline, she began to forge toward the channel dug by the wrecking tugs. A large crowd of spectators lined the piers and they knew the completion of the job was near as they saw the steamer move.
>
> Soon the **Argo** slid into the deep water and a mighty cheer went up. "Blow your whistle," shouted the enthusiastic onlookers and in response the captain pulled the cord and the whistle screeched forth. Other whistles joined in the din and gave the steamer quite an ovation.

The **Argo** was brought around and through the piers she had failed to make more than three months earlier and repairs were begun on her bent rudder stock. The **Aldrich** and **Salvor** laid up at Holland for the rest of the winter. During a spell of cold weather the sea-cock in the **Salvor** froze and burst and the tug sank. In the spring she was raised with the assistance of the **Aldrich**, but most of the furniture in her cabins was a total loss.

In the spring the **Argo** was ready for the trip to dry dock in Wisconsin. But, although Captain Tom Reid had American papers, both of the Reid Wrecking Co. tugs on the scene were of Canadian registry and a Canadian tug could not undertake a tow between two American ports. The penalty was fine and confiscation. Reid applied for special permission from the government but was denied.

"To hell with it!" he was reported to have said. "I'll sail her myself!" And with Reid in command, the damaged **Argo** arrived in Wisconsin under her own power.

Graham & Morton brought suit against the insurance companies charging them with undue delay in recovering the boat. After several complicated court maneuvers the company won and the **Argo** was sold, in 1910, to the Chicago, Racine and Milwaukee Line and renamed the **Racine**. In 1917 she was bought by New York City interests and later the same year was sold under the French flag and became the **Rene** of Brest.

Kate Lyons Beached in Storm

October 19, 1905
North of the Holland Piers

The **Kate Lyons** was a lumber schooner 201 gross tons, 122 feet in length. She had been launched in 1867 at Black River, Ohio. She was northbound on October 19, 1905, when she missed the entrance to Holland harbor and washed ashore north of the pier. The incident is described in the *Holland City News* for October 26, 1905:

> The schooner **Kate Lyons** in command of Captain Olsen of Grand Haven cleared light from Benton Harbor bound north and headed to this port for refuge shortly after 8 o'clock Thursday night. Baffled by the current and battered by the heavy seas she missed the harbor entrance and swung to the north of the north pier and in a short time was thrown upon the beach near the pier. The crew at no time were in danger as they could step to safety without great trouble.
>
> The life savers were at hand, but their services were not needed and when the wrecked crew finally decided to come ashore they went to the cottage of George Murphy where they dried their clothes and were served hot coffee.
>
> The **Lyons** stranded close to the shore line, and at that point about 200 feet of the pier was washed away. The schooner is a total wreck being practically broken in two but it forms a barrier to the waves and prevents them from washing the sand into the harbor. In spite of the destroyed cribwork the harbor is still navigable for the Graham & Morton steamers, there being about 14 feet of water.

Hundreds turned out to see the stranded schooner and a photograph was featured in a contemporary Christian magazine as an example of what can happen if you miss something as important as a harbor entrance, even by just a very little bit.

Kate Lyons
"The master of the vessel almost made the harbor, but not quite, and the little by which he missed was a bad as miles more would have been."

139

Five Die as **Naomi** Burns

May 21, 1907
Lake Michigan off Grand Haven

The Crosby line steamer **Naomi** caught fire mysteriously and burned her entire upperworks on May 21, 1907, nearly in midlake. She had left Grand Haven bound for Milwaukee about 11 p.m. the previous day with 52 passengers, a crew of 31, and five painters. Below, excerpts of the story as told in the May 21, 1907, *Grand Haven Daily Tribune*:

The fire on the **Naomi** was discovered at about 1:15 this morning when the steamer was about 35 or 40 miles from Grand Haven. The sleeping people in the state rooms were startled from pleasant dreams by the sound of running feet and by loud and continued pounding on the cabin doors. There was an odor of smoke. Some panic stricken passenger in one of the forward rooms was crying, "Fire. Fire." There was no pandemonium but there seemed to be an awful hurry and bustle in the main cabin. Cabin boys and officers were hurrying here and there, reassuring the passengers that there was no fear that there was a fire but it had been subdued, and then, in the same breath, calmly ordered the amazed people to strap on life belts and prepare for the worst.

Imagine if you can the horror of the situation. Smoke was piling up through the decks and the main cabin was one dense mass of smoke. In a few short moments it was impossible to remain in the cabins and the people hurried to the open air. The coolness and rare presence of mind displayed by the passengers was a feature. The women were especially cool. They cared for the children, allayed their fears and acted the part of brave mothers in every instance.

Outside and up above the crew were busy lowering the life boats, sending up signals, and aiding the precious lives in their care. There was little confusion. Outside the night was still, calm but chilly. The waters of Lake Michigan were smooth. This fact alone prevented a terrible tragedy . . .

Four life boats were lowered into the lake. Into the first one went all the women that it was possible to muster up on deck. The last boat off contained 14 men and three women.

The burning ship could be seen for miles and miles on the lake in the clear weather prevailing and passengers and crew shortly after the first alarm could see lights approaching. The **Naomi** in the meantime had been brought to and so placed that the wind would confine as much as possible the devouring flames to the forward part of the ship. But even this precaution upon the part of Capt. Traill could not of course prevent the fire from creeping aft through the cabin and while the work of rescue was going on the terrible fire was sweeping like a whirlwind through the light upper work of the once grand ship. . . .

The three specks of light far in the distance gradually crept closer. It seemed ages to the men of the crew and to the passengers, but as fast as steam could carry them these three steamers were hurrying to the assistance of the **Naomi**. The three ships proved to be the big steel freighters **Kerr** and **Saxonia** and the **Naomi's** sister line ship, the **Kansas**. The **Kansas**, being a wooden boat, was unable to draw up to the **Naomi's** side, but the commander of the **Kerr** put his ship's prow into the burning **Naomi** on the side least swept by flames, and thus enabled the balance of the crew and passengers, including Capt. Traill to leave the burning decks of the **Naomi**. . . .

Four poor fellows in the crew and one passenger lost their lives in the horrible accident. . . J. M. Rhodes of Detroit, a traveling representative of the Diamond Match Co., is the only passenger of the many on board who was lost. . . He was discovered with his clothes on fire by Purser Will Hanrahan. The purser at the time was in his last rounds over the burning ship to see that everybody was safe and was about to return to save his passenger list when he heard some one groaning on the deck above. he ascended the stairs hastily and discovered Rhodes laying in front of his cabin. His shirt was burning and he was unconscious. Rhodes was carried down below by the officer where he recovered consciousness and was in terrible pain. he gave his name and stated that he wanted the Diamond Match Co. apprised of his misfortune. All that could be done for the unfortunate man was done but he suffered so terribly that death must have come as a relief.

The four deckhands who were burned to death were caught in a terrible pen of fire. When the flames were discovered they were already shut off. Flynn, one of the crew, talked with one of these unfortunate fellows through a dead light. He gave Flynn his name and address and implored Flynn for aid, but the men caught in that trap were past all saving. . .

Frank Whalen, wheelsman, said: "I was on duty in the pilot house when the alarm was sounded. I told the lookout to notify the deckhands below. He wanted to call the crew first. I said, never mind the crew I will get them. I called the captain. The mate, Bob McKay, told me to put the wheel hard astarboard, toward the nearest light to be seen in the lake. Nearest boat was then about ten miles away. The smoke was so dense I could not stand it and I left pilot house to help lower the boats. I helped the second officer, Geo. Robertson. The first boat lowered contained the first wheelsman, Peter Boet and the second lookout, Joe Dysenaki and 14 passengers, mostly women and very excited. Then I helped second mate lower the second boat, and went with that boat to the front of boat where we could hear plainly the fireman, Peter Dyzenski, yelling in his room for help. He finally crawled through the front hole and we took him on our boat. We could hear the poor sailors who were caught in the forecastle and I told them to go down to the water ballast tanks where they could get in and close the doors. . ."

After leaving the **Naomi** the captain and Chief Engineer Barney Hopkins remained on board the **Kerr** and stayed with her until the **Kansas** arrived. The **Kansas** took all the passengers and members of the crew. The **Naomi** rapidly burned. As morning dawned after the cabin had dropped in, the **Kerr** and the **Saxonia** took the wreck of the **Naomi** in tow and brought her to within three miles of the harbor. The **Kansas** towed the **Naomi** into port and thousands of townspeople and many from outside were at the wharves when the **Kansas** and her ill-fated tow came up the river. The **Kansas** left the **Naomi** at her dock, all the time pouring streams of water upon her and the fire department was also called to aid in extinguishing the blaze. . . .

The flame beaten remains of the once proud and noble **Naomi** reached her dock at 10:30 a.m. . . . All the wood of her upperworks was consumed excepting a few charred and blackened stubs. Her immense smoke stack loomed up above her steel decks a lone and lofty sentinel above the blackened ruins that were still discharging here and there sullen rifts of smoke and steam. . . .

The scenes around the dock . . . bordered on the ridiculous. Men and women passengers walking around the streets but partially dressed, one shoe on and one off, and other articles missing, were common sights. Nearly every passenger lost part of their wearing apparel.

Standing out above everything else is the heroism and coolness displayed by Purser William Hanrahan and Steward Philip Rosbach of the **Naomi**. These men were everywhere. They helped awaken passengers, assisted many in putting on life belts and preservers, helped the women and children, even aided in getting out the small boats. They were heroes in the true sense of the term.

When the hull cooled the bodies of the four crew men were recovered. Two were in the forecastle and had suffocated. Two had walked through the fire and their badly burned remains were found on deck.

The cause of the fire was never discovered. Rumors that it was set by rats gnawing on a shipment of matches were probably the result of reports that the lone passenger victim was employed by a match company. On July 25 the hulk of the **Naomi** was towed to Ferrysburg, just upriver from Grand Haven, and there another body was found below decks. It was presumed to be a stowaway as all crew and passengers were accounted for. There was some speculation that it was a man named Harrington who had talked to one of the passengers and told him of dreaming that the boat would burn that evening.

The **Naomi** was 1,182 tons, 203 feet in length, and had been launched at Wyandotte, Michigan, in 1881, as the **Wisconsin** and sailed many years for the Goodrich Transit Co. She was sold to the Crosby Line in 1898, refitted in 1899 as a luxury liner and renamed **Naomi**. After her rebuilding following the fire, this time with steel upperworks, she was named **E. G. Crosby**. During World War I the steamer was taken over by the government and used as a hospital ship in New York harbor under the name **General Robert M. O'Reilly**. After the war she returned to Lake Michigan as the **Pilgrim**. In 1922 she returned to Goodrich hands and in 1924 they restored her original name **Wisconsin**. She continued on the Chicago to Milwaukee route until October 29, 1929, when she sank within sight of Kenosha, Wisconsin. Fishermen and a Coast Guard crew took off more than 60 survivors but 16 lives were lost including her captain and chief engineer.

The remains of the Naomi, still smoking, tied up at the Grand Haven pier.

Alert Strikes Bridge, Three Hurt

August 28, 1907
Kalamazoo River

The first bridge over the Kalamazoo River between Saugatuck and Douglas, built in 1868, was a wooden drawbridge. In 1903 this structure was replaced by an old steel swing span brought in from Buffalo, New York. Because of the narrow opening it was frequently nudged by passing steamers on their way to the Douglas Basket Factory just upstream. In August of 1907 one of the local excursion boats, impatient to get a group of excursionists back to Saugatuck, missed the opening with near-tragic results. The incident is reported in the August 30, 1907, *Commercial Record*:

> The young ladies of the Junior Choir of the First Cong'l Church, Chicago, took a trip up the river Wednesday to Purdy's Landing where they enjoyed a picnic.
>
> On their return about 7:30 o'clock the boat struck the end of the swing bridge when it was only partway open and three of the passengers were hurt quite badly and others more or less scared.
>
> S. P. Hitchcock who had charge of the bridge at the time claims that he did not have time to swing the bridge, Jas. K. Dole, engineer, and John Crock, wheelsman, claimed that they could not see the bridge but had blown for it to be open in plenty of time.
>
> Of course it is impossible to tell just how the affair happened and on whom the blame should be placed without a strict examination of all the witnesses obtainable but the fact that the boat struck her starboard bow against the up-stream corner of the bridge shows that she was in a peculiar position when the accident occurred.
>
> The young ladies who were hurt were sitting on the deck just in front of the wheelsman and thus received the force of the blow which also badly damaged the cabin.
>
> The boat owners will probably sue the township for damages. As far as can be learned both boat and bridge complied with the laws regarding the placing of lights.

A week later there was a rumor around town that one of the girls hurt in the accident had died, but officials at the Forward Movement camp assured the local edition that they had received a telegram from the ladies when on their arrival in Chicago and two had gone directly to their homes. One had been hospitalized, but her condition was not considered serious.

The **Alert** was owned by Henry Perkins of Saugatuck and was used for commercial fishing during the winter months.

City of Allegan Burns at the Dock

June 26, 1908
Kalamazoo River near Allegan

Navigation on the Kalamazoo River was always a struggle. The course was winding, the river was shallow and the competition from the railroads made it difficult to make a profit, but there was usually someone willing to take up the task. In the summer of 1908 three brothers from Millgrove, Allegan County, were about to begin service from Allegan 40 miles upriver to Saugatuck and Douglas near the mouth. The new river boat **City of Allegan** burned just as her commercial career was beginning on June 26, 1908. The *Allegan Gazette* reported in the July 4, 1908 issue:

> The Gardner brothers of Millgrove suffered a severe loss last Friday night when their new river boat, **City of Allegan**, valued at $4,000, was destroyed by fire. For the first time since the boat was finished no one stayed on it during the night, the reason being that the men had worked hard all day haying and were very tired.
>
> About twelve o'clock Charles Van Patten, who lives on the river just below where the boat was tied, was awakened by his dog. The animal barked and ran about in such an unusual way that Mr. VanPatten got up and saw at once that the boat was in flames. He hurried to the dock, the gasoline tank exploded while he was on his way and battered down the door of the room in which he knew the Gardner brothers were in the habit of sleeping, but flames burst out of the room so densely that he could not see whether anyone was sleeping there or not. All he could save was a row boat which was on the lower deck and that he pushed off into the river. Wm. Evans was aroused and the owners soon notified of their loss. They arrived at the ruins at about half-past one o'clock and found that the boat was a total loss. The gasoline engine, which cost about $1,300 was found to be ruined and the only part above the hull not burned entirely was the paddlewheel. . . .
>
> The Gardner brother fully believe that the boat was set on fire. They left no lamps nor fire of any kind upon the boat and they can not think of any way in which fire could have originated. It is a well known fact that there live in that vicinity some of the most lawless, low and vicious people to be found anywhere . . . there was a good deal of feeling against the Gardner brothers because they asked the township of Valley to place a swing in the Calkins bridge. This they had a perfect legal right to do, and it was a matter which entailed the outlay by the township of so small a sum that there should not have been any feeling about it. . . .
>
> It came to the owners of the boat in a roundabout way that "some of those on the other side of the river" were incensed at the necessity of repairing the bridge and consequent increased taxes, and yet, with all this feeling, there is a possibility that the boat caught fire somehow, and that no one had anything to do with its destruction. It attracted, however, so much attention that a detective agency immediately applied to the owners for a contract to investigate. The sheriff has had a man on the scene since the occurrence. . .

The following summer the Gardner brothers, using all they could salvage from the first **City of Allegan** built a second vessel, slightly larger than the first. The second river boat had serious trouble with the river bridges and never completed a trip. The second **City of Allegan** is recorded in the *Merchant Vessel* lists of 1910 as a total loss by fire at Allegan, November 5, 1910, but there are no newspaper accounts.

Burning of **Holiday** Blamed on Arson

September 19, 1908
Macatawa Park Docks Near Holland

Many saw a pattern when the **Holiday**, a gas screw passenger vessel of 10 tons, 47 feet in length, was destroyed by fire at her Macatawa Lake docks September 19, 1908. The small boat had been launched in 1906 in Chicago. In Holland she served as a ferry to connect the various venues around Lake Macatawa. There was only a short paragraph in the *Holland City News* for September 24, 1908:

> Fire, of unknown origin but believed from the circumstances to have been the work of an incendiary, destroyed the little ferry and pleasure boat **Holiday** early Saturday morning. The craft is the property of the Macatawa Park Association and is the third to burn under suspicious circumstances. The **Post Boy** and the **Pinta** are the other boats which were formerly destroyed. As in the other cases no trace of the perpetrators can now be discovered. The Association has offered $500 to the person securing the arrest and conviction of the guilty parties.

At Lake Macatawa (or Black Lake, the wide section of the river between the City of Holland on the east, and the mouth of the river at Lake Michigan) there were two rival resort developments. Ottawa Beach, begun by Grand Rapids railroad interests was on the north bank; Macatawa Park started by Holland investors was on the south bank. The rivalry was intense. In 1904 the "steamboat wars" began when Ottawa Beach tried to get the Macatawa ferries to pay for the privilege of landing on their side of the lake. They were not even allowed to land their passengers from the Graham & Morton boats. Persons bound for Macatawa had to cross from ferry to boat without stepping onto the dock.

In 1905 the Macatawa Park **Post Boy** was burned to the water level. In 1915 the Macatawa Park Association launches **Nina** (the reporter may have remembered that the a vessel previously burned was named after one of the boats sailed by Columbus, but he named the wrong one) and **Florence** were destroyed with several other boats when a row of boathouses burned. The newspaper did not mention arson in the previous reports, but in 1908 when the **Holiday** appeared to have been intentionally set on fire connections were drawn publicly with the earlier fires. The crime was never solved.

City of Kalamazoo Burns Again

May 29, 1911
South Haven Harbor

The fire aboard the **City of Kalamazoo** in 1896 remains one of the great Lakes tragedies of the port of South Haven, three members of the crew died in that fire. There must have been a special sense of horror 15 years later when the cry of fire went up again under almost exactly the same circumstances. The *South Haven Daily Tribune* for May 29, 1911, recounts the scene:

Damages amounting approximately to $2,000 were sustained by the Chicago-South Haven Transportation Co., in the fire which gutted the Steamer **City of Kalamazoo** in the process of fitting out for the approaching season at their docks in this city.

The men arrived last Wednesday and had been cleaning the machinery and yesterday had been testing the pumps. At 11 o'clock when the last round of the boat was made, everything apparently was all right. At about 2 o'clock one of the four men who were sleeping aboard the boat, an oiler by the name of Ernest Miller, was awakened by a feeling of suffocation to find that his stateroom was dense with smoke. He hastily roused his mates, the engineer, Bill Nice, assistant Lew Winkler and a fireman whose name was not learned.

Miller jerked on a pair of trousers and not halting for a more complete toilet, ran in his barefeet to the fire barn where he turned in the alarm. The shrill blast of the fire whistle and the incessant din of the bell, roused a large part of the population of the city at the weird hour of 2 o'clock in the morning, many of whom ran to the river's edge to watch the proceedings. Some understood the summons to have come from Kalamazoo street and a number wandered about that part of the city, trying to find the fire.

The flames only once or twice broke through so as to be seen above the hurricane deck, the firemen doing good work in keeping them subdued and finally extinguishing them before greater damage had been done.

The flames followed the large smokestack from the lower deck through the main cabin, consuming the forward side and completely ruining the jack. From there they spread to the ceiling and sides of the forward cabin badly charring them as well as the doors of the staterooms but a moment before occupied by Miller, Nice and Winkler. Cabin chairs stored in this cabin were also ruined by fire, while mattresses stored there during the winter were so drenched by the water that it is doubtful if they will ever be in a condition to be used.

The after cabin fared better, the ceilings and sides having been badly blistered, scorched and blackened with the smoke but not much burned. The starboard side of the boat is the least damaged the wind having come from the north . . .

There seems to be a feeling more or less of uncertainty as to the exact origin of the blaze, although those on the boat at the time believe it to have caught from the fire which had been burning under the small boiler used by the men in fitting out the boat.. . .

The **City of Kalamazoo** was expected to be put in commission in a very few weeks, with Capt. Gerald Stufflebeam as commanding officer.

In June the **City of Kalamazoo** was taken to Manitowoc, Wisconsin, and once again rebuilt and placed back into service. However, that fall the steamer burned a third time. On November 14, 1911, she sustained a serious fire at her dock at Little Manistee Lake and the four crewmen "jumped for their lives." This time she was rebuilt as a barge and continued in service on the Great Lakes until finally abandoned at Milwaukee, November 21, 1922.

Arundell Burns at Douglas

October 18, 1911
Kalamazoo River

The twin towns of Saugatuck and Douglas, two miles up the Kalamazoo River from Lake Michigan had been busy freight and passenger ports during the early days of fruit growing and were seeking water transportation for the growing resort business in 1909 when Andrew Crawford began direct service to Chicago with the **H. W. Williams**. The following year he renamed the **Williams** the **Tennessee** and purchased the **Arundell** a steamer of 339 gross tons, 257 net tons, 166.6 feet in length. On October 18, 1911, having completed a successful season she burned at her dock at Douglas. The *Commercial Record* published at Saugatuck, reported:

Wednesday morning at about four o'clock the people of Douglas and Saugatuck were aroused by the cry of "Fire" and awoke to find the str. **Arundell** all ablaze. The **Arundell** had been laying at the dock in Saugatuck since the resort season when there was no longer business for two boats, but it was decided to take her to Douglas and lay her up for the winter, and store her equipment in the large warehouse there, but before this could be done she was destroyed.

The Douglas fire department turned out and did good work but there is no fire fighting equipment that could have saved the boat but the dock and warehouse were saved although the boat lay close to the dock at the shore end so the warehouse was safe as long as the dock did not burn.

The **Arundell** was bought for $30,000 by the Crawford Transportation Co., two years ago and some $5,000 was spent on her, to put her in good shape. She was insured in the London Lloyds but not heavily, so there is a loss of about $10,000. Mr. Crawford is greatly pleased with the work of the Douglas fire department in saving the dock and warehouse. He says it hardly seems possible that the fire could be kept from spreading.

The Arundell right, and her sister ship the Tennessee, left.
This is the Red Dock in Douglas where the vessel later burned.

There was concern that a member of the crew had been sleeping aboard and may have lost his life in the fire. However, the hand was discovered in jail at Grand Haven on charges of public drunkeness.

In December of 1911 the burned-out hull was sold to Nessen & Kitsinger of Manistee, with plans to add her to the Pere Marquette fleet but there is no evidence that this was done. In the fall of 1912 the Crawford Transportation Co. filed for bankruptcy.

Manistee Burns at Winter Dock

June 28, 1914
Ferrysburg

The **Manistee**, a wooden passenger and package freight steamer, of 843 tons, 202 feet in length, had already experienced a long and varied career when she caught fire and burned at her winter berth in Ferrysburg on June 28, 1914, shortly after fitting out.

She had been launched at Benton Harbor in 1882 as the **Lora** for the Graham and Morton Transportation Co. when H. W. Williams was still a stockholder and named for his daughter, Lora. In 1897, other new owners, she was renamed the **Alice Stafford**, and underwent a second named change in 1905 when she was christened the **Manistee** and ran a triangular route from Manistee to Ludington to Milwaukee for the Nessen Transportation Company.

The Many Disasters of the **A. R. Heath**

1902-1916
Kalamazoo and Grand Rivers

The **A.R. Heath** was built in 1901 to run on the Kalamazoo River from Saugatuck to Allegan. Her career was a disaster from the beginning. Bridges across the river seemed to be especially treacherous to the vessel.

Near the end of July, 1902, she ran into the Huggins bridge near Allegan on the downstream trip and her port wheel house was broken off. Her captain and builder, Cal Heath had to lay up for emergency repairs and missed three days of service during the height of the season. He tried to collect damages of $225 from Allegan township because the boat ran into the ice break which the township had built.

The river steamer, A. R. Heath, with a deckload of passengers on an outing.

Two years later, again in July the **A. R. Heath** smashed one of her paddle boxes at Spring Lake on the Grand River. This time she struck a support for the bridge itself. The boat had gone north to take the Grand Rapids river committee and other distinguished guests on a tour of inspection.

In 1906, this time in August, she damaged one of her paddle wheels quite seriously trying to go through the draw bridge over the Kalamazoo River between Saugatuck and Douglas. After this accident she was repaired and put back in service.

There may have been other, unrecorded, mishaps. Part of her problem may have been her construction which coupled a very flat bottom, to get over the obstacles of a shallow river, with a two story upper structure that was prone to catch the wind. She was formally abandoned 1916 and was visible for many years, a wreck in the river on the north edge of Saugatuck where Moore's Creek enters the Kalamazoo River.

Delta Breaks Tow Line, Grounds

August 20, 1919
North of Holland Piers

The **Delta**, a bulk freight schooner-barge of 269 tons, 134 feet in length, was under tow of the steamer **Louis Pahlow** and headed for Holland harbor in a gale on August 21, 1919, when the tow line broke near the harbor entrance and before she could set sails went on the breakwater. According to the *Holland City News* of August 21, 1919 (which misunderstood and misspelled the name of the steamer):

> The steamer **"Dahlow"** of the Hamilton Transportation company went aground at Saugatuck yesterday and the barge **"Delta"** towed by the same steamer, after it had been taken off the sand bar, went aground north of the north breakwater at Macatawa late last night. This morning the barge loaded with 400,000 feet of lumber was pounded to pieces by the waves and the lumber was scattered along the beach at Ottawa Beach.
>
> The **Dahlow** with two lumber barges the **Interlaken** and the **Delta** in tow started out from Menominee. The **Interlaken** bound for Saugatuck and the **Delta** for Chicago. At 6 o'clock in the morning yesterday the steamer went aground at Saugatuck and the Holland Life Saving crew worked all day; finally releasing the steamer at 9:20 last night. The **Interlaken** was then safely taken into Saugatuck harbor, but the steamer, with the **Delta** in tow went on its way for Chicago.
>
> There was however, a heavy sea on and the vessel was compelled to turn back. At about 1:30 this morning it tried to make the harbor at Macatawa. The towline of the **Delta** parted when the barge caught behind the north breakwater, leaving the barge alone at the mercy of the waves. The **Delta** dropped her anchor and the Holland Life Saving Crew began work to take off the crew of seven persons, one of the crew a woman cook. Also some of the cargo was taken off to lighten the boat.
>
> This morning the barge dragged her anchor and the boat became fast on a sand bar where she was fully at the mercy of the pounding waves. She went aground about 9 o'clock this morning and the waves quickly began to pound her to pieces. The crew was taken off with the aid of the surf boat.
>
> The value of the barge is placed at about $15,000.

In stories in the Saugatuck newspaper the steamer was correctly identified as the

Louis Pahlow a vessel of 366 gross tons, 155.4 feet in length, 30.4 in beam that had been launched at Milwaukee in 1882. The Saugatuck reporter notes that the **Pahlow** also had a lot of trouble in Saugatuck harbor after she brought in the **Interlaken** with a cargo of coal. "The **Pahlow**, itself heavily loaded with lumber, grounded in Saugatuck harbor, and on again picking up the **Delta**." The **Pahlow** was under the command of Captain Higgie.

There was 400,000 feet of hardwood lumber in the hold of the **Delta** and the newspaper reported that "most of the cargo has been salvaged by the underwriters" and loaded on the **Interlaken** after she delivered her cargo of coal to Saugatuck. In approaching the beached barge the **Interlaken** parted its line and went on the beach exactly as the **Delta** had done, but was released by a Holland tug without much trouble."

The wreck also virtually closed the section of the Lake Michigan shoreline which served the Ottawa Beach resort at the height of the season because the water and sand was so full of lumber and pieces of the schooner. What remained of the vessel was further destroyed by resort operators trying to get it out of the way.

The schooner **Delta** had been launched in 1890 at Algonac.

Aliber Strikes Holland Pier

October 19, 1922
Black Lake Near Holland

The **John A. Aliber** was a between sizes boat. At 73 feet in length, 32.73 gross tons she was a little too big to be a river tug, although she did her share of towing. And at 18.60 net tons she didn't have the capacity to carry enough cargo on a regular basis to make her pay.

The vessel had been built in 1897 by Captain William P. Wilson and Cal Heath of Saugatuck. She carried fruit to Chicago early in the season when cargos were small, and during the height of harvest formed a connection between Saugatuck and the H. W. Williams Co. Chicago-bound boats at South Haven. But, by 1916 Captain Wilson had sold her to George W. Kelly and Elmer Weed of Saugatuck, and she was in use for short runs to Holland as well as towing gravel scows around Black Lake.

On October 19, under an inexperienced captain, she struck the pier trying to enter Holland harbor. According to the *Commercial Record* for October 20, 1922:

> The steamer **John A. Aliber,** with her stem broken and bow torn out, lies in shallow water on the bottom of Black lake at Macatawa. It is probable she will be towed to Saugatuck and rebuilt this winter.
>
> The **Aliber**, with Capt. James Pett of Grand Haven at the wheel, left Holland early yesterday morning for Saugatuck. Finding the going a little too rough in the heavy sea that was running, she put about to return to shelter. Under the strain of a hard over turn and the driving sea the rudder chain snapped and the little steamer dashed bow on into the pier. By herculean labor on the part of the crew and the coast guard she was worked into shallow water in the bay.
>
> The **Aliber** was built at Saugatuck in 1897 by Capt. W. P.

Wilson, and for many years plied between Saugatuck, the piers and South Haven, carrying both passengers and freight.

John A. Aliber

Ten days later Captain E. J. Harrington of the Harrington Coal Co. at Holland bought what was left of the steamer as she lay mostly submerged in the lake. It was first announced that he would raise the hull, remove the machinery and dismantle the remains. However, he changed his mind and rebuilt the **Aliber** into a work boat he named the **Mabel A.** She lay at a Macatawa dock, apparently seaworthy but little used until 1927 when her papers were surrendered with the note that she had been "dismantled and the hull was abandoned as unfit for further service."

Lady Hamilton Burns at Wilson's Dock

April 26, 1923
Kalamazoo River

The gas yacht **Lady Hamilton** was undergoing repairs on the shore of the Kalamazoo River, near the north end of downtown Saugatuck where Captain W. P.

Wilson had built a dock for his steamers **John A. Aliber** and **Anna C. Wilson,** when the vessel was totally destroyed by fire. The yacht was 21 gross tons, 54 feet in length. According to the *Commercial Record:*

> The yacht **Lady Hamilton** was completely destroyed by fire late on Thursday evening of last week. The boat, which belonged to Gus Jesiek of Jenison Park, was on the ways near Wilson's dock undergoing repairs. Origin of the fire is unknown. The department responded quickly, but Chief Coe was obliged to return to the engine house for extra lengths of hose. The blaze was quickly under control when reached by a stream, but only the charred skeleton of the boat remained. The fire burned so brilliantly in the still night that many who viewed it from a distance believed the warehouse buildings were burning.

There was plenty of water in the nearby Kalamazoo river, but it was difficult for the truck to get close enough to pump it. The week following the destruction of the **Lady Hamilton** the Saugatuck Village Board voted to purchase a chemical fire extinguisher mounted on a truck to aid in extinguishing similar fires.

Yacht **Merwyn** Explodes, Burns

July 15, 1924
Off South Haven

The yacht **Merwyn** was burned July 15, 1924, following an explosion as the passengers and crew escaped in her launches. The *South Haven Daily Tribune* for July 15, 1924, describes the scene:

> The cruising yacht **Merwyn**, the flagship of the Chicago Yacht club of which its owner Dr. W. L. Baum is Commodore, was completely destroyed by fire in Lake Michigan just off South Haven this forenoon.
> Fire starting just twenty minutes after the owner and his family had started on a cruise they expected would continue until September, swept the handsome craft giving the family and the crew barely time to get away in the two launches the **Merwyn** carried.
> All aboard escaped uninjured with the exception of the chief engineer, who was slightly burned about the head, and one of the sailors was burned on one hand. . . .
> The family with a crew of six on the yacht, captain, mate, engineer, steward and two sailors, left the yacht's mooring place in the local harbor at ten o'clock this morning. Twenty minutes later when the yacht was only a little over a mile north of the piers, and about a mile from shore, came the explosion that was to mean the complete loss of the beautiful craft.
> As nearly as captain and crew can determine, the explosion

came from a backfire that ignited some gasoline about the motor. Every fire extinguisher on board was hurriedly brought into play, without checking the flames, and those on board realized that speedy abandonment was the only chance to escape.

Breaking of one of the gasoline feeder lines released a flood of the fuel that removed the last vestige of hope of checking the flames.

Without losing a moment, the members of the crew whipped out their knives and slashed through the ropes on which the two power launches hung on either side of the craft. Family and crew were in the launches the moment they struck the water, and both dashed clear of the burning boat, not a moment too soon, as the flames had spread through the latter both ways from the engine room, in the few moments it took to release the launches.

The two launches remained near the flaming boat for a short time then headed for the harbor. The coast guard went out in the power boat and towed the **Merwyn** toward shore. It grounded on the outer sand bar about 150 feet from shore, directly west of the ravine between Eaton Park and Sleepy Hollow.

Dr. and Mrs. Baum and their two sons, Winston Lawrence and Merwyn, had planned a cruise to Mackinac Island, where they planned to spend about three weeks and where they were to be joined by Dr. and Mrs. Steinbach, who are old friends. From Mackinac Island they intended to go for a cruise among the myriad islands in and near Georgian bay and thence north into Lake Superior, being away until the first or second week of September.

*The yacht **Merwyn** in flames in 1924*

To prepare for the cruise, the three gasoline tanks, two of 500 gallons, had been filled, so there was an abundance of fuel to feed the flames that swept over the ship as it lay just off shore.

This was to be the first major trip taken on the **Merwyn** which had bee purchased by Dr. Baum in the spring. The vessel was brought from the Atlantic coast where it had been in service through the St. Lawrence and around the lakes. When the boat was delivered the motor was fed through an open pipe system and the new owner had a carburetor installed. A number of short trips showed that the new system was working well. The appointments of the yacht were luxurious for its day. It had a hot water heating plant, complete inter-room telephone system, equipment for showing movies aboard, and a radio receiving outfit. The **Merwyn** was valued at $50,000. In addition, both family and crew lost a great deal of clothing and personal effects.

The Baums had a summer residence in the "Doctor's Colony" on South Haven's south lake shore, about two miles south of the city limits. Captain Jensen, of South Haven, had served as master of Dr. Baum's yachts for 21 years when the fire occurred.

South American Burns at Dock

September 9, 1924
Black Lake near Holland

Beginning in 1919 the **South American** and the **North American** of the Georgian Bay Line wintered at Saugatuck. However, following the burning of the Ottawa Hotel at Holland in 1923 the insurance companies let it be known that they would not insure the vessels in the winter if they were moored near large wooden buildings, or too close together. Because no available sites in Saugatuck could meet these new guidelines new winter moorings were arrange for both boats at Black Lake, near the foot of 16th Street in Holland. The **South American** was just getting settled into her new dock, on September 9, 1924, when she was swept by a disastrous fire. According to the September 12, 1924, *Commercial Record*:

> The big steamer **South American** was burned to the water's edge Tuesday morning, while laying at the new dock built for winter quarters of the boats of the Chicago, Duluth and Georgian Bay Transit Co. on Black Lake, just outside the city limits of Holland. . .
> When Frank Amatuna, watchman gave the alarm, the flames which started amidships at about 1:30 a.m. had gained such headway that Capt. A. A. Anderson and the crew of 24, including three women, barely escaped with their lives. Miss Anna Kanera of Saugatuck, head waitress, found her escape through the hatchway cut off, and crawled through a porthole. Jerry Burkholter, cook, given up for lost, was the last person to leave the burning steamer, which at that time was ablaze from bow to stern.
> Twenty thousand gallons of fuel oil was stored in the hull, but it is said that was not burned, as at first reported.

156

*The **South American**, center, at her Holland dock along with
the **North American**, left, and the **Alabama**, right.*

During the progress of the fire a large tank of Naptha, standing
on the upper deck, exploded, the heavy container being hurled through
the air and tearing a hole through the porch and foundation of the
home of Mrs. George E. Merrell, 1,000 feet distant. A number of people
who were watching the fire from the Merrell house saw the tank coming
and ran to safety.

Capt. Anderson sustained serious burns about the hand and
arms, and was taken to the Holland hospital to have them dressed.
Some other members of the crew had slight burns or bruises.

City of Holland fire trucks rushed to the dock but had difficulty on some nearby
roads that had been dug up for installation of new fire hydrants. Although the steel hull
was largely intact most of the interior of the boat was gutted. When the metal cooled the
South American was towed to Ecorse where she had been built in 1914, and refurbished
in time for the 1925 summer season. The vessel was 321 feet long, 47.10 in beam and
had, along with her sister ship **North American**, been converted to fuel oil in 1922. The

South American would run another forty years after her near-death accident. In 1967 she sailed her last commercial excursion. She was then towed to Maryland where there were plans to convert her into a training ship for the Seafarer's Union.

The plans were abandoned and, in 1974, she was sold for scrap and towed to Camden, New Jersey. The cutting torches waited while various groups in Michigan tried to bring her back somewhere for use as a museum or a convention city or floating restaurant. In the end all of the schemes fell through and she was finally broken up for scrap in 1993.

All Rescued as **Hennepin** Sinks

August 18, 1927
Off South Haven

The barge **Hennepin** sank in a storm off South Haven, August 18, 1927. According to a report in the August 26, 1927, *Commercial Record*:

> The barge **Hennepin** owned by the Construction Materials Co. of Chicago and captained by Ole Hanson, went down in 203 feet of water out on Lake Michigan off South Haven, it was learned here upon arrival of the captain and a crew of 13 in the tug **Lotus** which was towing the barge back after taking a heavy cargo to Chicago.
>
> The barge left Chicago Saturday morning. At about 10:30 it was noticed the barge was taking water and at 2:30 it was necessary for the crew to leave the barge and board the tug, the former sinking at 6 p.m. All personal belongings were saved and no lives were endangered but the barge represents a loss of $100,000 according to company officials.
>
> The barge formerly was a package freighter, built in 1888 but several years ago its power machinery was removed and it reverted into barge use. It had valuable unloading apparatus and its replacement will be necessary immediately. It was breaking up when it went down and no efforts at salvage will be made.

The vessel was 1372 tons, 208 feet in length and had been launched in 1888 at Milwaukee as the steamer **George H.Dyer**.

Four Die as Boat Hits **City of Holland**

July 27, 1928
Black Lake Near Holland

Occasionally a shipwreck will have a greater effect on a community than a simple statement of the facts would indicate. That was the case when the **Norma** a 30-foot Chris-Craft was crushed under the big sidewheel of the **City of Holland** on Black Lake (later known as Lake Macatawa), July 27, 1928. Of the six young men on the powerboat, four died on impact with the wheel. The incident was described by the *Holland City News*:

> On Friday evening four well known and most popular young men of the city lost their lives on Black Like while riding in a high speed motor boat which crashed into the turning side-paddle of the Goodrich line steamer **City of Holland** and there was crushed like an eggshell and the frail craft with its human freight was sent to the bottom of Black Lake off Pine Creek Bay near Marigold Point.
>
> The steamer **Holland** had left her docks at the usual time Friday night when Paul Landwehr with the speedboat **Norma** sailed alongside of her to the north. Had the speedboat been to the south of the larger craft it would have been protected from the north wind and the heavier waves and the accident could never have happened.
>
> But being to the north the speedster was first drawn to the heavy paddle wheel by the tremendous suction. The strong north wind striking the small craft broadside could not help but bring added pressure that finally fed the **Norma** into the large steel paddle wheel of the outgoing steamer.
>
> There is no doubt that the waves of the steamer and the commotion of the water kicked up by the northwest wind combined and brought the stern and rudder of the motorboat out of the water and naturally the wheelsman could not help but lose all control of his craft, and the inevitable happened.
>
> Two men were miraculously saved since they sat in the rear of the boat and when the front end was crushed, according to eyewitnesses, the stern snapped into the air throwing the young men. Those who were forward were less fortunate and were no doubt killed almost instantly by the impact from the steel paddles of the large 30 foot side wheel for, according to the physicians, they were not drowned.

Captain D. A. McDonald of the **City of Holland** reported the accident and described how the speedboat had circled the departing steamer several times. He added, "I can't understand why they would come so near to our paddle wheel in a frail craft. They should have known the danger." He was not in a position to see the actual accident but said that he had heard the "thud." The big boat stopped and lowered two boats to search for survivors and bodies. The two men who were still alive were picked up by fishermen. When it became dark, the **City of Holland** went on to Chicago. "I regret the accident very much," Captain McDonald said in his report, "but there was nothing we could have done to avoid it."

The whole community, including the Sea Scouts turned out to scour Black Lake seeking the bodies of the four who died. These included Paul Landwehr, 20; his cousin, John Nystrom, 14; George Lyle, 21, of Los Angeles, a Holland pilot; and Robert Medrano, 30, who was a dancing partner of Paul's sister, Donna. Landwehr and Nystrom were both grandsons of John P. Kolla, who was one of the founders of the Holland Furnace Co., a major employer in Holland, and were probably slated for responsibility in the administration of the company. Following their death the leadership of the company was taken over by other hands and it fell into a mire of accusations concerning unfair sales practices and financial irresponsibility. The company ceased operations in 1966.

Small Collisions in a Crowded Harbor

Spring, 1929
Grand Haven Harbor

Grand Haven was a busy harbor and the size of the boats that either docked there on a regular basis, or called on special occasions added to the congestion. In the spring of 1929, the mouth of the harbor was not quite large enough for a car ferry and a government work boat.

On the last day of February the **Madison**, a car ferry for the Grand Trunk Milwaukee Car Ferry Co., struck the **Gen. G. G. Meade**, a U. S. Corps of Engineer's dredge that had spent the winter there. The **Madison** was headed into Grand Haven in fog and ice and the **Meade** was berthed on the south bank of the river for the winter. Damage was only slight.

But two weeks later, March 14, the **Madison** again ran into the **Meade** with more serious results. Remembering her previous problems, the car ferry was outbound proceeding slowly downstream hugging the north shore to give the dredge a wide berth. Unfortunately she was so near the north bank that when she was abreast of the **Meade** the ferry's prow went aground in the mud causing her stern to swing around striking the dredge. The helmsman on the car ferry realized the problem as soon as the boat began to drag and tried to stop the swing of the stern by ringing full speed ahead hoping to beach the vessel, but there was not time for the action to take effect. Both boats were promptly repaired.

Andaste Disappears, 25 Lost

September 9, 1929
Lake Michigan Somewhere Off Holland

The **Andaste**, a steel self-unloading steam sandsucker, was a strange looking boat. She was 1493 gross tons, 247 feet in length and had a slightly modified whaleback silhouette. She had been launched at Cleveland in 1892, and was under charter to the Construction Materials Company when she disappeared with a crew of 25, September 9, 1929, bound from Grand Haven to South Chicago with a load of gravel. According to a report in the September 19, 1929, *Holland City News*:

> The **Andaste** cleared the coast guard station at Grand Haven at 9:03 o'clock Monday night. An hour afterward a stiff wind arose, later taking on the velocity of a gale. . . .
> For several days nothing was heard of the stone boat which had no radio connections and while there were great fears that the ship had

gone down, it was not until 68 hours had passed that mute evidences of the terrible lake disaster began to pile up on the Lake Michigan beaches north and south of Holland harbor.

George F. Getz picked up an oar and other pieces of wreckage on the same beach where the piano, part of the wheel house and name plate of the **Alpena** had been picked up four decades ago.

Other wreckage was picked up further north of this port, and considerable wreckage was found in the neighborhood of the Felt estate and Castle Park, south of Holland harbor.

The shore for miles along is strewn with wreckage of the vessel. Washed up on the beach were the pilot's cabin and stairway, part of the cook's galley, an oar and a life preserver bearing the **Andaste's** name, letters addressed to crew members and innumerable pieces of wood.

The discovery of wreckage intensified the search for bodies and the first was located at Jenison Park wearing two life rings and a cork life preserver and was fully clothed. The coroner declared that physical evidence indicated that the sailor had been dead less than 24 hours. The crew of the Holland Coast Guard was joined in searching the shore by the yacht **Mizpah** from Chicago containing a search party sent by the *Chicago American* newspaper and the fish tug **Berthie G.**, commanded by Captain George Van Hall. Coast Guard boats were also sent from the Jackson Street Station, and the big yacht **Marj III**, owned by J. H. Oberfelder of the Chicago Yacht Club was placed at the disposal of the Old Chicago Coast Guard Station.

Former **Andaste** crew members identified many of the bodies as they were found. The first two were discovered off shore near Holland, the next 12 closer to Grand Haven. Then the wind shifted from the north and the area of search was extended to the south.

Andaste

Several men in the crew of the **Andaste** were from the area where the wreckage came ashore. The body of Fred Nienhouse washed ashore only a few hundred feet from the farm of his parents, Mr. and Mrs. Louis Nienhouse, where he had been born. Annie and William Kibby, the parents of crew member Claude Kibby, 35, of Benton Harbor, lived on the lakeshore south of Saugatuck and kept a keen eye on the shoreline. Claude's wife and five children joined them. The younger Mrs. Kibby was searching as well for the body of her father, James Bayless, who served on the same vessel. The steps from the cabin down to the deck of the vessel were found on the shore just north of Saugatuck.

A splintered board, thought to be part of the cabin siding, was washed ashore south of Macatawa Park on November 19. On it was scrawled, "Worse storm I have ever been in. Can't stay up much longer. Hope to God, we're saved." At the bottom of the words, barely decipherable in the grooves of the board, some saw the initials A. L. A., an indication that the message had been written by Captain Albert A. Anderson. Although at first considered authentic, it was later dismissed as a hoax by the coroner's jury on the basis that the board was far more battered than the message written upon it.

There were several accusations by former crew members that the boat was not operating safely. The *Holland City News* reported:

> Louis Broucek, a Chicago sailor who was a deck hand on the **Andaste** last season, said the vessel always had difficulty recruiting a full crew.
>
> "She used to pitch and roll so much," he said, "that it was hard to get a crew for her. Seaworthy and all that, but still the boys were afraid of her.
>
> "There's another thing about that boat -- she used to shift her cargo. That means that when she rolled about the gravel or rocks would slide to one side. Many times the crew would have to go down and trim the load even.
>
> "I think that is what happened Monday night. Her cargo probably shifted and she turned upside down. If that happened the boys didn't have a chance. They were inside and would not have been able to get to the lifeboats because the **Andaste**, with a heavy load, would go down in a few seconds."

In addition John Van Ingen, another former crew member, who in September of 1929 was a Coast Guard man based at the Holland station, told the coroner that he believed that the victims of the disaster were left to the mercy of the water because of their inability to launch lifeboats. "A year ago," he said according to the *Holland City News*, "the crew had been unable to lower the boats in the sinking of the tug **Liberty**. The davits were so rusted that they could not be used."

The boat had last been inspected on April 23 while she was docked at the Johnston Bros. Boiler Works at Ferrysburg, upriver from Grand Haven. At that time she had been pronounced in "good condition." The day after the inspection the **Andaste** was being towed in Spring Lake by the tug **Liberty** when the tug capsized. The starboard lifeboat of the **Andaste** had been swung out from the side of the vessel to lend assistance, but others had the situation under control and it was not needed, so it was not lowered.

But the incident, according to the inspectors, indicated that the davits were in good order, not rusted closed.

Another indication of safety efforts aboard was pointed out by the Construction Materials Co. Life belts on all the bodies except those of the two high ranking officers of the **Andaste** were found to be new equipment that had been purchased following the April 23 inspection when some of the life jackets aboard had been found to be faulty.

A second concern was the delay in searching for the vessel and any survivors. The boat had been expected in South Chicago on Monday, but it was not until Wednesday that the company had actually begun a full scale search for her. Part of the delay was caused by various indications that she might have been seen in sheltered places on Lake Michigan. When all of these tips had been followed-up and dismissed the search, which included aircraft from the Great Lakes Naval Training Station, was instituted. Later testimony, however, revealed that although many still felt the boat safe, the Coast Guard had been notified as early as Tuesday afternoon.

A coroner's inquest was convened about two weeks following the disappearance and heard 22 witnesses. The jury's findings were reported in the October 3, 1929, edition of the *Holland City News*:

> We are unable to locate the place of disaster, the reason for it, nor can we find any trace of laxity on the part of those in charge. However in the interest of safety of human life on the great lakes we make the following recommendations:
>
> 1. That all vessels of the size and type of the **Andaste** be equipped with wireless.
>
> 2. That a central marine office be established for reports of all ships overdue.
>
> 3. That proper facilities for the search for lost craft be set up on all of the great lakes.

Schoellkopf Grounds on Bar

November 28, 1936
South Haven Harbor

The **J. F. Schoellkopf Jr.** a steam-powered self-unloader of 7,263 gross tons, with more than 8,000 tons of coal on board ran aground November 28, 1936, in the South Haven channel. The news columns of Saturday, November 28, 1936, issue of the *South Haven Daily Tribune* detail the incident (while badly misspelling the name of the vessel):

> After having been dislodged from a sand bar directly to the south west of the harbor mouth the 500 foot **S. S. Schoellcoph Jr.** was again aground in the Black river near the Coast Guard lookout at 10:30 o'clock this morning. The boat was bringing a cargo of 8,200 tons of

coal for the Michigan Shore Lumber and Supply company. It sailed from Toledo, Ohio.

The **Schoellcoph Jr.** was visible at 5:25 o'clock. As it drew nearer the harbor it became apparent that the large boat would run aground on the sand bar. It seemed to settle on the bar shortly after 7:30 o'clock. Repeated attempts to push it off were of no avail. The boat signalled to the Coast Guard and Captain Fisher and men in the power boat pitched through the choppy lake to run slack lines from the boat to the piers. The slack lines were operated by a machine on the deck of the coaler.

After two hours work the long boat pulled off the sand bar and moved slowly between the piers. Full steam was necessary for the effort and the boat moved very slowly, partially because of the terrific pull and partly to permit careful progress through the harbor mouth in the face of the choppy lake.

Just outside the piers the coaler was drawing eighteen and a half feet of water. When it was grounded the second time it was only drawing sixteen feet.

This is the first time the **Schoellcoph, Jr.,** has brought a cargo to South Haven. The captain was unfamiliar with the local harbor. The Coast Guard was still at work on the slack lines at eleven o'clock this morning.

The cargo of coal was to be discharged at the Michigan Shore-Pomeroy yards, a block or so further up the river. The boat captain expressed his doubt as to how the **Schoellcoph Jr.** would be able to make the bend in the river after it was propelled from its grounded position.

Despite the doubts of her captain. James Herbert, the vessel was freed from the shallow water in the river and, at noon, finally arrived at the dock for unloading. She remained overnight and was escorted down river at about 6:30 a.m. Sunday by the Coast Guard cutter **Escanaba** which had been sent from Grand Haven arriving at 4:30 a.m. Sunday morning. The cutter paused briefly in South Haven to stand by in case help was needed by the **Farrendoc**, the last expected pulp boat of the season. Then the **Escanaba** turned north to assist with keeping the St. Mary's River and the Straits of Mackinac open despite the exceptionally cold weather until the boats on the open lake could return to their docks.

The **J. F. Schoellkopf Jr.** was launched in 1907 at Lorain, Ohio, as the **Hugh Kennedy**. She was 7,263 gross tons, 5,795 net tons, 532.2 in length, 56.2 in beam, 27.2 in depth. In 1930 she had been renamed **J. F. Schoellkopf Jr.** named for Jacob Frederick Schoellkopf Jr., a chemist and investor who was on the board of American Steamship Co. of Buffalo, New York. She was converted to a self-unloader in 1933.

After the incident at South Haven the **Schoellkopf** continued on the Great lakes for another for another 45 years, first for the American Steamship Co., later the Erie Sand Steamship Co. of Erie, Pennsylvania.

Low Water Claims the **Burlington**

December 6, 1936
North of the Holland Piers

When the **Burlington**, a freighter of 2024 tons, 255 feet in length left Toledo December 1, 1936, she was drawing 17 feet, 5 inches of water, but Captain James Woods was not concerned about the channel at Holland harbor, where they were to deliver a load of pig iron for the Holland Furnace Company, because the vessel had been loaded as much as four inches deeper, 17 feet, 9 inches, and made the harbor with no problems.

About 3 a.m., December 6, he squared away to enter Holland harbor. The captain described what happened next in testimony before federal inspectors two days later. The testimony was reported in the December 8, 1936, issue of the *Holland Sentinel*:

> Working down the midcenter, 200 feet from the piers, the boat struck bottom and then struck hard again as it entered the piers at a rate of about six miles an hour and stopped completely.
>
> The wind, Capt. Woods told the inspectors, was southwest at the time.
>
> "I realized that the water had dropped," he said, "and I made up my mind to back out and head for Muskegon."
>
> A "southwest sea was making" as he backed the **Burlington** up, he said, and was inclined to drive it to the north pier.
>
> Capt. Woods said he maneuvered the ship around an hour and a half, when he finally lined it up with the pier to the north.
>
> "On this last stage, I could do no more with her. She would not answer on go ahead or go stern and I blew the danger signals, signaling for the coast guard to come and take the crew off."

A surfman on lookout duty at the coast guard station, just inside the piers on the north side of the channel, realized the plight of the freighter when she began to back out and notified other members of the station. The surfboat was shoved out while the **Burlington** was still maneuvering. The December 7 issue of the *Holland Sentinel* describes the rescue:

> The crew left the boat after a futile attempt to pull her clear from the Ottawa beach shore. The heavy seas increased the hazard of rescuing the crew. Four trips were made in the surfboat to take the crew to land. Lines were swung overboard to the surfboat which bobbed like a cork at the freighter's side.
>
> Some of the crew gained the surfboat with the lines. Others were forced to jump. But while the seas pounded and snow bit harshly, the rescue was effected in about two hours with comparative precision.

As soon as the captain realized that the **Burlington** was grounded he ordered the mate and engineer to prepare to leave the ship, opening some of the sea cocks, and

165

closing all manholes, cargo holds and tanks. The dynamos were kept going to provide light to aid the coast guard, but finally as the last of the crew prepared to leave the motors were shut off. The temperature was about 14 degrees above zero. Removal of the crew was completed by 6:30 a.m.

*The **Burlington** during the winter of 1936-37*
the break amidships is clearly visible through the ice.

Coast Guard Captain E. J. Clemons told Captain Woods that the water in the channel was down two feet, seven inches below normal, mainly as the result of a strong southwest wind, but that there was no way of determining the depth of the channel ahead of time.

Captain Woods later testified that he had been master of the **Burlington** for six years and had entered Holland harbor 12 to 14 times with no trouble.

The crew was taken first to the Coast Guard station where they were served breakfast and at 10 a.m. the captain and 23 other members of the crew were taken to the Netherlands Hotel. One of the cooks was from Holland and went home.

By the second day the **Burlington** began to show evidence of a v-shaped split a little forward of midship. Viewed from the beach the bow of the freighter appeared to be down, and she was heavily coated with ice from waves breaking against her. The "broken back" was a result of the weight of her cargo, 2,200 tons of iron, and her position on the bar.

The **Burlington** was built by the Chicago Ship Building Co. and launched in 1897 as the steamer **Minneapolis**. From 1897 to 1916 she worked out of Cleveland, Buffalo, New York and Boston, Massachusetts, before being sold in 1916 to the Empress Navera

Co. of Havana, Cuba where she was renamed **Ramon Marimon.** In 1922 she returned to American registry as the **Burlington.** Her owner of record at the time of the accident was the Gartland Steamship Co. and her home port was Wilmington, Delaware. Her Great Lakes work was under the management of the D. Sullivan Company. The vessel was valued at $125,000.

The Coast Guard cutter **Escanaba,** usually stationed at Grand Haven, 20 miles north of Holland, was in the St. Mary's River, near Sault Ste. Marie, and not available to assist with the rescue. At the hearing Captain Woods testified that if the **Escanaba,** or a similar vessel, had been available it might have been possible to save the **Burlington.**

The **Antietam,** a 125 foot Coast Guard cutter, was sent from Milwaukee and arrived at noon on December 8, with a crew of 20 men, but there was little they could do. By that time the crack in the **Burlington** measured more than a foot in width. Some crew members who were allowed to board the boat in an attempt to rescue some of their personal belongings and ship's instruments, found many of the items destroyed by water which had gotten inside through the breach in the hull.

The **Burlington** was broken up by ice and waves over the winter. When the weather permitted scows and tugs, and a crane with an electro-magnet, removed some of the cargo which was taken to the Holland Furnace Co. and other metal machinery and pieces which were taken to the Louis Padnos Iron and Metal Company in Holland.

In the spring there was an attempt to refloat the hull by an Ionia company but the damage was too great and the pieces slid off the sand bar and sank. The scattered hull can still be located about 200 (some accounts say 400) feet north of the north breakwater where divers still find iron pigs.

Kreetan Struck by Barge

South of Grand Haven
November 15, 1939

The 15-ton gas screw propeller tug **Kreetan** was lost a mile south of Grand Haven, after it was struck by a barge and beached to avoid sinking on November 15, 1939. A news story in the *Grand Haven Daily Tribune* for Thursday, November 16, 1939, describes the incident:

> A gasoline motor from a 38-foot tugboat of Whitehall, the **Kreetan,** belonging to the Lyons Construction Co. is being salvaged from the boat which was beached Tuesday night along shore just south of the Hyland Gardens concessions.
>
> The boat was rammed by a barge in tow that was being taken to the Grand Rapids pipeline intake at the end of M-50 which is being constructed by the Lyons Co. A bad leak resulted and the boat was driven up onto the beach. There was no danger as the boat was not far from shore and after it was beached the crew jumped ashore. Capt. John Clark was in charge and the others aboard were George Clark, Clayton Kline and Peter Molenkamp.

After the machinery has been taken off the frame and hull of the boat, which is of wood construction, will be burned, it was reported by one of the crew working at the wreck this morning.

Powerless Sensibar Aground on Bar

December 7, 1939
South of Grand Haven

Even to the residents of Grand Haven, accustomed to boat traffic, the sight of a 537 foot boat anchored off shore was worth a look. The *Grand Haven Daily Tribune* for December 7, 1939, ran a long column of explanation:

> The 600 foot freighter **J. R. Sensibar**, owned by Construction Aggregates Co. is lying off shore about two miles, anchored to ride out the Lake Michigan gale which struck this shore during the early morning. The boat is not in immediate danger nor are the 13 men aboard, it was reported, as the ship is riding the waves that are piling up under a stiff wind that shifted from southwest to northwest at noon.
>
> The boat was being towed from Chicago by two powerful tugs owned by the Great Lakes Towing Co. to this port to go into winter quarters at the Construction Aggregates dock, where it is to be fitted out for gravel service next season.
>
> The tugs and tow arrived off shore about 5 a.m. and when near the pier entrance broke an eight-inch hawser. The **Sensibar** was swung around and the anchors were dropped The **Montana**. the flagship of the fleet of 60 tugs owned by the towing company, was in the lead, the most powerful tug in the fleet. Following was the **Wisconsin**. Capt. James Oakley is in charge of the **Montana** and Capt. Al Templeton is master of the other tug.
>
> After the **Sensibar** was anchored the tugs came into port. A call was made to Chicago telling of the experience and Capt. John E. Murrin, in charge of the Chicago fleet, is expected to arrive some time today to take charge. It is hoped that the wind will lay down within a few hours after which the two lines will be reset . . .

The **Sensibar** was built by the Great Lakes Engineering Works at Ecorse and was launched in 1906 as the **Frank C. Ball**. Her owner was the Globe Steamship Co. of Duluth. In 1930 she was purchased by the Sensibar Transport Co. of Chicago and renamed the **J. R. Sensibar**. She worked on the grounds created for the 1933-34 Chicago World's Fair. Most of this was fill land and included what later was Chicago's outer drive and Mieg's Field. She had been laid up at a South Chicago dock for three years. In 1935 the **Sensibar** became the property of the Midwest Vessel Co. of Delaware before being sold in 1942 to the Construction Materials Co., a predecessor of Construction Aggregates and it was decided to send her to Grand Haven to be reoutfitted as a gravel hauler.

J. R. Sensibar

All of these facts were carefully and quietly explained to *Tribune* readers, but at the head of the news column was a few lines of type that changed everything.

BULLETIN

The Sensibar broke loose from her anchor about 4 o'clock and drifted two miles south where it beached.

The following day the newspaper reported that as the wind direction changed to the northwest the tugs were radioed, or realized, the peril the big boat was in and attempted to go out into Lake Michigan to place a line aboard that would hold the vessel "up into the wind." The tugs got as far as the end of the pier "but the waves were too much" and they returned to the harbor. According to the December 8, *Grand Haven Daily Tribune*:

> When the lookout at the coast guard station yesterday reported the ship had broken loose from her anchor, coast guardsmen rushed into the big power life boat and headed into the lake. The **Sensibar** got into the trough of the sea and under the heavy gale made fast progress south. It appeared for a while that she would hit the shore broadside.

169

The wind shifting more and more to the north hit her freeboard and when she finally settled, her prow was pointed directly to shore. Coast guardsmen offered to take off the crew but after they were assured the ship was in no immediate danger agreed to stay aboard and the power boat returned to port. . .

The chief engineer was brought to the coast guard station this morning to get in touch with Chicago. A big centrifugal pump is expected to be sent over from Chicago and the underwriter will be here today, as the boat is reported to be insured. The amount was not given out. The boat is said to be worth $2,500,000. . .

Chief Boatswain E. J. Clemons who was aboard the **Sensibar** this morning, said there was seven feet of water in the engine room and he thought the plates were badly sprung, caused when the ship listed far over as she struck shallow water.

The Coast Guard brought the breeches buoy apparatus to the shoreline Friday to rescue the crew should the boat begin breaking up and pumps were set aboard, powered by a steam line from the **Montana**, to keep up with the water leaking through strained seams. When the accident first happened the Coast Guard vessel **Escanaba** which was stationed at Grand Haven was inoperative because it was having some machinery overhauled, and a call was sent to Milwaukee for the Coast Guard patrol boat **Antietam**. By Saturday the **Escanaba** was back in business and it was this crew that actually used the Lyle gun to send a line to the **Sensibar** to set up the breeches buoy. Two investigators, one from Construction Aggregates and another from the insurance company, rode out to the vessel on the breeches buoy Saturday and two of the crew came ashore. The insurance man received a good dunking on his return trip when he was struck by a big wave as he neared shore.

Coast Guard officers reported that it was believed that it was the first time the breeches buoy had been sent to a distressed vessel at Grand Haven since the **Clara Parker** grounded south of Grand Haven November 15, 1883. Later writers would claim that it was also the last time the breeches buoy apparatus was used on the Great Lakes.

On Monday it was decided that the **Montana** and **Wisconsin** were not strong enough to pull the **Sensibar** free and the tug **Favorite** of Sault Ste. Marie was called to the scene. After several false stars and delays, caused by the weather, work began in earnest Wednesday afternoon. The *Grand Haven Daily Tribune* reported:

The **J. R. Sensibar**, beached three miles south of the piers for one week, was drawn off the shoals about 4 a.m. today and is now docked at the foot of Washington street, where the 600-foot vessel occupies the greater share of both the Robbins and Grand Trunk docks.

The choppy sea yesterday afternoon laid down later in the evening and the three tugs, **Favorite, Montana** and **Wisconsin** renewed their efforts to release the ship. The smooth water was favorable to the continued effort to free the stern from sand, the three tug boats working all night. . .

170

After considerable dredging was done around the ship she floated and with little or no effort she was drawn to deep water. Pumps were kept working to keep water out of the hold and as there was no sea the tugs had no difficulty in bringing her into port about 6:30 a.m.

The ship is one of the largest ones ever to enter this port. She looks old and rusty now as she has been laid up at South Chicago for three years and is minus considerable paint. The engines, all electrically driven, are said to be in good condition as they have been smeared with inches of grease.

Tom Mahon, former local resident and veteran diver at Muskegon arrived here at noon with his tug the **Tee-Zee-Lee**, and will begin diving this afternoon to determine what if any damage has been done to the bottom of the ship. If the damage is considerable she will be towed across Lake Michigan again to dry dock at Manitowoc.

The **Sensibar** was taken to Wisconsin where the repair and conversion work was completed. She was sold to Canadian registry in 1981 and renamed the **Conallison** but worked only briefly in Canada before being sold again in 1984 to Descguaces Vige, a Spanish salvage company. The vessel was towed across the Atlantic by the **George M. Carl** and broken up.

Explosion Rocks the **Chambers Bros.**

October 6, 1945
Off Holland

A simple mistake can spell disaster in the unforgiving environment of Lake Michigan. The **Chamber Bros.**, a fishing tug docked at Macatawa Park, went out on a regular run in early October, 1945.

*The **Chambers Bros.** at Saugatuck after conversion to a stern trawler.*

171

They were about 15 miles out of Holland harbor at 10:45 p.m. Saturday, October 6, when Frank Nehis, one of the crew, added some fuel to the light machine tank and it overflowed. The gas spilled out onto a hot exhaust pipe and the rolling sea spread it around on the pipe until it ignited. The fire spread rapidly to Nehis' clothing and the cabin of the tug.

The rest of the crew rushed to his aid with Neil Sandy, suffering second degree burns on his hand and forearm. Captain Clifford Chambers and his brother, Lloyd were also burned as they tried to help Nehis and extinguish the fire on the boat.

Nehis suffered second and third degree burns to his face, arms and chest. When the fire was extinguished it was apparent that he needed medical attention quickly and the vessel turned toward Holland. Their light machine was not working and they made the 15 mile trip in the dark. The tug landed at about 12:15 a.m. and the injured man was rushed to the hospital, but he died the following week.

The **Chamber Bros.** was built and launched by the Sturgeon Bay Boatworks in 1928. Her owner of record was Clifford D. Chambers, 1928 to 1934 with a home port of Kenosha, Wisconsin; Lloyd L. Chambers, 1934 to 1951, homeport, Grand Marais, Michigan; and Clifford D. Chambers, 1951 to 1961, homeport, Holland.

The year after her launch the **Chamber Bros.** was docked at Kenosha, Wisconsin, September 29, 1929, when the Goodrich steamer **Wisconsin** foundered a mile off shore. When he saw the big boat on her way down crewman Clarence Ferris went directly to the **Chambers Bros.** and began heating torches to fire up the semi-diesel engine. When Clifford and Lloyd came to see what was happening, they jumped aboard with other volunteers and headed directly into the wreckage toward a chorus of cries for help. As fast as they pulled the men from the water, crew members and volunteers help them below decks where a fire was going in the steam boiler usually used to lift nets. Fifty-nine of the estimated 74 passengers and crew who were on board the **Wisconsin** were saved by volunteer vessels, such as the Chambers brothers' boat, and two Coast Guard boats.

After the 1945 accident the cabin and light machine were repaired and the **Chambers Bros.** continued in service for many years. She was sold in 1961 to Keith Winton who converted her to a stern trawler to harvest alewives. When the alewife industry played out the **Chambers Bros.** was sold to Roger Chapman of Milwaukee, Wisconsin in 1977 and renamed the **Recovery**.

Fish Tugs Lost in 'Big Storm'

November 11, 1940
North of Holland

Two fishing tugs from South Haven were among the many victims of the great storm of November 11, 1940, sometimes referred to as the Armistice Day Storm because it occurred on the anniversary of the day the peace treaty for World War I was signed. As boats that went to search for the lost boats failed to return, anxiety among those who waited helplessly on shore increased. The Tuesday, November 12, 1940, issue of the *South Haven Daily Tribune* reported:

Coast guardsmen who had kept a futile, all night vigil along gale-swept Lake Michigan, today virtually gave up all hope for the safety of 12 men who disappeared into the lake yesterday in three boats and have been unreported since.

Missing were two fishing tugs, the **Indian**, owned by James Madsen, the **Richard H.**, owned by Captain John C. McKay, who was not aboard, and a coast guard power lifeboat which put out at 2:50 p.m. yesterday in an attempt to locate the missing craft.

Aboard the **Richard H.** were John McKay Jr., 28, Stanley White, 33, and John Taylor, 35. The boat put out at approximately 9 a.m. yesterday to set nets for trout and whitefish, on which the season opened yesterday. The craft left harbor only a few minutes before the coast guard storm warning was posted.

Aboard the **Indian** were James Madsen, 55, Harold Richter, 35, Bill Bird, 30, Chris Wakild, 56, and Art Reeves. The boat left harbor at 7:35 a.m. for an all day fishing excursion.

At about 1:30 p.m., shortly before the second terrific gale hit this area the **Richard H.** was sighted about five miles out. A steamer, the **Justin C. Allen**, was sighted at the same time. Then the waters of the lake were whipped into an inferno by a 60-mile gale which rolled up mountainous waves and spread a milky mist over the water in which visibility was blacked out. When the storm's fury had spent from 20 to 30 minutes later, neither the **Richard H.** nor the steamer were to be seen.

At 2:50 p.m. a coast guard power lifeboat . . . put out to search for the missing boats. The craft moved steadily out into the wind tossed lake and has not been reported since.

Extra coast guard men were rounded up from St. Joseph, Grand Haven, Holland and South Haven and beach patrols extended from St. Joseph to Saugatuck. The Coast Guard boat **Escanaba** was reported in dry dock and unable to assist.

The Coast Guard boat from South Haven arrived in Chicago at 6 p.m. Tuesday after a 27 hour search. About the same time the wrecked hull of the **Indian** was discovered by men from the Coast Guard patrolling the beach between Grand Haven and Holland. Identification was made by the imprint of the Berger Boat Company on the pilot house which was located in Little Pigeon creek, ten miles north of Holland. Wreckage, including the fish tug's smokestack, was reported over a four mile area. It was unusual for tug owner Madsen to be along, but he had joined the party for the first day of whitefish season. Richter and Wakild owned the smaller fish tug, **Three Juan**, but worked for Madsen on the larger vessel in the winter.

The tug **Indian** was 26 tons, 48 feet in length. It was described as "a sturdy craft with a powerful diesel engine, and considered by sailing men here to be a highly seaworthy boat." The newspaper noted that the **Indian** had survived a similar storm in 1939, finally putting in at Chicago.

The hull of the 19 ton tug **Richard H.** was never located. Some wreckage and the name plate of the vessel was discovered at Grand Haven State Park on Tuesday. No bodies ever came ashore from either boat.

Gotham Founders on Fishing Trip

The Saugatuck-based fishing tug **Gotham** was unusual for its time. It was a steel-hulled tug handmade by her owner, Lewis Gotham, and his two sons, Fred and Sam. No bolts were used in her construction, all seams were welded. She was launched in 1940 and registered at 57 gross tons, 39 net tons, 56.3 feet in length.

The **Gotham** left Saturday morning, December 11, on a regular fishing run for trout and whitefish with the three Gothams aboard and F. Harley Jones and his teenage son, Billy. That night lights were sighted headed for the Saugatuck pier. According to Saugatuck's *Commercial Record*:

> During the heavy windstorm of Saturday night when a 60 mile gale was blowing on Lake Michigan, the **Gotham**, steel fishing tug belonging to Lou Gotham and his sons, in trying to make the harbor at Saugatuck apparently struck the north pier and was sunk.
>
> Lights were seen by the coast guard on watch at Holland about 9 o'clock, but disappeared soon after. It is thought when the boat struck the pier it rolled on its side and dismantled the cabin as the first thing washed ashore was the ring buoy. Later all four life preservers were found in a bunch, about 25 fish boxes, the sidelights and decking were found.
>
> Fred Davis, who had been on the beach most of the night, Sunday morning picked up Mr. Gotham's pipe and tobacco and Sam's cigarettes, where they had been washed ashore. About 50 feet north of the pier fuel oil came up indicating that the tanks were broken and water was driving the oil to the surface. . . .
>
> Conflicting stories gave various theories on how the crash occurred. There were no eyewitnesses, but some think the boat crashed into the north pier. Others think the vessel may have struck bottom, tearing a hole in the steel hull. Other commercial fishermen in the vicinity said the depth of the lake in that area is about 12 feet but when the sea is high the depth between waves is sometimes as little as three feet. The boat had a seven foot draft.
>
> The **Gotham** was built in 1940. Having an enclosed structure, it resembled a submarine, and was highly publicized when she was completed. Power was provided by diesel engines and the vessel had capacity for 1,000 gallons of crude oil.
>
> Sam Gotham was ill of the flu with a temperature of 104 when he left with the crew Saturday morning according to friends. Some believe the elder Gotham, a hardy seaman, who ordinarily rode out the storms, was trying to make port on his son's account whose condition may have become worse.

*The **Gotham** shortly after her launch.*

A diver checking for damage and bodies reported that the hull was intact, refuting the idea that the vessel struck the pier or the bottom. However the rear doors were caved in. A former employe noted that this was the boat's weakest part because they never completed closing in the engine room.

Three bodies were found during the winter and the last two discovered within the hull of the ship when she was finally raised in May of 1944. The Gotham was reoutfitted as a regular tug boat, with a cabin and open decks, and continued in operation until at least 1993, first in Detroit and later in Port Huron.

Motor Yacht **Verano** Founders

August 28, 1946
Off Glenn

The 92-foot motor yacht **Verano** foundered for still unexplained reasons about eight miles north of South Haven, near the Allegan County community of Glenn on August 28, 1946. A number of local residents actually saw the boat go down, but reported no sign of the three men who were known to be aboard. The *South Haven Daily Tribune* describes the sinking:

> The fate of three crewmen aboard the ill-fated 92-foot motor yacht **Verano** remained a mystery today as South Haven Coast Guardsmen, State Police, three local pilots, a Coast Guard plane and local Sea Scouts continued their search for the men and the yacht which sank seven miles off South Haven Wednesday. Battling heavy seas the vessel went down in 60 feet of water approximately a half mile off the shore at 5:52 p.m.

The vessel . . . put out of Chicago at 6 a.m. Wednesday for the Jesiek Boat Yard at Holland where repairs were to be made on the keel.

At 3:50 p.m. William Merriel of Ganges notified the South Haven Coast Guard that he had sighted a ship in distress from one-half to three-quarters of a mile off shore. The local guardsmen left immediately for the spot in the station life boat and reached the **Verano** about 17 minutes before she sank in 60 feet of water.

Chief Boatswain's Mate William Herbet reported that no survivors were seen and that the lifeboat was gone. It is believed the men abandoned the vessel after it became apparent it was doomed. The big yacht reared and sank stern first. "It went down before our eyes," he said.

A bulletin at the top of the story reported that the Coast Guard had discovered the dinghy of the **Verano** with the oars still lashed to the boat indicating that no attempt had been made to use it. The Michigan State Police were notified and two officers responded to the scene and searched the beach on horseback, but found no bodies or wreckage.

Aboard the vessel at the time of her foundering were Captain Chester Granath, a business partner of the vessel's owner Maynard Dowell; a Japanese-American cook, Ben Murakoshi; and the engineer, Fred Stenning, all of Chicago.

The **Verano** was one of the largest yachts on the Great Lakes, at 102 gross tons, and was valued at $75,000. She had been built in New York in 1925 and had been purchased by Dowell about six weeks before the sinking from J. R. Baumgartner of Milwaukee. The vessel was powered by twin gas motors and normally carried a power launch in addition to the small lifeboat, but the launch had been left behind on this trip.

The day after the sinking the wife of Captain Granath, came to South Haven and offered a reward for the recovery of her husband's body. She told reporters that it was her feeling that the vessel had developed engine trouble and that all three aboard had been in the engine room when she foundered. She based her theory on the report of the Coast Guard that before the **Verano** sank a chair was seen stuck into the steering wheel. Mrs. Granath said this was a device often resorted to when the pilot needs to go below and check on the engines.

On Saturday, August 31, the body of Captain Granath was discovered on the beach near Daybreak Farm, eight miles north of South Haven, by a couple walking on the beach about 11:30 a.m. The same afternoon the body of the cook was sighted about 40 feet from shore in Lake Michigan 12 miles north of South Haven. The engineer's body was never recovered.

The site of the sinking was marked with a buoy and divers searched the wreckage for bodies and to try to determine a cause for the accident. Later there was a serious effort to refloat the vessel, but it was not successful and resulted only in further damage to the hull. In 1993 the hull was rediscovered by local divers Tom Conczos and Robert Trowbridge who report that wreckage is now strewn over a quarter of a mile. A large piece lies to one side of the main vessel body, possibly as a result of the aborted salvage operation. About 200 feet from the **Verano** the sailboat **Francie** sits, nearly intact. Both wrecks would be included in the proposed Southwest Michigan Underwater Preserve.

176

*The yacht **Verano***

Eagle Sinks in Flooded River

April 5, 1947
South Haven Harbor

The 13 ton gas screw fishing tug **Eagle** sank in a rain swollen river at South Haven on April 5, 1947. The *South Haven Daily Tribune* for April 7, 1947, reported:

> The fishing tug "**Eagle**" broke loose from its moorings upstream from the South Haven bridge about 4:30 Saturday afternoon, capsized, hit the bridge piers and sank about 100 feet west of the bridge. For almost six hours the Coast Guard searched the river using grappling hooks but were unable to find a trace of the boat. Witnesses said the cabin of the **Eagle** was ripped off when it struck the bridge piers.
>
> The value of the fishing tug was estimated at $4,000 by the owner Henry Damgard of Racine, Wis. Ten boxes of nets worth about $1,000 were also lost. Coast Guard men were unable to find these on the Black River bed. Boatswain Mate First Class Frank Rydlewicz, head of the local station, said the river had been flowing along at eight or 10 miles per hour when the boat broke loose.
>
> The barge to which the **Eagle** was tied sank where it was moored about 300 feet upstream from the bridge.

B & L a Picturesque Hulk

Abandoned 1954
Kalamazoo River near Douglas

Before the Gotham family of Saugatuck constructed the **Gotham** the welded iron tug they were working on when she sank in 1943, they fished from the **B & L**, a more traditional wooden fishing boat built in 1931 by Hank Perkins of Saugatuck.

After the death of both Lewis and his sons on the **Gotham**, the old **B & L** (named for the elder Gotham and his wife, Berthie and Lewis) was sold several times. In 1952 she ended up in the hands of a Fennville farmer who leased the **B & L** on a summer-long charter to resorters who so damaged the hull that the vessel sank. She was dragged up on the edge of the Kalamazoo River, just west of the Blue Star Highway bridge near the entrance to Douglas, but there was never enough money for repairs and the old boat was formally abandoned in 1954.

The rotting hull remained a picturesque part of the harbor, frequently photographed and painted by visitors and pupils at the Ox-Bow Summer School of Painting and other organized summer classes until it was obliterated by the high water of the mid-1970's.

Kling Wins in Collision with Dock

April 25, 1962
Grand Haven Harbor

The strange thing about the collision of the sand carrier **John A. Kling** with a dock at Grand Haven, April 25, 1962, was the near total absence of damage to the boat. The dock was left with a large v-shaped hole and the impact was so great that it damaged a road and buckled part of the parking lot. The cost to repair the damage was estimated to be $10,000.

The accident occurred at about 1:10 a.m. when the **John A. Kling**, a 6,800 ton lake freighter, was entering the harbor of Grand Haven and headed for the Construction Aggregates dock. She some how got off course coming around the curve in the channel and hit the Harbor Industries dock just a few feet from the shoreline.

Her bow pushed a large, ragged "V" nearly ten feet into the dock and the parking lot behind it, buckling the pavement 30 feet from the shoreline and narrowly missing the firm's boiler house. A spokesman for Harbor Industries said the damage would cost at least $10,000 to repair. More if there was serious undermining in the paved areas.

Captain Malcom A. Johns of Detroit, master of the **Kling** was questioned by the Grand Haven city police and the local Coast Guard, but was unable to explain why the vessel strayed from the channel. She came right next to shore and clipped off some old pilings south of the dock before she buried her bow in the parking lot. She was barely moving, Captain Johns said. He backed the **Kling** off the scene of the accident and continued to the Construction Aggregates dock upstream. Johns said that his ship was the only one in the harbor at the time of collision.

The damage was discovered by Harbor Industries personnel coming to work Wednesday morning.

The **Kling** was loaded and left Grand Haven at 9:50 a.m. Coast Guard officers in Grand Haven notified the Coast Guard marine inspection service at Cleveland where the **Kling** was expected to dock on Friday, for a closer inspection of the boat's hull.

At the time of the accident the vessel was owned by Rockport Steamship Co. of Sheboygan, Wisconsin.

Barge, Crane Go to Bottom

July 27, 1972
South of Holland

A work barge with a crane sank in Lake Michigan south of Holland for reasons that have never been publicly explained on July 27, 1972. The July 29 *Holland Evening Sentinel* reported:

> The Coast Guard is alerting boaters of a barge and crane that sank in Lake Michigan about a quarter mile off shore in 35 feet of water between Holland and Saugatuck Thursday morning.
>
> The 20 by 40 foot barge with a 20 foot crane aboard was being towed by a 26-foot cabin cruiser from Glenn when the barge sank. The cabin cruiser and those aboard arrived safely at Holland.
>
> The owner of the crane and barge and those aboard the cabin cruiser were not identified by the Coast Guard. The cause of the mishap was not learned.
>
> Attempts were being made to locate the sunken barge and crane and mark the spot with a buoy. The location was given as 42'43" north and 86'13" west.

The barge was later located but there was no attempt at salvage. The crane and barge appear on several shipwreck maps and have become a favorite spot for SCUBA divers. The wreck is in 35 feet of water.

Algorail Sinks at Holland

October 6, 1972
Holland Channel

When the Canadian freighter **Algorail** struck the Holland channel wall and sank in October of 1972, the shallow water in the harbor mouth turned a serious incident into a minor convenience.

On October 6, 1972, the 640-foot vessel was entering Holland with 17,000 tons of rock salt intended for winter use on the roads. According to the October 12, 1972, issue of the *Holland City News*:

The **Algorail** was entering the harbor about 6:30 p.m. Friday when a gust of wind caught her and sent the bow into the pier.

Captain Dougal Campbell, of Gore Bay, Ontario, said he apparently struck bottom on entering the channel, used another engine to maneuver and the bow was sent into the pierhead. . .

The disabled **Algorail** blocked Holland Harbor to all commercial shipping and the coal carrier **Nicolet**, 513 feet long, waited off the harbor entrance Saturday morning with a load of coal for the Holland Board of Public Works.

The Coast Guard said the channel is dredged to a depth of 22 feet and the **Algorail** reported a draft of 21 feet three inches, allowing a slight clearance.

While on the bottom Friday evening and Saturday, crewmen attempted to rig a canvas and plywood patch over the hole but later welded bolts to the hull and fasted a piece of conveyor belting over the opening and bolted the patch tight. Water that entered the gash was pumped out and the vessel refloated.

When the **Algorail** was floated Captain Campbell backed the vessel into the spilling basin of the breakwater to get a proper angle to enter the walled channel. She was then taken to Brewer's City Coal Dock to unload her cargo and assess the emergency repairs. The journey from the harbor mouth to the docks usually takes less than an hour. The **Algorail**, proceeding carefully, took nearly three hours.

After the cargo of salt was removed, the patched area floated high above the waterline and the **Algorail** was cleared to proceed to Thunder Bay, Ontario, for repairs but was delayed an additional day due to rough seas and high winds.

The **Algorail**, part of the Algoma Central Steamship fleet, was rated at 16,157 gross tons, 11,114 net tons and was a self-unloader with a 250-foot boom. She was launched at the Collingwood Shipyards at Collingwood, Ontario in December of 1967. She was the second vessel by that name. The first **Algorail** had been launched in 1901 as the **William S. Mack**, was renamed the **Home Smith** when first acquired by Algoma Central in 1917, but after extensive refurbishing was renamed the **Algorail**. The vessel remained in active service until 1963 when she was scrapped. The first boat to carry the name was rated at 3,720 gross tons, and the new **Algorail** could carry as much coal in one hold as the oldest vessel did in an entire load.

Fire Follows Explosion on the **Sea Castle**

May 13, 1974
In Holland Channel

Quick thinking by the captain of the tug **John M. Selvick** averted disaster when the barge she was towing was rocked by explosion and fire, May 13, 1974, in the Holland channel. An account was published in the Fall, 1974, edition of *Inland Seas*, written by J. W. Bissell who was an eye witness to the event.

On May 6th the barge **Sea Castle** in tow of the tug **John M. Selvick** arrived in Holland, Michigan, from Petoskey, with 17,500 barrels of cement for the Penn-Dixie Cement Company. Unloading would normally take about thirty hours with the size lines at the Holland facility. However, with unloading about two-thirds completed, mechanical failure with some of the unloading equipment delayed complete unloading and subsequent departure until Monday, May 13.

Just as the **Selvick** with the **Sea Castle** in tow was about to enter the channel joining the west end of Lake Macatawa with Lake Michigan, an explosion occurred on deck at the stern of the **Sea Castle**. Subsequent investigation showed that an air compressor apparently overheated, exploded, and set fire to a diesel fuel line. Within seconds the fire started spreading forward toward the bow of the barge fanned by a strong east wind.

Capt. Roy Eliason of the **Selvick**, with what seemed to this observer to be a superb bit of seamanship, brought the tug and barge about after clearing the pierhead, but within the breakwall leading out into Lake Michigan, without striking either side of the narrow channel. He apparently realized that he would have to get the barge headed into the wind in a hurry to keep the fire from completely engulfing the barge and possibly spreading to the tug.

The crew of both the tug and barge could be seen frantically trying to secure the **Sea Castle** to the seawall of the channel so that the fire could be fought from land as well as from the Coast Guard boat that had arrived by this time and was spraying water on the stern area of the barge. With the wind seeming to increase with each passing moment, the barge broke a mooring line and started to drift stern first and broadside out the channel toward Lake Michigan! The tug was helpless at this point, being upwind of the barge and without a towline attached anymore. The steering had been damaged on the barge also, in the explosion. Finally, a line was passed from the barge to the tug and things were brought under control, but not before the wind dealt one more blow to the **Sea Castle** by driving her into the pierhead, punching a two-foot hole in the stern section about three feet above the water.

The **Sea Castle** was once again brought alongside the channel wall, secured, and the fire brought under control. After inspection, to insure that the fire was out and that there was no oil leakage, the Coast Guard cleared the **Selvick** to tow the **Sea Castle** back to the Penn-Dixie dock in Holland where repairs could be made.

Fortunately, no one was at the stern of the **Sea Castle** when the explosion occurred; however, two crewmen were slightly injured when a line broke while attempting to stop the drifting barge.

Repairs to the **Sea Castle** took about three days, and she then left in tow of the **Selvick** without further ado.

Collision in Lake, One Vessel Lost

June, 1980
Off Saugatuck

Even the vastness of Lake Michigan is sometimes not enough. In June of 1980 two pleasure craft, both under 40 feet collided in conditions of poor visibility about 20 miles off Saugatuck on a course of 273 degrees.

The 33-foot **EMM'EL** sank and her passengers and crew were taken aboard the other vessel, a 36-foot Trojan boat named **Outdoorsman IV**. The **Outdoorsman** was bound from Saugatuck to Racine, Wisconsin, at the time of the collision.

Four Lost as **Sea Mar III** Disappears

September 26, 1980
Off South Haven

A four day search of southern Lake Michigan failed to find any trace of the four men who were aboard the **Sea Mar III**, a gas screw Trojan cabin cruiser 32 feet in length that apparently sank between Chicago and Holland in September of 1980.

The yacht, with the four men aboard, left Montrose Bay at Chicago at 5:30 p.m. Thursday, September 25. The trip from Chicago to Holland on a boat that size would normally take six to seven hours to complete and they were expected to arrive at a Holland marina about midnight. When they had not arrived by Friday morning the Coast Guard was notified.

An immediate search was instituted over more than 30,000 square miles in the southern part of Lake Michigan by two helicopters from Chicago and Traverse City, the Holland Coast Guard Station's 140 foot vessel **Mobile Bay** and about 70 seamen from the stations at Holland, Grand Haven, South Haven and Michigan City, Indiana. In addition hundreds of civilian boats assisted in the search. The effort was under the direction of the Coast Guard Rescue Coordination Center regional office at Cleveland, Ohio.

On Sunday afternoon a Coast Guard vessel discovered a pair of orange life jackets 14 miles southwest of Holland and eight miles off shore. The items were picked up at the site and flown by helicopter to Tulip City Airport near Holland, then taken by truck to the Holland Coast Guard station where they were positively identified by Claude Boles of Winetka, Illinois, who was the owner of the lost vessel.

Later Sunday several items from the boat including an engine cover, seat covers, a fire extinguisher and an unopened emergency flare kit were found floating in the water 12 miles south of where the life jackets had been located. The Coast Guard reported that none of the items appeared to be burned or broken apart as if a fire or explosion had occurred.

Aboard the vessel were Curtis Anderson of Holland, an ex-Coast Guard seaman who was a part time salesman at Bay Haven marina and a part owner of Ottawa Beach marina, and was expected to be the principal pilot of the cruiser. Others were Steven Brower of Holland, a salesman at Bay Haven Marina; Michael Stevenson of Holland, manager of the ship's store at the marina; and Harvey Willsey of Lexington, Ohio, a friend of the other three who docked his boat in Holland.

Coast Guard reports said that although there were storm warnings posted Thursday night only for the northern two-thirds of Lake Michigan, the southern portion of the lake was experiencing winds of 23 to 33 knots and waves of two to five feet. The water temperature was about 55 degrees.

On Tuesday the Coast Guard announced that they were suspending search efforts pending further developments. Later a side scan sonar was used on the most likely area to attempt to locate the hull, but no bodies were recovered and the remains of the vessel has never been located. It was speculated that the vessel may have had engine trouble, then capsized in the waves.

The following spring the discovery of additional wreckage caused searchers to renew their efforts, but the second search was not successful and was officially abandoned July 3, 1981.

Index

189

Illustration Credits

p.37,44	Samuel Ward Stanton
p.65,161	St. Clair Collection of the Great Lakes Historical Society
p.78,124	C. Patrick Labadie
p.92	Robert Wolbrink Collection
p.103,109, 126,130,155	Appleyard Collection, South Haven
p.111	From *History of the Great Lakes*
p.117,143,149, 166,169	Institute for Great Lakes Research
p.128	Manistee County Historical Museum
p.157,171	Commercial Record Collection
p.177	Lois J. Koyes Collection of the Michigan Maritime Museum